The Thrilling Prophecies of

Mr. Z and Jesus

Jerusalem, the Jew, and You

The Thrilling Prophecies of

Mr. Z and Jesus

Jerusalem, the Jew, and You

Jerry Johnston

First Family Inspirations

Overland Park, Kansas

Library of Congress Card Number 2007922011

ISBN-13 978-1-934438-09-1
ISBN-10 1-934438-09-x

All inquiries should be addressed to:
First Family Inspirations
7700 W. 143rd Street
Overland Park, Kansas 66223

Printed in USA

To Christie, my wife and best friend.
Thank you for your endless patience
for my many hours in study.
You have captured me.

Contents

Preface

Since the early days of my Christian life I have been intrigued by prophecy. There is no more challenging book of prophecy in the Bible than Zechariah. The entire book seems like a limitless treasure. I could have spent a year teaching in this one book. Again I want to thank the wonderful people of First Family Church who showed their avid interest in Zechariah by listening thoughtfully to each sermon with a yearning to discern every prophetic element. Attendance for this series was remarkably strong - another reminder that pastors and teachers should be diligent to teach exegetically the prophetic sections of Scripture. I want to encourage the reader to obtain my book on DANIEL which correlates a number of the Old Testament prophetic truths in Zechariah with a harmony that is stunning! The sermonars from this series in the back section of this book provide helpful study outlines to make this a perfect study for churches, Bible studies, home cell groups, and personal enrichment. Zechariah reminds us clearly that the Bible is an inspired book designed primarily to be studied, not just read. Roll up your sleeves and dig in to this phenomenal book of prophecy from a fireball young prophet.

Jerry Johnston
Kansas City

Using This Book

This book is designed for three primary audiences, although, as things inevitably change, we can envision other uses being discovered for its pages.

The simplest use of this book will be as straight-forward reading. Such a use requires little if any explanation from the author. You might be tempted to jump ahead to a chapter title that seems especially compelling. After all, who wouldn't want to know "What the world will be like someday"? In order to make your reading meaningful, however, you are encouraged to read chapter one first as it provides a good overview of Zechariah's entire body of work.

It is also hoped that these pages will provide a strong curriculum for small-group studies. If you choose to use it in that fashion, let me suggest that you avail yourself of the extra information to be found in the Sermonars pages beginning on page 207. These Sermonars began as sermon outlines, provided to our church members. Teachers will find them useful as teaching guides and class plans. Also, notice that each chapter ends with a set of "Discussion Questions." Most of these questions are open questions without set, brief answers. In active classes, they should provide a great deal of discussion fodder. However you use these resources, be sure to approach such a group teaching situation with considerable prayer and Bibles at the ready.

The final way in which we envision this book being employed is as ready-made sermons for a pastor hoping to cover this same material. God has blessed the author with a very supportive and well resourced church. It is his prayer that some of those blessings might then bless others if they provide other pastors with materials, usable as they are or adapted to fit your particular needs. The Sermonars were the original sermon outlines provided in our church. You are invited to use those notes for your own church or simply as a guide for your preaching.

Chapter One

The Panorama of the Prophetic in Zechariah

12 Then the Angel of the Lord answered and said, "O Lord of hosts, how long will You not have mercy on Jerusalem and on the cities of Judah, against which You were angry these seventy years?"

13 And the Lord answered the angel who talked to me, with good and comforting words. 14 So the angel who spoke with me said to me, "Proclaim, saying, 'Thus says the Lord of hosts:

"I am zealous for Jerusalem
And for Zion with great zeal." (Zech. 1:12-14)

One of the truly unique distinctives about Christianity is that God says a great deal about the future and that He always keeps His word! Everything that God promised would happen in the past has come to pass just as He predicted. Therefore, we can also have confidence that everything God has revealed about the future will also be perfectly fulfilled at the right time. God is the sovereign ruler of the universe. In Him there is no deceit. He is in control of the future, and nothing happens outside of His control or knowledge.

Prophecy: A God Who Remembers

Not surprisingly, at least twenty-eight percent of the Bible is prophetic in nature. What constitutes prophetic material? A prophecy is a specific prediction that has literally been fulfilled or that points to a definite future time when it will come true. Some of the prophecies we find in the Bible were made hundreds and even thousands of years before their fulfillment. The precision of these prophecies makes it practically impossible for them to be explained away as merely the product of man's creativity or some random coincidence.

What is even more astounding is that all the prophecies of the Bible that have been fulfilled so far have come to pass with absolute accuracy. In the Old Testament, for instance, there are more than 100 prophecies about the coming of the Messiah to the earth. Through the testimony of these prophecies, we know that Jesus Christ was truly the Messiah, since He fulfilled every one of the prophecies related to His first coming.

Introducing Mr. Z

Although not classed among the major prophets, Zechariah stands out as a giant of prophecy. What is especially astonishing about the prophetic book of Zechariah is that it contains five times more prophecies about Jesus' Second Coming than about His first coming. With the exception of Isaiah, there is more prophecy about Jesus in Zechariah than in any other Old Testament book—more than in any other minor prophet. Because of its focus on Jesus and on His Second Coming, many scholars believe that Zechariah is to the Old Testament what the book of Revelation is to the New. Homer Heater comments, "Zechariah is second only to Isaiah in frequency of citations in the passion narratives and has the greatest influence of all the prophets in John's apocalypse."[1]

Because its prophecies can be hard to understand at times, many people think that the book of Zechariah is one of the most difficult books in all of the Old Testament. However, if we study this book with diligence and approach God's Word as a whole, with a proper understanding and attitude, we can definitely gain a better appreciation of the message of Zechariah. C. I. Scofield writes:

> Zechariah, like Haggai, was a prophet to the remnant which returned after the 70 years. There is much of symbol in Zechariah, but these difficult passages are readily interpreted in the light of the whole body of related prophecy. The great Messianic passages are, upon comparison with the other prophecies of the kingdom perfectly clear. Both advents (comings) of Christ are in Zechariah's prophecy (9:9 with Mt. 21:1-11 and Zech. 14:3-4). More than Haggai or Malachi, Zechariah gives us the mind of God about the Gentile world-powers surrounding the restored remnant.[2]

Timetable

Haggai, Zechariah, and Malachi are the last of the prophetic books in the Old Testament, not only in the order in the Bible but in their date of composition. This trio of prophets brought the Word of the Lord to the Jews after they returned to Jerusalem from Babylon. Nebuchadnezzar had captured Jerusalem and completely destroyed the Jewish Temple, burning it to the ground. As traumatic as these events must have been, they did not bring the Jews to national repentance. In reading Ezra, we find that when Cyrus, king of Persia, issued a decree permitting all the captives to return to Jerusalem and rebuild their Temple, only about 50,000 took the opportunity to return. Most of those 50,000 were priests, Levites, and the poorer among the people. Al-

3

though the Jews increased in power and numbers, they never re-established their political independence. They remained a subject people under Gentile rulers from that time on.

Before God raised up Haggai, the Jews had returned to their own land under Zerubbabel. The returnees set to work rebuilding the Temple (Nehemiah 12), but their enthusiasm soon waned. They made no progress beyond laying the foundation of the temple. The Samaritans and other neighboring enemies were determined that Jerusalem should not be rebuilt. The combination of apathy and opposition meant that the work lay unfinished for fifteen years. During that time, the people became more interested in building their own private homes, places where they could live with their families, than in rebuilding the house of God. It was in those days that Haggai and Zechariah preached their messages in order to encourage the people to keep building the Lord's Temple.

The book of Zechariah was written beginning in 520 BC. Zechariah's ministry began two months after Haggai's (Haggai 1:1 and Zechariah 1:1). Their joint ministry resulted in the completion of the Temple in 515 BC. Zechariah prophesied for three years, while Haggai ministered for four months.

Zechariah: The Priest & Prophet

Zechariah is a book of comfort for God's people of the past, present, and future. We see this very clearly in Zechariah 1:12–14,

> Then the Angel of the LORD answered and said, "O LORD of hosts, how long will You not have mercy on Jerusalem and on the cities of Judah, against which You were angry these seventy years?" And the LORD answered the angel who talked to me, with good and comforting words. So the angel who spoke with me said to me, "Proclaim, saying, 'Thus says the LORD of hosts: 'I am zealous for Jerusalem and for Zion with

great zeal.'"

The name Zechariah means "Jehovah remembers." In the midst of their struggles, the Lord wanted to remind His people of His promises to them. Even though the Jews had no Temple, and even though they had to fight against their enemies and against their own complacency, the Lord remained faithful. He comforted them by giving them precious promises that they should hold on to as they yielded their lives to Him.

Zechariah was a young prophet when he worked alongside the aged Haggai. Zechariah 2:4 relates the beginning of Zechariah's ministry when an angel instructs him to "Run, speak to this young man, saying: 'Jerusalem shall be inhabited as towns without walls, because of the multitude of men and livestock in it.'" Zechariah, born in pagan Babylon, wrote his book in Palestine and was murdered as a result of his faith at the end of faithful ministry. Jesus refers to Zechariah's martyrdom in Matthew 23:35 when he pronounces woes upon the Pharisees: "That on you may come all the righteous blood shed on the earth, from the blood of righteous Abel to the blood of Zechariah, son of Berechiah, whom you murdered between the temple and the altar."

The Panorama of Prophecy in Zechariah Regarding Jesus Christ

There are many key prophecies in the book of Zechariah. For instance, this unique book gives us God's revelation about:

• The birth of children during the Millennium

• The need for evangelism in the Millennium

• The complete destruction of the Antichrist

• The description of the battle of Armageddon

• The martyrdom of believers in the Great Tribulation

- The ultimate salvation of the nation Israel

- Alexander the Great's world domination, which began the Grecian world empire (9:1–10)

- The staggering vision of angels patrolling the earth in Zechariah 1:11

Jesus Christ is the main character of Zechariah. He is the One seen comforting God's people throughout the book. Not surprisingly, there are several Christophanies (pre-incarnate appearances of Jesus Christ) all throughout the book. Below are just a few:

1. Jesus is described as the branch in Zechariah 3:8, "Hear, O Joshua, the high priest, You and your companions who sit before you, for they are a wondrous sign; for behold, I am bringing forth My Servant the BRANCH." The Bible teaches us these facts about the Branch:

   - The Branch will be a man: Isaiah 4:2, "In that day the Branch of the LORD shall be beautiful and glorious; and the fruit of the earth shall be excellent and appealing for those of Israel who have escaped."

   - The Branch will be from Israel: Isaiah 53:2, "For He shall grow up before Him as a tender plant, and as a root out of dry ground. He has no form or comeliness; and when we see Him, there is no beauty that we should desire Him."

   - The Branch will build His temple: Ezekiel 40–43; Haggai 2.

2. Zechariah also described Jesus' entry in the Jerusalem on a colt in Zechariah 9:9, "Rejoice greatly, o daughter of Zion! Shout, o daughter of Jerusalem! Behold, your King is coming to you; He is just and having salvation, lowly and riding on a donkey, a colt, the foal of a donkey." This is exactly what happened when Jesus entered Jerusalem on Palm Sunday according to Matthew 21:1–5.

3. Jesus is described as God's smitten Shepherd, a clear reference to Jesus' torture and death, in Zechariah 13:7, "'Awake, o sword, against My Shepherd, against the Man who is My Companion,' says the LORD of hosts. 'Strike the Shepherd, and the sheep will be scattered; then I will turn My hand against the little ones.'"

4. Zechariah mentions Judas' betrayal of Jesus for thirty pieces of silver in Zechariah 11:12, "Then I said to them, 'If it is agreeable to you, give me my wages; and if not, refrain.' So they weighed out for my wages thirty pieces of silver."

5. Zechariah predicted that Jesus' hands would be pierced in His crucifixion death. Zechariah 12:10 states, "And I will pour on the house of David and on the inhabitants of Jerusalem the Spirit of grace and supplication; then they will look on Me whom they pierced. Yes, they will mourn for Him as one mourns for his only son, and grieve for Him as one grieves for a firstborn."

6. The prophet predicted that the Jews, Christ's own people, would ultimately be saved. We see this very clearly in Zechariah 13:1, "In that day a fountain shall be opened for the house of David and for the inhabitants of Jerusalem, for sin and for uncleanness."

7. Zechariah mentions that Jesus would be rejected by His own people in his first coming (Zechariah 13:6, "And one will say to him, 'What are these wounds between your arms?' Then he will answer, 'Those with which I was wounded in the house of my friends.'").

8. Zechariah also predicts that Jesus' Second Coming will take place on the Mount of Olives. Zechariah 14:3-4 reads, "Then the LORD will go forth and fight against those nations, as He fights in the day of battle. And in that day His feet will stand on the Mount of Olives, which faces Jerusalem on the east. And the Mount of Olives shall be split in two, from east to west, making a

very large valley; half of the mountain shall move toward the north and half of it toward the south."

More Prophecy in Zechariah

Besides mentioning this long list of facts that pertain directly to Jesus Christ, Zechariah also reveals to us several other prophecies about the future of the world in general. Take a look:

1. **The restoration and protection of Israel.** In Zechariah 8:8, we read "I will bring them back, and they shall dwell in the midst of Jerusalem. They shall be My people and I will be their God, in truth and righteousness," while 10:9 continues, "I will sow them among the peoples, and they shall remember Me in far countries; they shall live, together with their children, and they shall return."

2. **The evil reign of the Antichrist.** Zechariah 11:16 relates, "For indeed I will raise up a shepherd in the land who will not care for those who are cut off, nor seek the young, nor heal those that are broken, nor feed those that still stand. But he will eat the flesh of the fat and tear their hooves in pieces."

3. **The role of Jerusalem in the final battle of Armageddon.** In Zechariah 14:2 we learn, "For I will gather all the nations to battle against Jerusalem; the city shall be taken, the houses rifled, and the women ravished. Half of the city shall go into captivity, but the remnant of the people shall not be cut off from the city." Zechariah 12:3 echoes this theme: "And it shall happen in that day that I will make Jerusalem a very heavy stone for all peoples; all who would heave it away will surely be cut in pieces, though all nations of the earth are gathered against it."

4. **Two-thirds of the Jews will perish in the Tribulation.** In Zechariah 13:8 we read, "And it shall come to pass in all the land,' says the LORD, 'that two-thirds in it shall be

cut off and die, but one- third shall be left in it."

5. **Gentiles will worship God.** Zechariah 14:16 relates, "And it shall come to pass that everyone who is left of all the nations which came against Jerusalem shall go up from year to year to worship the King, the LORD of hosts, and to keep the Feast of Tabernacles."

6. **Jesus will build His Temple.** "Yes, He shall build the temple of the LORD. He shall bear the glory, and shall sit and rule on His throne; so He shall be a priest on His throne, and the counsel of peace shall be between them both" (Zechariah 6:13).

Zechariah's Eight Night Visions

One additional feature in the pages of Zechariah is the account of eight remarkable visions the prophet received directly from the Lord in just one night. His eight visions were the following:

1. **The rider on the red horse in Zechariah 1:7–17.** Zechariah 1:8 states, "I saw by night, and behold, a man riding on a red horse, and it stood among the myrtle trees in the hollow; and behind him were horses: red, sorrel, and white." This vision seems to refer to an appearance of Jesus Christ Himself, along with some angels, while they kept watch over Jerusalem.

2. **The four horns and the four craftsmen in Zechariah 1:18–21.** The horns are instruments of discipline that God used to scatter his people. These were foreign nations that oppressed Israel: Assyria (which captured the northern kingdom); Babylon (which captured the southern kingdom); Persia (which plotted against all the Jews according to the book of Esther); and Rome (which has scattered Israel and will do so again in the future).

3. **The man with the measuring line in Zechariah 2:1-13.** This is a reference to the measuring of Jerusalem during

the Millennium (cf. Ezekiel 40:1–5; 48:30–35).

4. **The clothing of Joshua, the high priest, in Zechariah 3:1–10.** Joshua represented the nation of Israel. In this passage, Satan was pointing out Israel's unfaithfulness and its unworthiness of God's favor. But God's answer was that He had chosen Israel and that His people would be saved in the end. Joshua's dirty clothes are symbolic of the nation's sinfulness and apostasy. By putting clean clothes on the high priest, God was declaring that he would cleanse the entire nation of Israel in the future. He will accomplish this through the Branch, Jesus Christ.

5. **The golden lampstands and the two live trees in Zechariah 4:1-14.** This vision seems to have two possible meanings. Historically, it probably referred to the anointed team of Zerubbabel and Joshua. Prophetically, it probably refers to the anointed team of Moses and Elijah during the Tribulation in Revelation 11:3-12.

6. **The flying scroll in Zechariah 5:1–4.** Zechariah saw a scroll with the same measurements as the tabernacle flying through the land. This scroll had writing on both sides. Its purpose was to curse the land of those who swore and stole.

7. **The woman in the ephah in Zechariah 5:5–11.** Zechariah saw an ephah or commercial measuring device, which further confirmed the sinfulness of the nations and the need for judgment. The woman he described was the personification of evil, so he slammed the lid back down on the basket. In verses 9-11 two women with stork wings came and flew away with the basket and put it on a pedestal in Shinar (where the tower of Babel was built).

8. **The four chariots in Zechariah 6:1–8.** There were four heavenly spirits (angels) driving the chariots, proceeding from two brass mountains. The chariots may represent the first four plagues of Revelation 6 and the mountains the judgment of God.

Hopefully, this chapter has given you a basic overview of the background and the prophetic content of the book of Zechariah. In the remaining chapters of this volume, we will explore Zechariah's book in more depth. May the Lord sanctify you and cause you to grow as you diligently study and apply His Word.

Discussion Questions

1. When does Zechariah's ministry occur in the history of Israel? What parallels can you draw between this time in Israel's history and current society?

2. What is a prophecy? Why is prophecy important to the Christian faith?

3. What does prophecy teach us about God's character?

4. What is the meaning of the name "Zechariah"? Why is this significant?

5. Who is the main character of the book of Zechariah? What does the book teach us about Him?

6. What other prophecies mentioned in this chapter caught your attention? Why?

That's Not All

You can find sermon outlines and other extras in the "Sermonars" section at the back of the book. These pages may be freely reproduced, either from the book or from the accompanying CD-ROM for any devotional or ministry use.

Mr. Z and Jesus

Chapter Two

The Rider on the Red Horse

1 In the eighth month of the second year of Darius, the word of the LORD came to Zechariah the son of Berechiah, the son of Iddo the prophet, saying, 2 "The LORD has been very angry with your fathers. 3 Therefore say to them, 'Thus says the LORD of hosts: "Return to Me," says *the LORD of hosts, "and I will return to you," says the LORD of hosts. 4 "Do not be like your fathers, to whom the former prophets preached, saying, 'Thus says the LORD of hosts: "Turn now from your evil ways and your evil deeds."' But they did not hear nor heed Me," says the LORD.*

5 " Your fathers, where are they?
And the prophets, do they live forever?
6 Yet surely My words and My statutes,
Which I commanded My servants the prophets,
Did they not overtake your fathers?
"So they returned and said:
' Just as the LORD of hosts determined to do to us,
According to our ways and according to our deeds,
So He has dealt with us.""'"

7 On the twenty-fourth day of the eleventh month, which is the month Shebat, in the second year of Darius, the word of the LORD came to Zechariah the son of Berechiah, the son of Iddo the prophet: 8 I saw by night, and behold, a man rid-

ing on a red horse, and it stood among the myrtle trees in the hollow; and behind him were horses: red, sorrel, and white. 9 Then I said, "My lord, what are these?" So the angel who talked with me said to me, "I will show you what they are." 10 And the man who stood among the myrtle trees answered and said, "These are the ones whom the LORD has sent to walk to and fro throughout the earth."

11 So they answered the Angel of the LORD, who stood among the myrtle trees, and said, "We have walked to and fro throughout the earth, and behold, all the earth is resting quietly."

12 Then the Angel of the LORD answered and said, "O LORD of hosts, how long will You not have mercy on Jerusalem and on the cities of Judah, against which You were angry these seventy years?"

13 And the LORD answered the angel who talked to me, with good and comforting words. 14 So the angel who spoke with me said to me, "Proclaim, saying, 'Thus says the LORD of hosts:

> *" I am zealous for Jerusalem*
> *And for Zion with great zeal." (Zech 1:1-14)*

Promises are to be kept no matter the cost. This is true of us; this is especially true of God. The book of Zechariah is all about God keeping His promises to His chosen nation and people. God always keeps His word. He does not lie or make mistakes. What God says will happen can be counted on to come to pass.

Chastisement and Comfort

Because of their disobedience, the Jews had been in captivity in Babylon for seventy years, just as the Lord had promised them years earlier through the prophet Jeremiah in Jeremiah 29:10-14,

> For thus says the LORD: after seventy years are completed at Babylon, I will visit you and perform My good word toward you, and cause you to return to this place. For I know the thoughts that I think toward you, says the LORD, thoughts of peace and not of evil, to give you a future and a hope. Then you will call upon Me and go and pray to Me, and I will listen to you. And you will seek Me and find Me, when you search for Me with all your heart. I will be found by you, says the LORD, and I will bring you back from your captivity; I will gather you from all the nations and from all the places where I have driven you, says the LORD, and I will bring you to the place from which I cause you to be carried away captive.

It is interesting to note that seventy years in captivity was not all the Lord had promised the Jews through Jeremiah in the passage above. He promised them future deliverance and restoration as well. In His kindness and faithfulness to His chosen people, the Lord promised them not only punishment but also healing and forgiveness. Not surprisingly, this is the same type of message we find in Zechariah—both chastisement and a call to repentance. Read carefully Zechariah's opening words in 1:1–14.

> In the eighth month of the second year of Darius, the word of the LORD came to Zechariah the son of Berechiah, the son of Iddo the prophet, saying, "The LORD has been very angry with your fathers. Therefore say to them, 'Thus says the LORD of hosts: "Return to Me," says the LORD of hosts, "and I will return to you," says the LORD of hosts. "Do not be like your fathers, to whom the former prophets preached, saying, 'Thus says the LORD of hosts: "Turn now from your evil ways and your evil deeds." 'But they did not hear nor heed Me,' says the LORD. "Your fathers, where are they? And the prophets, do they live forever? Yet surely My words and My statutes, which I commanded My servants the

prophets, did they not overtake your fathers? So they returned and said: 'Just as the LORD of hosts determined to do to us, according to our ways and according to our deeds, so He has dealt with us.'" On the twenty-fourth day of the eleventh month, which is the month Shebat, in the second year of Darius, the word of the LORD came to Zechariah the son of Berechiah, the son of Iddo the prophet: I saw by night, and behold, a man riding on a red horse, and it stood among the myrtle trees in the hollow; and behind him were horses: red, sorrel, and white. Then I said, "My lord, what are these?" So the angel who talked with me said to me, "I will show you what they are." And the man who stood among the myrtle trees answered and said, "These are the ones whom the LORD has sent to walk to and fro throughout the earth." So they answered the Angel of the LORD, who stood among the myrtle trees, and said, "We have walked to and fro throughout the earth, and behold, all the earth is resting quietly." Then the Angel of the LORD answered and said, "O LORD of hosts, how long will You not have mercy on Jerusalem and on the cities of Judah, against which You were angry these seventy years?" And the LORD answered the angel who talked to me, with good and comforting words. So the angel who spoke with me said to me, "Proclaim, saying, 'Thus says the LORD of hosts: "I am zealous for Jerusalem and for Zion with great zeal."'"

Comfort Only by Repentance

Zechariah makes it very clear that only through repentance we can receive God's comfort. This requirement exists because sin separates us from God, building a barrier between our total depravity and God's perfect holiness. Therefore, unless we repent and confess our rebelliousness before the Lord, He cannot take us back. Otherwise, God would be denying His own nature. Sin rightfully brings the anger and judgment of God. We see this very clearly in Zechariah 1:2-4. Read it again:

> The LORD has been very angry with your fathers. Therefore say to them, "Thus says the LORD of hosts: 'Return to Me,' says the LORD of hosts, 'and I will return to you,' says the LORD of hosts. 'Do not be like your fathers, to whom the former prophets preached, saying, "Thus says the LORD of hosts: Turn now from your evil ways and your evil deeds." 'But they did not hear nor heed Me,'" says the LORD.

What was true in the days of Zechariah remains true today. There is no comfort from God in our lives unless we turn from sin. Isaiah 59:1-2 states, "Behold, the LORD's hand is not shortened, that it cannot save; nor His ear heavy, that it cannot hear. But your iniquities have separated you from your God; and your sins have hidden His face from you, so that He will not hear." This was true in Isaiah's and Zechariah's time, and it is still true today. After all, God does not change.

We must break the sins of our past and cancel the generational sins that may have plagued our families in previous generations. But how exactly do we do that? We accomplish this by turning our backs on sin and our hearts to God. Zechariah 1:5-6 reads,

> Your fathers, where are they? And the prophets, do they live forever? Yet surely My words and My statutes, which I commanded My servants the prophets, did they not overtake your fathers? So they returned and said: "Just as the LORD of hosts determined to do to us, according to our ways and according to our deeds, so He has dealt with us."

Let's be very clear about the meaning of this passage for us today. If you return to God, He is faithful enough to forgive whatever you have done in the past. There is no bondage the Lord cannot break.

God's promises mean that He will both bless and curse us depending on our obedience or disobedience to Him. When God, in Jeremiah 29:7-12, promised Israel that they would be in captivity for seventy years, He was declaring to the people of Israel that His judgment on their disobedience was a sure thing. It was going to happen. They were going to face some serious consequences for their repeated disloyalty to God.

But at the same time, God also declared to them that He would not punish them forever. If they returned to Him, He would take them back and forgive all their transgressions. In the same way that God's judgment is sure, so are His promises of forgiveness and healing. We see this very clearly in 2 Chronicles 36:14-23. Read it very carefully:

> Moreover all the leaders of the priests and the people transgressed more and more, according to all the abominations of the nations, and defiled the house of the LORD which He had consecrated in Jerusalem. And the LORD God of their fathers sent warnings to them by His messengers, rising up early and sending them, because He had compassion on His people and on His dwelling place. But they mocked the messengers of God, despised His words, and scoffed at His prophets, until the wrath of the LORD arose against His people, till there was no remedy. Therefore He brought against them the king of the Chaldeans, who killed their young men with the sword in the house of their sanctuary, and had no compassion on young man or virgin, on the aged or the weak; He gave them all into his hand. And all the articles from the house of God, great and small, the treasures of the house of the LORD, and the treasures of the king and of his leaders, all these he took to Babylon. Then they burned the house of God, broke down the wall of Jerusalem, burned all its palaces with fire, and destroyed all its precious possessions. And those who escaped from the

sword he carried away to Babylon, where they became servants to him and his sons until the rule of the kingdom of Persia, to fulfill the word of the LORD by the mouth of Jeremiah, until the land had enjoyed her Sabbaths. As long as she lay desolate she kept Sabbath, to fulfill seventy years. Now in the first year of Cyrus king of Persia, that the word of the LORD by the mouth of Jeremiah might be fulfilled, the LORD stirred up the spirit of Cyrus king of Persia, so that he made a proclamation throughout all his kingdom, and also put it in writing, saying, Thus says Cyrus king of Persia: All the kingdoms of the earth the LORD God of heaven has given me. And He has commanded me to build Him a house at Jerusalem which is in Judah. Who is among you of all His people? May the LORD his God be with him, and let him go up!

Comfort, therefore, is one of the major themes of the book of Zechariah. In fact, we can outline the entire book around this theme. Take a look:

• Comfort by a call to repentance - 1:1-6

• Comfort to Israel through visions - 1:7-6:15

• Comfort through counsel regarding fasts - 7:1-8:23

• Comfort in the coming events and Jesus' first and second comings - 9:1-14:21

With the above outline in mind, let us continue our journey through the book of Zechariah by taking a look at the prophet's first vision. First, we notice that the vision was the word of the Lord. We see this very clearly in Zechariah 1:7, which states, "On the twenty-fourth day of the eleventh month, which is the month Shebat, in the second year of Darius, the word of the LORD came to Zechariah the son of Berechiah, the son of Iddo the prophet."

A prophetic vision is an awareness of reality beyond the human senses. It is extra-spiritual and physical insight that allows the person having the vision to look into the future before it happens. Zechariah had a vision, as did many Old Testament prophets and patriarchs. Through this vision, the Lord revealed to him a special message that He wanted the prophet to proclaim to the Jewish people.

What Does It Mean?

Zechariah's first vision revealed to him part of God's divine plan for Jerusalem and for Israel. Zechariah 1:8-9 describes what it was that the prophet saw, "I saw by night, and behold, a man riding on a red horse, and it stood among the myrtle trees in the hollow; and behind him were horses: red, sorrel, and white. Then I said, 'My lord, what are these?' So the angel who talked with me said to me, 'I will show you what they are.'"

First, we notice that Zechariah saw a man. Even though some scholars debate the identity of this man, the Scriptures seem to indicate that this is a reference to an Old Testament appearance of the second person of the Trinity, Jesus Christ Himself. Thus, Jesus appeared to Zechariah riding on a red horse. In the Bible, horses often represent war. Coincidently, we also see a rider on a red horse in the book of Revelation. Take a look at Revelation 6:1-4.

> Now I saw when the Lamb opened one of the seals; and I heard one of the four living creatures saying with a voice like thunder, "Come and see." And I looked, and behold, a white horse. He who sat on it had a bow; and a crown was given to him, and he went out conquering and to conquer. When He opened the second seal, I heard the second living creature saying, "Come and see." Another horse, fiery red, went out. And it was granted to the one who sat on it to take peace from the earth, and that people should kill one another; and there was given to him a great sword.

Verse 8 also states that the man stood among the myrtle

trees in the hollow. This type of tree was the most common bush in Israel. It can grow up to eight feet tall, and it is the plant promised in the Millennium (Isaiah 49:19; 55:13). In this particular vision, the myrtle tree seems to represent Jerusalem. The Angel of the Lord was thus standing in the midst of Israel, rousing the angelic squadron on her behalf ("and behind him were horses: red, sorrel, and white"). This seems to imply that angels keep a protective watch over Jerusalem and Israel. The white horse reminds us of the ultimate victory of Israel.

Zechariah 1:10 states, "And the man who stood among the myrtle trees answered and said, 'These are the ones whom the LORD has sent to walk to and fro throughout the earth.'" This is fascinating! God's angels walk to and fro throughout the earth, keeping watch on the people. This is true not only of holy angels, but also of Satan himself. We see this in Job 1:6-7, "Now there was a day when the sons of God came to present themselves before the LORD, and Satan also came among them. And the LORD said to Satan, 'From where do you come?' So Satan answered the LORD and said, 'From going to and fro on the earth, and from walking back and forth on it.'" There is a spiritual battle that goes on continually in the unseen world. We must never forget that.

Verse 11 reveals to us that the focus of this vision is on the Angel of the Lord. It reads, "So they answered the Angel of the LORD, who stood among the myrtle trees, and said, 'We have walked to and fro throughout the earth, and behold, all the earth is resting quietly.'" As briefly mentioned above, the angel of the Lord is God the Son, the pre-incarnate Jesus Christ. In the Old Testament times, every Jew knew that the Angel of the Lord was the protector of Israel. He is always before the Father pleading on behalf of His people. The slave Hagar called the Angel of the Lord the "God Who Sees" in Genesis 16:13. In the midst of her despair, the Angel had seen her suffering and came to help her. This is clearly in agreement with Psalm 34:7, which states, "The angel of the LORD encamps all around those who fear

Him, and delivers them."

We see the Angel of the Lord's interceding ministry very clearly in Zechariah 1:12-14.

> Then the Angel of the LORD answered and said, "O LORD of hosts, how long will You not have mercy on Jerusalem and on the cities of Judah, against which You were angry these seventy years?" And the LORD answered the angel who talked to me, with good and comforting words. So the angel who spoke with me said to me, "Proclaim, saying, 'Thus says the LORD of hosts: "I am zealous for Jerusalem and for Zion with great zeal.""'"

We can make at least two key observations based on the verses above. First, the Angel pleaded before God the Father, asking for mercy on Jerusalem and Judah. Second, we also notice that God is greatly jealous of Jerusalem and Zion. He will not sit back and let Israel be ultimately destroyed. God has a very special place in His heart for the Jew, Israel, and Jerusalem. He will not let anything or anyone (not even the Jews themselves) thwart His plans for them.

Therefore, Zechariah's first night vision teaches us at least four main things:

1. Jesus is the Protector and Deliverer of Israel.

2. Jesus intercedes for Israel.

3. Jesus will comfort Israel.

4. In many ways, Jesus' protective ministry to Israel parallels His relationship with the church. In 1 John 2:1 we read, "My little children, these things I write to you, so that you may not sin. And if anyone sins, we have an Advocate with the Father, Jesus Christ the righteous."

Discussion Questions

1. How were both chastisement and comfort part of God's message to the Jews through the prophets? Explain.

2. Explain in your own words why we can only receive God's comfort through personal repentance.

3. What does it mean to repent? How exactly can we do that? (Take a look at 2 Corinthians 7:9–11 before answering)

4. What is a prophetic vision?

5. Who is the Angel of the Lord? What is part of His role?

6. Identify some other examples of a pre-incarnate appearance of Christ in the Old Testament.

That's Not All

You can find sermon outlines and other extras in the "Sermonars" section at the back of the book. These pages may be freely reproduced, either from the book or from the accompanying CD-ROM for any devotional or ministry use.

Mr. Z and Jesus

Chapter Three

The Times of the Gentiles: Horns, Craftsmen, and Israel

Then I raised my eyes and looked, and there were four horns. And I said to the angel who talked with me, "What are these?" So he answered me, "These are the horns that have scattered Judah, Israel, and Jerusalem." Then the LORD showed me four craftsmen. And I said, "What are these coming to do?" So he said, "These are the horns that scattered Judah, so that no one could lift up his head; but the craftsmen are coming to terrify them, to cast out the horns of the nations that lifted up their horn against the land of Judah to scatter it."

These are the words of Zechariah's second vision from Zechariah 1:18-21. These images combine to create one of the most fascinating prophecies in the entire Old Testament. Among other things, this powerful passage implies that God uses ungodly nations ("the horns") to accomplish His purposes.

God's Protective Hand

Our God is so powerful that He can guide the nations—including those that do not know Him—in order to accomplish His plans. This assurance of God's power should give us great comfort, especially in our day and age, when the political situation in the Middle East is so volatile. No matter how dangerous or hopeless Israel's situation might seem, we can have the confidence that God will preserve His people until the end. This assurance should not lead us to conclude that God will never allow hardships to befall the Jews. Instead, this means that even when the Jews are attacked by their enemies, the Lord remains in control and will not let those attacks go too far.

God's preservation of the Israeli nation can be easily seen throughout history. Several nations and leaders have tried to exterminate Israel, but none has ever succeeded. What has hindered their success? Various explanations might be offered, but believers understand that God's unseen hand is on His people, functioning as a protective wall on their behalf. Nothing can ever penetrate God's protective wall without the Lord's permission.

The Times of the Gentiles

The most prominent feature in Zechariah's second vision is the horns. These horns represent nations, in this case the nations that would come and scatter Judah, Israel, and Jerusalem. This vision fits perfectly with what Jesus stated in Luke 21:24: "And they will fall by the edge of the sword, and be led away captive into all nations. And Jerusalem will be trampled by Gentiles until the times of the Gentiles are fulfilled." Even though they used different terminology, both Jesus and Zechariah referred to a period of time called the "Times of the Gentiles." This is a period in history when the nation of Israel is constantly under some degree of bondage to Gentile world powers. This long period of time began with the Babylonian captivity that we read about in the Old Testament, and it will end with the Second Coming of Jesus Christ. This means that we are living right now in the Times of the Gentiles. We can be sure of that interpretation for several reasons:

1. The Babylonian captivity, which began the Times of the Gentiles, took place thousands of years ago.

2. The Second Coming of Christ, which will end the Times of the Gentiles, is still future.

3. Israel has never possessed the fullness of its inheritance as promised in the Palestinian Covenant of Deuteronomy 30:3.

4. Israel does not dwell in peace in its land.

5. Gentile nations have dominated that part of the world since Nebuchadnezzar, and they will—to some degree—hold power over it until Jesus comes again.

6. The rule of the Antichrist will end the Times of the Gentiles at the Second Coming of Christ. Dr. J. Dwight Pentecost comments, "In Luke 21:24 the Lord indicates that Jerusalem will continue in Gentile domination 'until the times of the Gentiles be fulfilled.' Zechariah 12:2 and 14:2, 3 indicate that this will not be until the Second Advent, when the armies of the Beast are destroyed by the Lord, as He is seen to do in Revelation 19:17-19."[1]

The Four Horns in Zechariah 1:18-19

In Zechariah 1:18-19, the horns are symbols of power referring to both Gentile Kings and nations. This same symbolism—horns as powerful nations—appears several places in the Bible. Take a look:

- Jeremiah 48:25, "'The horn of Moab is cut off, and his arm is broken,' says the LORD."

- Lamentations 2:3, "He has cut off in fierce anger every horn of Israel; He has drawn back His right hand from before the enemy. He has blazed against Jacob like a flaming fire devouring all around."

- Psalm 75:10, "All the horns of the wicked I will also cut off, but the horns of the righteous shall be exalted."

- Zechariah 1:19 states, "And I said to the angel who talked with me, 'What are these?' So he answered me, 'These are the horns that have scattered Judah, Israel, and Jerusalem.'"

The verb "scattered" in this last verse is in the past tense. In Hebrew, the verb was originally in the perfect tense, referring to a completed action in the past, present, and future. As He gave this vision to Zechariah, God treated this prophecy as a certain event, even though at that time most of its fulfillment was still future.

Commenting on Zechariah's second vision, Dr. Henry Halley writes,

> The Four Horns represent the Nations that had destroyed Judah and Israel. The Four Smiths ('carpenters') represent God's Destroyers of those nations. It was a figurative way of saying that prevailing World-Powers would be broken, and Judah again be exalted. God is on the throne, even when His people are temporarily vanquished.[2]

Thus, the horns in this passage represent Gentile nations that have afflicted and conquered Israel throughout its history. Significantly, this is the same type of language and prophecy we find featured in the book of Daniel. Bible teacher Warren Wiersbe explains the historical realities behind Zechariah's vision:

> The concept of four horns (nations) reminds us of Daniel's visions of the image (Daniel 2) and the beasts

(Daniel 7), both of which speak of four empires: Babylon, Medo-Persia, Greece, and Rome. In 722, Assyria devastated the Northern Kingdom of Israel, but God raised up Babylon to defeat Assyria (Jer. 25:9; 27:6) and eventually take Judah in captivity in 586. Babylon did indeed oppress the Jews, but then God raised up Cyrus to conquer Babylon in 539 (Isa. 44:28; 45:1); and in 538, he permitted the Jews to return to their land. The Persians were conquered by the Greeks under Alexander the Great, and Greece was conquered by Rome.[3]

Historically, therefore, Israel's four afflicting nations or horns were the following:

1. The Babylonian Empire

2. The Medo-Persian Empire

3. The Greek Empire

4. The Roman Empire and the future, revived Roman Empire

Horns & Little Horns in Daniel

The four empires mentioned above are the same four nations that Daniel described in his prophecy. Daniel 7:21, for instance, states, "I was watching; and the same horn was making war against the saints, and prevailing against them." Contextually, this verse seems to refer to the Antichrist, who will align himself with the revived Roman Empire in order to make final war against the Tribulation saints and against Israel. Consider also the following key passages from the book of Daniel:

> The ten horns are ten kings who shall arise from this kingdom. And another shall rise after them; he shall be different from the first ones, and shall subdue three kings (Daniel 7:24).

You, O king, were watching; and behold, a great image! This great image, whose splendor was excellent, stood before you; and its form was awesome. This image's head was of fine gold, its chest and arms of silver, its belly and thighs of bronze, its legs of iron, its feet partly of iron and partly of clay. You watched while a stone was cut out without hands, which struck the image on its feet of iron and clay, and broke them in pieces. Then the iron, the clay, the bronze, the silver, and the gold were crushed together, and became like chaff from the summer threshing floors; the wind carried them away so that no trace of them was found. And the stone that struck the image became a great mountain and filled the whole earth. This is the dream. Now we will tell the interpretation of it before the king. You, O king, are a king of kings. For the God of heaven has given you a kingdom, power, strength, and glory; and wherever the children of men dwell, or the beasts of the field and the birds of the heaven, He has given them into your hand, and has made you ruler over them all—you are this head of gold. But after you shall arise another kingdom inferior to yours; then another, a third kingdom of bronze, which shall rule over all the earth. And the fourth kingdom shall be as strong as iron, inasmuch as iron breaks in pieces and shatters everything; and like iron that crushes, that kingdom will break in pieces and crush all the others. Whereas you saw the feet and toes, partly of potter's clay and partly of iron, the kingdom shall be divided; yet the strength of the iron shall be in it, just as you saw the iron mixed with ceramic clay (Daniel 2:31–41).

Many people find this sort of prophetic symbolism to be baffling; however, one of the reasons that God uses such symbolism is to provide a visual cue to readers. It makes sense, then, that we should employ a visual representation, the diagram on the next page, to better understand what

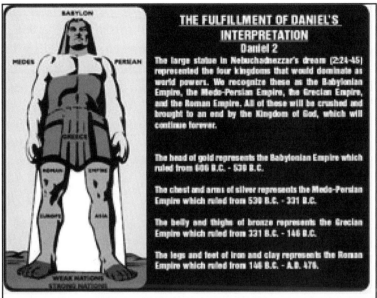

THE FULFILLMENT OF DANIEL'S
INTERPRETATION
Daniel 2

The large statue in Nebuchadnezzar's dream (2:24-45) represented the four kingdoms that would dominate as world powers. We recognize these as the Babylonian Empire, the Medo-Persian Empire, the Grecian Empire, and the Roman Empire. All of these will be crushed and brought to an end by the Kingdom of God, which will continue forever.

The head of gold represents the Babylonian Empire which ruled from 606 B.C. - 539 B.C.

The chest and arms of silver represents the Medo-Persian Empire which ruled from 539 B.C. - 331 B.C.

The belly and thighs of bronze represents the Grecian Empire which ruled from 331 B.C. - 146 B.C.

The legs and feet of iron and clay represents the Roman Empire which ruled from 146 B.C. - A.D. 476.

Daniel was describing in the verses we read previously. The Empires that make up the statue are the same horns Zechariah referred to in his second vision.

Besides giving us more details about the horns that Zechariah mentioned in Zechariah 1:18-21, Daniel provides one more piece of information, the mention of a final empire—God's own kingdom. At His Second Coming, Jesus Christ will set up His kingdom, defeat the Antichrist, and bring the Times of the Gentiles to an end. Daniel wrote, in Daniel 2:44, "And in the days of these kings the God of heaven will set up a kingdom which shall never be destroyed; and the kingdom shall not be left to other people; it shall break in pieces and consume all these kingdoms and it shall stand forever."

The Four Craftsmen in Zechariah 1:20-21

Besides the horns, the Lord also showed Zechariah four craftsmen. To understand this image, let us refer back to Zechariah 1:20-21 once again.

Then the LORD showed me four craftsmen. And I said,

'What are these coming to do?' So he said, 'These are the horns that scattered Judah, so that no one could lift up his head; but the craftsmen are coming to terrify them, to cast out the horns of the nations that lifted up their horn against the land of Judah to scatter it.'"

Commenting on these verses, John Phillips writes:

> Next Zechariah saw four 'carpenters' (1:20)—that is, ironsmiths—and again he requested an explanation. The 'carpenters' symbolize those who would be raised up to "fray [terrify]" the world powers responsible for terrifying the Jews through the centuries (1:21). In the vision the Jews were so maltreated "that no man did lift up his head." The Lord showed Zechariah that God has His own instruments for cutting even superpowers down to size. The repatriated Jews were living proof. The Babylonian empire, which had deported them, had collapsed like a house of cards. God eventually pulls down all nations that persecute or ill-treat the Jews.[4]

Who were the craftsmen? The four craftsmen represent four leaders who have or will defeat or master the nations represented by the four horns. Historically, there are three rulers that seem to adequately fit the roles prescribed for them by Zechariah. The fourth ruler's triumph is the only one that remains in the future. The four craftsmen, then, can be identified with great confidence as follows:

1. Cyrus, who defeated Babylon (Daniel 5)

2. Alexander the Great, who defeated Persia

3. Various Roman generals who subdued Greece

4. Jesus Christ, who will destroy the revived Roman Empire under Antichrist's reign

This second vision of Zechariah represents an important truth for the believer. God's powerful protection extends over the nation of Israel even through the centuries when He has allowed the Gentile nations to chastise and dominate His chosen people. God has raised up four horns, or nations, who have dominated Israel. He has already raised up three craftsmen, or leaders, who have defeated the first three of those horns. We can, with absolute confidence, trust in God's promise that the fourth craftsmen, Jesus Christ Himself, will appear to bring an end to the fourth horn, the Antichrist's revived Roman Empire. God's promises never fail and His power is absolute.

Discussion Questions

1. Zechariah 1:13 describes God's words to the prophet as "good and comforting." What comfort can we find in Zechariah's second vision?

2. What is the Time of the Gentiles?

3. What are the beginning and ending points for the Time of the Gentiles?

4. How do we know we are living in the Time of the Gentiles right now?

5. How do we know that the word "horn" refers to nations?

6. What are the four main nations that have afflicted Israel throughout its history?

7. How do we know that the word "craftsman" refers to leaders?

8. Who are the four craftsmen identified in Zechariah's prophecy.

9. Explain in your own words the connection between Zechariah's second vision and Daniel's prophecy.

That's Not All

You can find sermon outlines and other extras in the "Sermonars" section at the back of the book. These pages may be freely reproduced, either from the book or from the accompanying CD-ROM for any devotional or ministry use.

Chapter Four

A Wall of Fire: Discovering God's Protection

1 Then I raised my eyes and looked, and behold, a man with a measuring line in his hand. 2 So I said, "Where are you going?"

And he said to me, "To measure Jerusalem, to see what is its width and what is its length."

3 And there was the angel who talked with me, going out; and another angel was coming out to meet him, 4 who said to him, "Run, speak to this young man, saying: 'Jerusalem shall be inhabited as towns without walls, because of the multitude of men and livestock in it. 5 For I,' says the LORD, 'will be a wall of fire all around her, and I will be the glory in her midst.'"

6 "Up, up! Flee from the land of the north," says the LORD; "for I have spread you abroad like the four winds of heaven," says the LORD. 7 "Up, Zion! Escape, you who dwell with the daughter of Babylon."

8 For thus says the LORD of hosts: "He sent Me after glory, to the nations which plunder you; for he who touches you touches the apple of His eye. 9 For surely I will shake My hand against them, and they shall become spoil for their servants.

Then you will know that the LORD of hosts has sent Me.

10 "Sing and rejoice, O daughter of Zion! For behold, I am coming and I will dwell in your midst," says the LORD. 11 "Many nations shall be joined to the LORD in that day, and they shall become My people. And I will dwell in your midst. Then you will know that the LORD of hosts has sent Me to you. 12 And the LORD will take possession of Judah as His inheritance in the Holy Land, and will again choose Jerusalem. 13 Be silent, all flesh, before the LORD, for He is aroused from His holy habitation!" (Zech 2:1-13)

The Apple of God's Eye

We live in an age when prophecy is being fulfilled before our very eyes. Unfortunately, many skeptics prefer to explain away the fulfillment of significant prophetic events, denying that they have been brought about by God Himself. But what do we make of the fact that the nation of Israel, for instance, is still in existence even though it is surrounded by enemy nations, nations that have attacked it time and time again? I believe that it takes more faith to attribute the preservation of Israel throughout history to fate than to God. The Lord's promise to protect Israel becomes very evident as we consider Zechariah's second vision.

> Then I raised my eyes and looked, and behold, a man with a measuring line in his hand. So I said, "Where are you going?" And he said to me, "To measure Jerusalem, to see what is its width and what is its length." And there was the angel who talked with me, going out; and another angel was coming out to meet him, who said to him, "Run, speak to this young man, saying: 'Jerusalem shall be inhabited as towns without walls, because of the multitude of men and livestock in it. For I,' says the LORD, 'will be a wall of fire all around her, and I will be the glory in her midst.'" "Up, up! Flee from the land of the north," says the LORD;

"for I have spread you abroad like the four winds of heaven," says the LORD. "Up, Zion! Escape, you who dwell with the daughter of Babylon." For thus says the LORD of hosts: "He sent Me after glory, to the nations which plunder you; for he who touches you touches the apple of His eye. "For surely I will shake My hand against them, and they shall become spoil for their servants. Then you will know that the LORD of hosts has sent Me. "Sing and rejoice, O daughter of Zion! For behold, I am coming and I will dwell in your midst," says the LORD. "Many nations shall be joined to the LORD in that day, and they shall become My people. And I will dwell in your midst. Then you will know that the LORD of hosts has sent Me to you. And the LORD will take possession of Judah as His inheritance in the Holy Land, and will again choose Jerusalem. Be silent, all flesh, before the LORD, for He is aroused from His holy habitation." (Zechariah 2:1-13)

Isaiah's Stunning Prophecies

One of the most important principles of Bible interpretation is that "Scripture interprets Scripture." This means that when we come across certain Bible passages that we find difficult to understand, the best thing we can do is to allow other portions of Scripture to guide us. In other words, clearer biblical passages help us better comprehend and appreciate more obscure passages. This is especially important concerning Zechariah's vision. In order to better understand what this second vision means, we must allow the prophet Isaiah to come to our aid with his own prophetic material. After all, the messages preached by both prophets (Zechariah and Isaiah) are closely connected. In fact, we could even say that these two prophets complement each other.

Many people call Isaiah the "Mount Everest of the Old Testament," since it seems to resemble the content of the entire Bible. In many ways, Isaiah's first thirty-nine chapters correspond to thirty-nine books of the Old Testament, stressing the righteousness, holiness, and justice of God. Isaiah's last twenty-seven chapters, on the other hand, seem to correspond to the twenty-seven books of the New Testament, portraying God's glory and giving us many prophecies concerning the promised Messiah. Not surprisingly, therefore, Isaiah has been called the Old Testament equivalent of the Apostle Paul.

Isaiah was a contemporary of Hosea and Micah. He prophesied the doom of the Northern Kingdom of Israel, a prophecy that was fulfilled in 722 BC. He also warned Judah of impending judgment, not by Assyria but by Babylonia, even though at that time Babylonia had not yet even risen to power. Like Zechariah, Isaiah predicted that the Lord would preserve His people even as they were chastised for their disobedience. Consider carefully the following interesting prophecies made by Isaiah:

1. **Paths in the sea:** Isaiah 43:15–16, "I am the Lord, your Holy One, the Creator of Israel, your King. Thus says the Lord, who makes a way in the sea and a path through the mighty waters."

2. **The earth is round:** Isaiah 40:22, "It is He who sits above the circle of the earth, and its inhabitants are like grasshoppers, who stretches out the heavens like a curtain, and spreads them out like a tent to dwell in."

3. **Nuclear warfare predicted:** Isaiah 24:6, "Therefore the curse has devoured the earth, and those who dwell in it are desolate. Therefore the inhabitants of the earth are burned, and few men are left." Interestingly enough, Zechariah's prophecies also seem to include nuclear warfare in Zechariah 14:12, which states, "And this shall be the plague with which the Lord will strike all the people who fought against Jerusalem: Their flesh shall dissolve while they stand on their feet, their eyes shall dissolve in their sockets, and their tongues shall

dissolve in their mouths."

4. **The destruction of Tyre:** Isaiah 23:1, "The burden against Tyre. Wail, you ships of Tarshish! For it is laid waste, so that there is no house, no harbor; from the land of Cyprus it is revealed to them."

5. **The Jewish Babylonian captivity and return:** Isaiah 39:6, "'Behold, the days are coming when all that is in your house, and what your fathers have accumulated until this day, shall be carried to Babylon; nothing shall be left,' says the LORD." See also Isaiah 44:28 and 13:19, where Isaiah identified the name of Cyrus, a key Persian king, years before he was born and Babylon's future destruction by Persia.

6. **Numerous prophecies about Jesus:** Isaiah 7:14, "Therefore the Lord Himself will give you a sign: behold, the virgin shall conceive and bear a Son, and shall call His name Immanuel."

7. **The future rebirth of the nation of Israel:** Isaiah 66:8, "Who has heard such a thing? Who has seen such things? Shall the earth be made to give birth in one day? Or shall a nation be born at once? For as soon as Zion was in labor, she gave birth to her children."

Jerusalem: God's Eternal City (Zechariah 2:1-4)

One of the key areas of agreement among all of the Old Testament prophets is God's guarantee that He will forever preserve the existence of His chosen people. In fact, this is seen throughout the Old Testament. At many points, for instance, God makes it very clear that He has chosen Jerusalem to be His eternal city. This is exactly what we see in the first four verses describing Zechariah's second vision.

Then I raised my eyes and looked, and behold, a man with a measuring line in his hand. So I said, "Where are you going?" And he said to me, "To measure Jerusalem, to see what is its width and what is its length." And there was the angel who talked with me, going out; and another angel was coming out to meet him, who said to him, "Run, speak to this young man, saying: 'Jerusalem shall be inhabited as towns without walls, because of the multitude of men and livestock in it.'"

Jerusalem is the place the Lord has chosen to be His Holy City, the location that will serve as the center of Jesus' millennial kingdom on earth. Consider also the following key verses that reveal God's passion for David's City:

- Psalm 132:13-14, "For the LORD has chosen Zion; He has desired it for His dwelling place."

- Psalm 137:4, "How shall we sing the LORD's song in a foreign land? If I forget you, O Jerusalem, let my right hand forget its skill! If I do not remember you, let my tongue cling to the roof of my mouth—if I do not exalt Jerusalem above my chief joy."

- Psalm 48:2-3, "Beautiful in elevation, the joy of the whole earth, is Mount Zion on the sides of the north, the city of the great King. God is in her palaces; He is known as her refuge."

- Psalm 102:13, 16, "You will arise and have mercy on Zion; for the time to favor her, yes, the set time, has come. For the LORD shall build up Zion; He shall appear in His glory."

- Daniel 9:26, "And after the sixty-two weeks Messiah shall be cut off, but not for Himself; and the people of the prince who is to come shall destroy the city and the sanctuary. The end of it shall be with a flood, and till the end of the war desolations are determined."

Besides being God's eternal city, Jerusalem will also be the location of the final battle of Armageddon. Mankind's darkest hour and greatest war have not happened yet. Armageddon will happen outside of Jerusalem in the plain of Megiddo. That will be mankind's most severe war. The Scriptures state that the blood shed on that battle will be as deep as the bridle of a horse, stretching for 200 miles. This unique catastrophe in human history will only be brought to an end by the return of Jesus Christ Himself. Zechariah wrote about those dark days in Zechariah 12:2-4.

> "Behold, I will make Jerusalem a cup of drunkenness to all the surrounding peoples, when they lay siege against Judah and Jerusalem. And it shall happen in that day that I will make Jerusalem a very heavy stone for all peoples; all who would heave it away will surely be cut in pieces, though all nations of the earth are gathered against it. In that day," says the LORD, "I will strike every horse with confusion, and its rider with madness; I will open My eyes on the house of Judah, and will strike every horse of the peoples with blindness."

Not even the battle of Armageddon, however, will be able to utterly destroy the city of Jerusalem. God's Holy City will be glorified and remodeled after Jesus' Second Coming. Zion will then become the central location of Jesus' millennial kingdom:

- Isaiah 1:26, "I will restore your judges as at the first, and your counselors as at the beginning. Afterward you shall be called the city of righteousness, the faithful city."

- Isaiah 4:3-4, "And it shall come to pass that he who is left in Zion and remains in Jerusalem will be called holy—everyone who is recorded among the living in Jerusalem. When the Lord has washed away the filth of the daughters of Zion, and purged the blood of Jerusalem from her midst, by the spirit of judgment and by the spirit of burning."

• Isaiah 62:2, 4, 11–12, "The Gentiles shall see your righteousness, and all kings your glory. You shall be called by a new name, which the mouth of the Lord will name. You shall no longer be termed Forsaken, nor shall your land any more be termed Desolate; but you shall be called Hephzibah, and your land Beulah; for the Lord delights in you, and your land shall be married. Indeed the Lord has proclaimed to the end of the world: 'Say to the daughter of Zion, "Surely your salvation is coming; behold, His reward is with Him, and His work before Him."' And they shall call them The Holy People, The Redeemed of the Lord; and you shall be called Sought Out, A City Not Forsaken."

What do we learn from these verses? Someday an unfathomable multitude will be gathered in to dwell in the millennial Jerusalem. Even animals will dwell there, as seen in Zechariah 2:2–3 (above) and the city will be established as God's special possession, as we described in Zechariah 2:12: "And the Lord will take possession of Judah as His inheritance in the Holy Land, and will again choose Jerusalem."

A Wall of Fire around Her (Zechariah 2:4–5)

But how is it possible for Jerusalem to be preserved when it has gone through so many attacks in the past and will go through even worse things in the future? This is because God has placed a spiritual wall, a wall of fire, which surrounds and protects His city. This is exactly what Zechariah was referring to in Zechariah 2:4–5: "Who said to him, 'Run, speak to this young man, saying: "Jerusalem shall be inhabited as towns without walls, because of the multitude of men and livestock in it. For I," says the Lord, "will be a wall of fire all around her, and I will be the glory in her midst."'"

Even after the Babylonian captivity, when the physical walls of Jerusalem were destroyed, the Lord continued to protect His Holy City with a spiritual wall of fire. The

Jewish remnant that decided to leave Babylon and return to their destroyed city enjoyed sixty-six years of protection from God until Nehemiah rebuilt the walls of Jerusalem. Those who decided to stay out of God's will in Babylon, however, were killed when Babylon fell before the Persian Empire. This historical lesson stands as a great reminder that when we are walking in obedience, God has a wall of fire around us. When we are out of his will—when we choose Babylon over Jerusalem– however, we are placing ourselves outside of His care for us.

The idea of a protective wall of fire around us reminds me of the amazing story we read in 2 Kings 6:11-17.

> Therefore the heart of the king of Syria was greatly troubled by this thing; and he called his servants and said to them, "Will you not show me which of us is for the king of Israel?" And one of his servants said, "None, my lord, O king; but Elisha, the prophet who is in Israel, tells the king of Israel the words that you speak in your bedroom." So he said, "Go and see where he is, that I may send and get him.' And it was told him, saying, "Surely he is in Dothan." Therefore he sent horses and chariots and a great army there, and they came by night and surrounded the city. And when the servant of the man of God arose early and went out, there was an army, surrounding the city with horses and chariots. And his servant said to him, "Alas, my master! What shall we do?" So he answered, "Do not fear, for those who are with us are more than those who are with them." And Elisha prayed, and said, "LORD, I pray, open his eyes that he may see." Then the LORD opened the eyes of the young man, and he saw. And behold, the mountain was full of horses and chariots of fire all around Elisha.

Land of the North: God's Punishment (Zechariah 2:6-8)

It is also important to notice that God's protection over Jerusalem did not mean that He was going to overlook the disobedience of His people. In other words, the Lord was not promising to protect Jerusalem from the coming conflicts but through those conflicts. We can see this very clearly in Zechariah 2:6-8, "Up, up! Flee from the land of the north," says the Lord; "for I have spread you abroad like the four winds of heaven," says the Lord. "Up, Zion! Escape, you who dwell with the daughter of Babylon. For thus says the Lord of hosts: 'He sent Me after glory, to the nations which plunder you; for he who touches you touches the apple of His eye." God made it very clear in these verses that He was the One who had spread the Jews abroad because of their sinfulness. But even in the midst of God's judgment, the Jews found grace and were preserved from complete destruction.

God's Man: The Messiah (Zechariah 2:1, 8-11)

Zechariah's second vision goes on to describe God's ultimate plans for His people. The prophet recorded these plans in Zechariah 2:9-11:

> "For surely I will shake My hand against them, and they shall become spoil for their servants. Then you will know that the Lord of hosts has sent Me. Sing and rejoice, O daughter of Zion! For behold, I am coming and I will dwell in your midst," says the Lord. "Many nations shall be joined to the Lord in that day, and they shall become My people. And I will dwell in your midst. Then you will know that the Lord of hosts has sent Me to you."

In this passage and elsewhere, God has promised that someday he will literally dwell among His people. But how exactly is that possible if God is spirit and no one can see Him? It is possible because God will dwell with the Saints through the incarnation of God the Son, Jesus Christ. After all, Jesus' name is Immanuel, which means "God with us" (Matthew 1:23).

As we read this promise of God dwelling with His people in the form of Jesus Christ, it seems reasonable to infer that the man Zechariah mentioned in 2:1 ("Then I raised my eyes and looked, and behold, a man with a measuring line in his hand.") was a reference to Jesus Christ Himself. This is not the only time this man appears in Zechariah's book. Actually, we see Him repeatedly throughout the book:

- Zechariah 2:1, "Then I raised my eyes and looked, and behold, a man with a measuring line in his hand."

- Zechariah 2:8, "He sent Me after glory..."

- Zechariah 2:9, "Then you will know that the Lord of hosts has sent Me."

- Zechariah 2:10, "'Sing and rejoice, O daughter of Zion! For behold, I am coming and I will dwell in your midst,' says the LORD."

- Zechariah 2:11b, "Then you will know that the Lord of hosts has sent Me to you."

God's Ultimate Victory: Christ's Kingdom (Zechariah 2:11-12)

After describing some of the hardships God's people will go through, Zechariah closes his second vision with a reference to God's ultimate victory at the End Times. Zechariah 2:11-12 states, "Many nations shall be joined to the LORD in that day, and they shall become My people. And I will dwell in your midst. Then you will know that the LORD of hosts has sent Me to you. And the LORD will take possession of Judah as His inheritance in the Holy Land, and will again choose Jerusalem."

The millennial kingdom (spanning 1,000 years) will take place in Jerusalem after the battle of Armageddon and Jesus' Second Coming (cf. Isaiah 49:19; 44:26; Jeremiah 31:23–25). Jesus Himself, God's Messiah, will reign in His Temple from the New Jerusalem. What a great reminder that God's plans will triumph over man's sinfulness. His peace will overcome our wars. Someday, God will dwell with us, and His presence will be our constant wall of fire!

Discussion Questions

1. In your own words, explain the principle of biblical interpretation that states that "Scripture interprets Scripture." What does that mean? Why is this important?

2. Why is it important to study Zechariah's prophecies in light of other prophetic books, including Isaiah?

3. Explain the concept of God's "wall of fire." How can we apply this to our lives? What are the limits to this wall of fire? Looking back, in what ways have you seen God's wall of fire in your own life? What difference did it make?

4. Who was the man measuring Jerusalem in Zechariah 2:1? Why was he measuring the city?

5. Read Zechariah 2:11–12 one more time paying attention to the promises made.

6. How should these promises make a difference in the way you live your life today?

That's Not All

You can find sermon outlines in the "Sermonars" section at the back of the book. These pages may be freely reproduced, either from the book or from the accompanying CD-ROM for any devotional or ministry use.

Chapter Five

The Angel of the Lord: Who Is It?

1 Then he showed me Joshua the high priest standing before the Angel of the LORD, and Satan standing at his right hand to oppose him. 2 And the LORD said to Satan, "The LORD rebuke you, Satan! The LORD who has chosen Jerusalem rebuke you! Is this not a brand plucked from the fire?"

3 Now Joshua was clothed with filthy garments, and was standing before the Angel.

4 Then He answered and spoke to those who stood before Him, saying, "Take away the filthy garments from him." And to him He said, "See, I have removed your iniquity from you, and I will clothe you with rich robes."

5 And I said, "Let them put a clean turban on his head."

So they put a clean turban on his head, and they put the clothes on him. And the Angel of the LORD stood by.

6 Then the Angel of the LORD admonished Joshua, saying, 7 "Thus says the LORD of hosts:

> *'If you will walk in My ways,*
> *And if you will keep My command,*
> *Then you shall also judge My house,*

And likewise have charge of My courts;
I will give you places to walk
Among these who stand here.
8 ' Hear, O Joshua, the high priest,
You and your companions who sit before you,
For they are a wondrous sign;
For behold, I am bringing forth My Servant the
BRANCH.
9 For behold, the stone
That I have laid before Joshua:
Upon the stone are seven eyes.
Behold, I will engrave its inscription,'
Says the LORD of hosts,
' And I will remove the iniquity of that land in one
day.
10 In that day,' says the LORD of hosts,
' Everyone will invite his neighbor
Under his vine and under his fig tree.'" (Zechariah
3:1-10)

The 10 Greatest Prophecies Regarding Israel/Jews

Before we take a look at Zechariah's fourth vision, it is
important for us to keep in mind the magnitude of God's
promises to judge the nation of Israel because of their rebellion. Consider, therefore, the ten greatest Old Testament
prophecies regarding the Jews, paying special attention to
the nature of each individual prophecy (i.e., did it promise
a blessing or a curse?).

1. Jesus prophesied that the Temple would be destroyed
   in Matthew 24:1-2, "Then Jesus went out and departed
   from the temple, and His disciples came up to show
   Him the buildings of the temple. And Jesus said to
   them, 'Do you not see all these things? Assuredly, I say
   to you, not one stone shall be left here upon another,
   that shall not be thrown down.'" This prophecy was

recorded in AD 30 and fulfilled 40 years later, in AD 70 when a Roman army razed the temple.

2. Jesus said that Jerusalem would be destroyed in Luke 21:24, "And they will fall by the edge of the sword, and be led away captive into all nations. And Jerusalem will be trampled by Gentiles until the times of the Gentiles are fulfilled." This prophecy was also recorded in AD 30 and fulfilled 40 years later, in AD 70 by the same Roman army.

3. Like Jesus, Daniel also foretold the destruction of Jerusalem and the Temple in Daniel 9:26, "And after the sixty-two weeks Messiah shall be cut off, but not for Himself; and the people of the prince who is to come shall destroy the city and the sanctuary. The end of it shall be with a flood, and till the end of the war desolations are determined." This prophecy was made in 530 BC, centuries before its fulfillment in AD 70.

4. The prophet Micah predicted that Jerusalem would be destroyed and "plowed like a field." We find this prophecy in Micah 3:11-12, "Her heads judge for a bribe, her priests teach for pay, and her prophets divine for money. Yet they lean on the LORD, and say, 'Is not the LORD among us? No harm can come upon us.' Therefore because of you Zion shall be plowed like a field, Jerusalem shall become heaps of ruins, and the mountain of the temple like the bare hills of the forest." Micah wrote these words between 750 and 686 BC, and they were fulfilled centuries later in AD 135.

5. The Bible foreshadowed Rome's destruction of Israel in Deuteronomy 28:49-52:

"The LORD will bring a nation against you from afar, from the end of the earth, as swift as the eagle flies, a nation whose language you will not understand, a nation of fierce countenance, which does not respect the elderly nor show favor to the young. And they shall eat the increase of your livestock and the produce of your land, until you are destroyed; they shall not leave you grain or new wine or oil, or the increase of your cattle or the offspring of your flocks, until they have destroyed you. They shall besiege you at all your gates until your high and fortified walls, in which you trust, come down throughout all your land; and they shall besiege you at all your gates throughout all your land which the LORD your God has given you."

Moses wrote these words about 1400 BC, and they were fulfilled when the Romans attacked Jerusalem in AD 70.

6. Moses also foretold that Israel would become a wasteland in Deuteronomy 29:23, "The whole land is brimstone, salt, and burning; it is not sown, nor does it bear, nor does any grass grow there, like the overthrow of Sodom and Gomorrah, Admah, and Zeboim, which the LORD overthrew in His anger and His wrath." This prophecy was also written about 1400 BC and fulfilled between AD 135 and 1800.

7. God promised through Moses that the people of Israel would be exiled, scorned, and ridiculed in Deuteronomy 28:36-37, "The LORD will bring you and the king whom you set over you to a nation which neither you nor your fathers have known, and there you shall serve other gods—wood and stone. And you shall become an astonishment, a proverb, and a byword among all nations where the LORD will drive you." This was predicted about 1400 BC and fulfilled between AD 135 and 1900.

8. The land of Israel would be inhabited by enemies. We find this prophecy in Leviticus 26:31-32, "I will lay your cities waste and bring your sanctuaries to desolation, and I will not smell the fragrance of your sweet

aromas. I will bring the land to desolation, and your enemies who dwell in it shall be astonished at it." This prophecy was also written by Moses about 1400 BC. Its fulfillment started in AD 135, continuing to this day.

All of the prophecies listed above have to do with God's judgment on Israel because of their sins. But all hope is not lost. God has also promised to preserve His people and to restore them in the future.

9. The prophet Isaiah foretold that the people of Israel will never cease to be a nation in Jeremiah 31:33, "But this is the covenant that I will make with the house of Israel after those days, says the LORD: I will put My law in their minds, and write it on their hearts; and I will be their God, and they shall be My people." This prophecy was written between 626 and 586 BC.

10. The exiled people of Israel would return to Israel. We find this prophecy in several places throughout the Old Testament, including Jeremiah 32:37-41:

"Behold, I will gather them out of all countries where I have driven them in My anger, in My fury, and in great wrath; I will bring them back to this place, and I will cause them to dwell safely. They shall be My people, and I will be their God; then I will give them one heart and one way, that they may fear Me forever, for the good of them and their children after them. And I will make an everlasting covenant with them, that I will not turn away from doing them good; but I will put My fear in their hearts so that they will not depart from Me. Yes, I will rejoice over them to do them good, and I will assuredly plant them in this land, with all My heart and with all My soul."

The Cleansing & Restoration of Israel

God's promise to cleanse and restore Israel in the future gives us the background against which we can understand every other Old Testament prophecy regarding the Jews. Without the certainty of Israel's future restoration (prophecies 9 and 10, above), all the other prophecies (prophecies 1-8) lose their true meaning. This is why Zechariah's fourth vision is so important. It gives us a better understanding of God's future plans for His people after they have been disciplined for their iniquities. Read carefully Zechariah 3:1-10.

> Then he showed me Joshua the high priest standing before the Angel of the LORD, and Satan standing at his right hand to oppose him. And the LORD said to Satan, "The LORD rebuke you, Satan! The LORD who has chosen Jerusalem rebuke you! Is this not a brand plucked from the fire?" Now Joshua was clothed with filthy garments, and was standing before the Angel. Then He answered and spoke to those who stood before Him, saying, "Take away the filthy garments from him." And to him He said, "See, I have removed your iniquity from you, and I will clothe you with rich robes." And I said, "Let them put a clean turban on his head." So they put a clean turban on his head, and they put the clothes on him. And the Angel of the LORD stood by. Then the Angel of the LORD admonished Joshua, saying, "Thus says the LORD of hosts: 'If you will walk in My ways, and if you will keep My command, then you shall also judge My house, and likewise have charge of My courts; I will give you places to walk among these who stand here. Hear, O Joshua, the high priest, you and your companions who sit before you, for they are a wondrous sign; for behold, I am bringing forth My Servant the BRANCH. For behold, the stone that I have laid before Joshua: upon the stone are seven eyes. Behold, I will engrave its inscription,' Says the LORD of hosts, 'And I will remove

the iniquity of that land in one day. In that day,' says the LORD of hosts, 'Everyone will invite his neighbor under his vine and under his fig tree.'"

The main theme of Zechariah's fourth vision is God's promise that He will cleanse His people some time in the future and make them a holy nation once again. This holiness is precisely what the high priest's clothes represent. Before the Lord intervened, the high priest, representing the whole nation of Israel, was dressed in filthy garments (i.e., their sins). But the Lord gave the high priest clean clothes, restoring him—and the entire nation—to a new relationship with Him.

Whereas the first three visions we have studied deal primarily with the physical elements of the Temple, the fourth vision speaks of Israel's future cleaning and restoration. Dr. J. Vernon McGee comments:

> This vision of Joshua the high priest actually goes beyond the man himself. We will learn that this vision gives us the answer to a very difficult question. This is the problem: We have learned so far that God is going to return the nation of Israel to the land and that He will dwell in the midst of them. They will be totally restored as His people. That hasn't happened yet, but He says He is going to do that.[1]

The Accused: Joshua the High Priest

According to Zechariah 3:1–2, there are three main characters in Zechariah's fourth vision: Joshua the high priest, Satan, and the Angel of the Lord. As Israel's representative, Joshua was being accused by Satan and defended by the Angel of the Lord. All the charges that Satan was presenting against Joshua also applied to the entire nation of Israel.

Joshua, whose name means "Jehovah saves," is the same person as Jeshua, who appears in the books of Ezra and Nehemiah (Haggai 1:1; Ezra 5:1; Zechariah 6:11). He was the current high priest at the time. As such, Joshua represented the sinful nation of Israel, viewed as covered with sin. Along with the other priests, God wanted to use Joshua as a sign to all the Jews. This is why we read in verse 8, "Hear, O Joshua, the high priest, you and your companions who sit before you, for they are a wondrous sign; for behold, I am bringing forth My Servant the BRANCH." H. C. Leupold explains:

> He represents and practically impersonates Israel in his holy office. For the nation he prays; for it he enters the Holy Place, he bears the nation's guilt. We must, therefore, not refer the issues and implications of this chapter to Joshua as an individual, nor merely to Joshua, the high priest. We must conclude that his condition is Israel's condition, his acquittal a typical way of expressing theirs; the words of comfort and assurance given him apply with equal validity to them.[2]

In Zechariah 3:1 we read that Joshua the high priest was standing before the Angel of the Lord. This seems to be a reference to his role as a representative of the entire Jewish people. Among other things, it was Joshua's job to "stand" before God, to offer sacrifices, to sprinkle the blood of atonement, and to intercede daily as he offered incense before the veil. Unfortunately, Joshua was not truly ready in God's eyes to perform his priestly duties. Zechariah 3:3-5 describes Joshua as being clothed with filthy garments. He was so polluted by sin that he could not do his job. This is why the Lord commanded him to take away his filthy clothes so he could put on new ones.

The Hebrew word commonly translated filthy also meant "excrement." This is one of the strongest words in the Hebrew language, describing something detestable and loathsome. But by God's grace, all that filth will be removed some day and pure garments will clothe God's people. In order for that to happen, however, Israel will have to come to the point of truly repenting from their sins. We see this in

Zechariah 3:6-7, "Then the Angel of the LORD admonished Joshua, saying, 'Thus says the LORD of hosts: "If you will walk in My ways, and if you will keep My command, then you shall also judge My house, and likewise have charge of My courts; I will give you places to walk among these who stand here.""""

Thus, God made it very clear that there is cleansing where there is genuine repentance from sin! This principle applies not only to Joshua and Israel but also to believers today. God replaces our sins with His royalty when we forsake our iniquity and return to Him with broken hearts. Once again, McGee explains, "Joshua represented not only the nation of Israel, he represents us today. In him we see the sin of the believer. Joshua was a priest before God – God appointed priests in the Old Testament. In our day every believer is a priest before God, but some of us are standing in dirty garments."[3]

The Accuser: Satan

Joshua was not the only one standing before God in Zechariah's fourth vision. According to verse 1, Satan was also there in order to oppose him. The name Satan means "adversary," which describes his primary work against believers. Therefore, Satan seeks to oppose, accuse, and destroy God and all that belongs to Him. We also see this very clearly in John 8:44, "You are of your father the devil, and the desires of your father you want to do. He was a murderer from the beginning, and does not stand in the truth, because there is no truth in him. When he speaks a lie, he speaks from his own resources, for he is a liar and the father of it."

Satan is constantly seeking to destroy us. The most appropriate response to demonic warfare in our lives, therefore, is to draw closer to the Lord and let Him rebuke Satan. We are not strong enough to fight against Satan and His demons apart from God's power. Take a look:

• Zechariah 3:2, "And the LORD said to Satan, "The

LORD rebuke you, Satan! The LORD who has chosen Jerusalem rebuke you! Is this not a brand plucked from the fire?"

- 1 John 2:1, "My little children, these things I write to you, so that you may not sin. And if anyone sins, we have an Advocate with the Father, Jesus Christ the righteous."

- 1 John 4:4, "You are of God, little children, and have overcome them, because He who is in you is greater than he who is in the world."

- James 4:7–8, "Therefore submit to God. Resist the devil and he will flee from you. Draw near to God and He will draw near to you. Cleanse your hands, you sinners; and purify your hearts, you double-minded."

The Angel of the Lord: Jesus Christ

Besides Joshua and Satan, there is also a third key character mentioned in Zechariah's fourth vision: The Angel of the Lord. Take a look at Zechariah 3:8–10 one more time:

> "Hear, O Joshua, the high priest, you and your companions who sit before you, for they are a wondrous sign; for behold, I am bringing forth My Servant the BRANCH. For behold, the stone that I have laid before Joshua: upon the stone are seven eyes. Behold, I will engrave its inscription," says the LORD of hosts, "And I will remove the iniquity of that land in one day. In that day," says the LORD of hosts, "Everyone will invite his neighbor under his vine and under his fig tree."

The "Branch" in verse 8 represents Jesus Christ, the Angel of the Lord and our Messiah. Take a look:

- Isaiah 11:1–2, "There shall come forth a Rod from the stem of Jesse, and a Branch shall grow out of his roots.

The Spirit of the LORD shall rest upon Him, the Spirit of wisdom and understanding, the Spirit of counsel and might, the Spirit of knowledge and of the fear of the LORD."

• Jeremiah 23:5-6, "'Behold, the days are coming,' says the LORD, 'That I will raise to David a Branch of righteousness; a King shall reign and prosper, and execute judgment and righteousness in the earth. In His days Judah will be saved, and Israel will dwell safely; now this is His name by which He will be called: THE LORD OUR RIGHTEOUSNESS.'"

Jesus is also represented as a "stone" in verse 9. Jesus is the foundation and chief cornerstone of the church (Ephesians 2:19-22). The Prophet Daniel also described the Messiah as a stone in Daniel 2:34-35.

You watched while a stone was cut out without hands, which struck the image on its feet of iron and clay, and broke them in pieces. Then the iron, the clay, the bronze, the silver, and the gold were crushed together, and became like chaff from the summer threshing floors; the wind carried them away so that no trace of them was found. And the stone that struck the image became a great mountain and filled the whole earth.

To the Jews at His first coming, Jesus was a stumbling block and a rock of offense (Isaiah 8:13-15; Psalm 118:22-23; Matthew 21:42; 1 Peter 2:7-8). Upon the stone there were also "seven eyes" (verse 9). This seems to be a reference to the fullness of the Holy Spirit, symbolizing infinite intelligence and omniscience.

Verse 9 ends with the promise that the Lord will remove the iniquity of the land in one day. How exactly is He going to accomplish that? God will—and in fact already has—removed the iniquity of those who believe in Jesus through Calvary, where Jesus died for our sins. This cleansing will be consummated through Christ's Second Coming, when

Jesus will vindicate God's justice and establish His Millennial kingdom.

Discussion Questions

1. What is the basic content of the top eight prophecies listed above? Why did the Lord promise that Israel would go through those things? What do the last two prophecies promise?

3. What is the basic content of Zechariah's fourth vision? Explain it in your own words.

4. Who were the three main characters in this fourth vision? Who was Joshua? What did he symbolize?

6. What is significant about Joshua's garments? How was the Lord going to cleanse them?

7. What is Satan's role in Zechariah's fourth vision? How can we stand against Satan today?

9. Who is the Angel of the Lord in this vision? What is his role in God's plan?

That's Not All

You can find sermon outlines in the "Sermonars" section at the back of the book. These pages may be freely reproduced, either from the book or from the accompanying CD-ROM for any devotional or ministry use.

Chapter Six

God's Two Olive Trees

1 Now the angel who talked with me came back and wakened me, as a man who is wakened out of his sleep. 2 And he said to me, "What do you see?"

So I said, "I am looking, and there is a lampstand of solid gold with a bowl on top of it, and on the stand seven lamps with seven pipes to the seven lamps. 3 Two olive trees are by it, one at the right of the bowl and the other at its left." 4 So I answered and spoke to the angel who talked with me, saying, "What are these, my lord?"

5 Then the angel who talked with me answered and said to me, "Do you not know what these are?"

And I said, "No, my lord."

6 So he answered and said to me:

> *"This is the word of the* Lord *to Zerubbabel:*
> *'Not by might nor by power, but by My Spirit,'*
> *Says the* Lord *of hosts.*
> *7 'Who are you, O great mountain?*
> *Before Zerubbabel you shall become a plain!*
> *And he shall bring forth the capstone*
> *With shouts of "Grace, grace to it!"'"*

8 Moreover the word of the Lord *came to me, saying:*

9 " The hands of Zerubbabel
Have laid the foundation of this temple;
His hands shall also finish it.
Then you will know
That the LORD of hosts has sent Me to you.
10 For who has despised the day of small things?
For these seven rejoice to see
The plumb line in the hand of Zerubbabel.
They are the eyes of the LORD,
Which scan to and fro throughout the whole earth."

11 Then I answered and said to him, "What are these two olive trees—at the right of the lampstand and at its left?" 12 And I further answered and said to him, "What are these two olive branches that drip into the receptacles of the two gold pipes from which the golden oil drains?"

13 Then he answered me and said, "Do you not know what these are?"

And I said, "No, my lord."

14 So he said, "These are the two anointed ones, who stand beside the Lord of the whole earth." (Zechariah 4:1-14)

The Interrogation in Chapter Four

As we move on to the fifth of the prophet Zechariah's visions, we find ourselves facing a passage full of questions. Chapter four opens with this next vision, one very different from those that have gone before. Read these verses carefully, paying special attention to the series of eight intriguing questions that are posed to the prophet:

Now the angel who talked with me came back and wakened me, as a man who is wakened out of his sleep. And he said to me, "What do you see?" So I said, "I am looking, and there is a lampstand of solid gold with a bowl on top of it, and on the stand seven lamps with seven pipes to the seven lamps. Two olive trees are by it, one at the right of the bowl and the other at its left." So I answered and spoke to the angel who talked with me, saying, "What are these, my lord?" Then the angel who talked with me answered and said to me, "Do you not know what these are?" And I said, "No, my lord." So he answered and said to me: "This is the word of the LORD to Zerubbabel: 'Not by might nor by power, but by My Spirit,' says the LORD of hosts. Who are you, O great mountain? Before Zerubbabel you shall become a plain! And he shall bring forth the capstone with shouts of "Grace, grace to it!"'" Moreover the word of the LORD came to me, saying: "The hands of Zerubbabel have laid the foundation of this temple; his hands shall also finish it. Then you will know that the LORD of hosts has sent Me to you. For who has despised the day of small things? For these seven rejoice to see the plumb line in the hand of Zerubbabel. They are the eyes of the LORD, which scan to and fro throughout the whole earth." Then I answered and said to him, "What are these two olive trees—at the right of the lampstand and at its left?" And I further answered and said to him, "What are these two olive branches that drip into the receptacles of the two gold pipes from which the golden oil drains?" Then he answered me and said, "Do you not know what these are?" And I said, "No, my lord." So he said, "These are the two anointed ones, who stand beside the Lord of the whole earth."

If you kept track correctly, you should have identified the following eight questions:

1. What do you see? (v. 1)

2. What are these, my Lord? (v. 3)

3. Do you know what these are? (v. 5)

4. Who are you, O great mountain? (v. 7)

5. For who has despised the day of the small things? (v. 10)

6. What are the two olive trees—at the right of the lampstand and at its left? (v. 11)

7. What are these two olive branches that drip into the receptacles or the two gold pipes from which the golden oil drains? (v. 12)

8. Do you know what these are? (v. 13)

To say that this passage sounds both intriguing and obscure is a serious understatement. When we first read the verses above we tend to become overwhelmed with so many different symbols, wondering what they actually mean. Not surprisingly, many Bible scholars consider this to be one of the hardest chapters to understand in the entire Bible. Even Zechariah was confused at first; hence all the questions we find in the passage. As we slowly make our way through these verses, however, answering these eight questions along the way, we can better understand Zechariah's fifth vision.

Why Was Zechariah Asleep? (4:1)

Chapter four opens by informing the reader that the prophet was asleep when the angel appeared to reveal this new vision to him. Zechariah's spiritual exhilaration from the previous visions wore him out, leading him to fall asleep. But after he got some much needed rest, the angel woke him up so he could receive a new vision. The news that Zechariah was awakened by the angel is important, because it tells us that God revealed His truth to Zechariah through visions, not dreams. His eyes were wide open when he saw God's revelation.

Why the Unique Lampstand? (4:2-4)

The first thing Zechariah saw after he woke up was a

very unique lampstand. Zechariah 4:2-4 reads,

> And he said to me, 'What do you see?' So I said, 'I am looking, and there is a lampstand of solid gold with a bowl on top of it, and on the stand seven lamps with seven pipes to the seven lamps. Two olive trees are by it, one at the right of the bowl and the other at its left.' So I answered and spoke to the angel who talked with me, saying, 'What are these, my lord?'

The lampstand Zechariah saw is based on the lampstand familiar to all the Jews from its use in Solomon's Temple and the Tabernacle before it. But at the same time, this specific lampstand is strangely different. On close examination, we will notice four differences. Zechariah's lampstand (1) had a bowl on top of it; (2) had pipes; (3) had two olive trees strategically placed at its right and left; and (4) also carried two distinct golden spouts or pipes.

The lampstand was made of solid gold, which suggests both purity and preciousness. There were seven lamps to the lampstand and seven pipes to each lamp. Therefore, the lampstand boasted a total of forty-nine pipes. The whole picture of this most unusual lampstand is intended to convey the thought of an unlimited supply which needed no human priests for replenishing the oil or wicks, completely unlike the lampstands in the Tabernacle or in the Temple, which the priests attended on a daily basis. Besides being self-sufficient, this lampstand was also incredibly luminous. After all, the larger the number of oil pipes, the brighter the light from the lampstand.

What, after all, did this amazing lampstand symbolize? It seems that the lampstand represented Israel as a holy nation, God's chosen vessel to shine forth the amazing light of the gospel in our dark world. From the very beginning of their existence, God designed the entire nation of Israel to be a kingdom of priests (Exodus 19:6, "'And you shall be to Me a kingdom of priests and a holy nation.' These are the words which you shall speak to the children of Israel.").

Through this vision, therefore, God was telling Zechariah that someday He would restore His people and fulfill His purpose through them.

In this vision, God was also communicating through Zechariah that the prophet Zerubbabel was going to get the project of rebuilding the Temple completed. This would happen not through the might or strength of man. Instead, the Temple would be completed through the power of the Holy Spirit alone. There was a bowl of oil on top of that unique lampstand. Neither a priest nor any other human being had to replenish the oil necessary to produce light. Spiritually, this signifies that the light we need comes directly from God the Father through the power of the Holy Spirit. What a great reminder that man's weakness is no hindrance to the work of God, since God supplies the power of the Holy Spirit to those who seek Him. The Apostle Paul reflected on this truth in 2 Corinthians 4:7, "But we have this treasure in earthen vessels, that the excellence of the power may be of God and not of us."

If the lampstand represented the nation of Israel, its light represented the true light of the world, the Lord Jesus Christ. Repeatedly throughout the Scriptures Jesus is described as God's true light. Take a look at just a few examples(emphases added):

- Isaiah 49:5, "And now the LORD says, who formed Me from the womb to be His Servant, to bring Jacob back to Him, so that Israel is gathered to Him (For I shall be glorious in the eyes of the LORD, and My God shall be My strength), indeed He says, 'It is too small a thing that You should be My Servant to raise up the tribes of Jacob, and to restore the preserved ones of Israel; I will also give You as a light to the Gentiles, that You should be My salvation to the ends of the earth.'"

- Luke 1:78, "Through the tender mercy of our God, with which the Dayspring from on high has visited us."

- Luke 2:32, "A light to bring revelation to the Gentiles, and the glory of Your people Israel."

- John 8:12, "Then Jesus spoke to them again, saying, 'I am the light of the world. He who follows Me shall not walk in darkness, but have the light of life.'"

To summarize what we have covered thus far:

- The lampstand represented Israel.

- The bowl full of oil symbolized the Holy Spirit. Oil can bring healing, light, and warmth to our lives. The same is also true of the Holy Spirit.

- The forty-nine channels (pipes) symbolized an unlimited supply of power from the Holy Spirit.

- The light that shone forth from the lampstand represented Jesus Christ.

Who Are the Olive Trees? (4:3, 11-14)

Another key element of this vision is the two olive trees placed on the right and left of the lampstand. Zechariah 4:3 tells us that "two olive trees are by it, one at the right of the bowl and the other at its left." In verses 11-14, we read more about the trees:

> Then I answered and said to him, 'What are these two olive trees—at the right of the lampstand and at its left?' And I further answered and said to him, 'What are these two olive branches that drip into the receptacles of the two gold pipes from which the golden oil drains?' Then he answered me and said, 'Do you not know what these are?' And I said, 'No, my lord.' So he said, 'These are the two anointed ones, who stand beside the Lord of the whole earth.'

A common Old Testament comparison is that of a man

to a tree (cf. Psa 1:3; 52:8; Jer 17:8; Dan 4:10). We know from verse 6 that the golden oil referred to in verse 12 represents the Holy Spirit. So who are these two human figures who are filled by the Spirit and play key roles in Israel's history?

Because of the historical context surrounding this passage, many scholars believe that the two witnesses were two men who played key roles in Israel's history at the time Zechariah had this vision. Some scholars, for instance, identify the two olive trees as Zechariah and Haggai, due to their great prophetic ministry at that time. Old Testament scholar Charles Feinberg, on the other hand, identifies the two olive trees as Joshua and Zerubbabel in their official capacities as God's channel through whom the Holy Spirit evidenced power and grace to the entire Israelite nation. J. Vernon McGee seems to agree with Feinberg when he writes, "The two olive trees were identified in Zechariah's day. Zerubbabel, who was the king in the line of David, is one of the olive trees. The other olive tree was Joshua, the high priest. They would be the two instruments God would use to bring light back into the nation of Israel and make them a light to the world."

But besides having a historical meaning, this vision also seems to have a prophetic (futuristic) interpretation. We see this very clearly in Revelation 11:1–5:

> Then I was given a reed like a measuring rod. And the angel stood, saying, "Rise and measure the temple of God, the altar, and those who worship there. But leave out the court which is outside the temple, and do not measure it, for it has been given to the Gentiles. And they will tread the holy city underfoot for forty-two months. And I will give power to my two witnesses, and they will prophesy one thousand two hundred and sixty days, clothed in sackcloth. These are the two olive trees and the two lampstands standing before the God of the earth. And if anyone wants to harm them, fire proceeds from their mouth and devours their enemies. And if anyone wants to harm them, he must be

killed in this manner."

Thus, prophetically the two olive trees referred to the two witnesses who will minister to the Jewish nation during the Tribulation in Revelation 11. Many understand these two men to be Moses and Elijah because of their unparalleled roles as two of Israel's greatest prophets.

Who was Zerubbabel? (4:6-10)

After focusing on the lampstand and on the two olive trees, Zechariah's attention was turned to Zerubbabel in Zechariah 4:6-10:

> So he answered and said to me: "This is the word of the LORD to Zerubbabel: 'Not by might nor by power, but by My Spirit,' says the LORD of hosts. 'Who are you, O great mountain? Before Zerubbabel you shall become a plain! And he shall bring forth the capstone with shouts of "Grace, grace to it!"' Moreover the word of the LORD came to me, saying: "The hands of Zerubbabel have laid the foundation of this temple; His hands shall also finish it. Then you will know that the LORD of hosts has sent Me to you. For who has despised the day of small things? For these seven rejoice to see the plumb line in the hand of Zerubbabel. They are the eyes of the LORD, which scan to and fro throughout the whole earth."

Whereas Joshua the high priest, whom we studied in the previous chapter, served as Israel's religious head, Zerubbabel was their main civil leader. He was the head of the tribe of Judah at the time when the Jews returned to Jerusalem after seventy years in captivity. In fact, it was Zerubbabel who led the first group of Jews to return to Jerusalem from Babylon.

Zerubbabel's great work was that of rebuilding the Temple. This important task, however, was constantly threatened by danger from the outside and discouragement from within. Israel's enemies were trying to keep the Temple from being rebuilt, while the people were struggling with internal motivation to get the Lord's work done. Thus, God was giving this vision to Zerubbabel through the prophet Zechariah to strengthen his faith as he led the people. God wanted to remind Zerubbabel that he should not depend on human efforts alone to get the work done. In verse 6, the Lord specifically told Zechariah that it was not by might (the strength of many) or by power (the strength of one) that the Temple would be rebuilt, but by His Spirit. This verse serves as a great reminder that the Lord always enables us to accomplish what He was called us to do through the enabling ministry of the Holy Spirit.

What Is Your Mountain? (4:7)

In light of God's promise to enable Zerubbabel to get the work done through the power of the Spirit, God asked a very reassuring question in Zechariah 4:7, "Who are you, O great mountain? Before Zerubbabel you shall become a plain! And he shall bring forth the capstone with shouts of 'Grace, grace to it!'"

The mountain in this verse represents the adversity and opposition that Zerubbabel faced as he led those Jewish exiles back to Jerusalem from Babylon to rebuild the Temple. At several times in his book, Ezra records the mountain of opposition Zerubbabel faced and overcame by God's Spirit. The following are just a few:

- Ezra 4:1-4, "Now when the adversaries of Judah and Benjamin heard that the descendants of the captivity were building the temple of the LORD God of Israel, they came to Zerubbabel and the heads of the fathers' houses, and said to them, 'Let us build with you, for we seek your God as you do; and we have sacrificed to Him since the days of Esarhaddon king of Assyria, who brought us here.' But Zerubbabel and Jeshua and the rest of the heads of the fathers' houses of Israel said to them, 'You may do nothing with us to build a house for our God; but we alone will build to the LORD God of Israel, as King Cyrus the king of Persia has commanded us.' Then the people of the land tried to discourage the people of Judah. They troubled them in building."

- Ezra 4:6, "In the reign of Ahasuerus, in the beginning of his reign, they wrote an accusation against the inhabitants of Judah and Jerusalem."

- Ezra 4:24, "Thus the work of the house of God which is at Jerusalem ceased, and it was discontinued until the second year of the reign of Darius king of Persia."

By asking where the great mountain was, the Lord was promising Zerubbabel that there was no adversity too strong for him to overcome. But if victory was such a sure thing, why did God allow Zerubbabel to face so much opposition in the first place? He did so because through those struggles Zerubbabel and the entire Jewish nation were forced to turn to God and to rely on Him for strength. Even though we might hate facing the mountains of opposition in our lives, it is in the process of overcoming them that we get rid of all attempts to be self-sufficient and that we are able to experience God in a new way. Paul put this profound biblical truth so well in Philippians 4:13: "I can do all things through Christ who strengthens me."

Discussion Questions

1. Why is it significant that Zechariah was asleep at the beginning of chapter 4?

2. Describe the unique lampstand Zechariah saw. What was it like? What was it made of? How was it unique?

3. What elements made this lampstand different from the one that stood in Solomon's Temple?

4. Explain in your own words the meaning of the following: the lampstand, the light, the bowl full of oil, the forty-nine pipes.

5. Who are the two Olive Trees both historically and prophetically? What role will they have in the Tribulation?

6. Who was Zerubbabel? What was his task? Why did the Lord want to encourage him?

7. What is your "great mountain"? What has God called you to do and what is keeping you from accomplishing it? How do you think God wants you to overcome that (cf. Zech 4:6)?

That's Not All

You can find sermon outlines and other extras in the "Sermonars" section at the back of the book. These pages may be freely reproduced, either from the book or from the accompanying CD-ROM for any devotional or ministry use.

Chapter Seven

The Flying Scroll: What in the World Is It?

1 Then I turned and raised my eyes, and saw there a flying scroll.
2 And he said to me, "What do you see?"
So I answered, "I see a flying scroll. Its length is twenty cubits and its width ten cubits."
3 Then he said to me, "This is the curse that goes out over the face of the whole earth: 'Every thief shall be expelled,' according to this side of the scroll; and, 'Every perjurer shall be expelled,' according to that side of it."

> *4 " I will send out the curse," says the LORD of hosts;*
> *" It shall enter the house of the thief*
> *And the house of the one who swears falsely by My name.*
> *It shall remain in the midst of his house*
> *And consume it, with its timber and stones."*

5 Then the angel who talked with me came out and said to me, "Lift your eyes now, and see what this is that goes forth."
6 So I asked, "What is it?" And he said, "It is a basket that is going forth."
He also said, "This is their resemblance throughout the earth:
7 Here is a lead disc lifted up, and this is a woman sit-

71

ting inside the basket"; 8 then he said, "This is Wicked-ness!" And he thrust her down into the basket, and threw the lead cover over its mouth. 9 Then I raised my eyes and looked, and there were two women, coming with the wind in their wings; for they had wings like the wings of a stork, and they lifted up the basket between earth and heaven. 10 So I said to the angel who talked with me, "Where are they carrying the basket?" 11 And he said to me, "To build a house for it in the land of Shinar; when it is ready, the basket will be set there on its base." (Zechariah 5:1-11)

God's Impending Judgment

In previous chapters, we have studied the first six of Zechariah's visions. The prophet had a total of eight night-time visions. In chapter five of his book we find visions six and seven.

Then I turned and raised my eyes, and saw there a fly-ing scroll. And he said to me, "What do you see?" So I answered, "I see a flying scroll. Its length is twenty cubits and its width ten cubits." Then he said to me, "This is the curse that goes out over the face of the whole earth: 'Every thief shall be expelled,' according to this side of the scroll; and, 'Every perjurer shall be expelled,' according to that side of it. I will send out the curse," says the LORD of hosts; "It shall en-ter the house of the thief and the house of the one who swears falsely by My name. It shall remain in the midst of his house and consume it, with its timber and stones." Then the angel who talked with me came out and said to me, "Lift your eyes now, and see what this is that goes forth." So I asked, "What is it?" And he said, "It is a basket that is going forth." He also said, "This is their resemblance throughout the earth: Here is a lead disc lifted up, and this is a woman sitting inside the basket"; then he said, "This is Wickedness!" And he thrust her down into the basket, and threw the lead cover over its mouth. Then I raised my eyes and looked, and there were two women, coming with the wind in their wings; for they had wings like the wings of a stork, and they lifted up the basket between earth and heaven. So I said to the angel who talked with me, "Where are they carrying the basket?" And he said to me, "To build a house for it in the land of Shinar; when it is ready, the basket will be set there on its base" (Zech 5:1–11).

Leonardo da Vinci once stated that "He who does not punish evil, commands it to be done." Unfortunately, da Vinci's words reflect in a very powerful way the reality of the world in which we live today. Wickedness and sin not only go unpunished in our day and age, but they are even glamorized by different segments of our society. However, such a permissive attitude toward sin and rebellion against God will not go on forever. Zechariah's vision of the flying scroll makes it very clear that God will one day judge all the nations for their sins. Moreover, at repeated times throughout the Scriptures we read about God's promise of future judgment on sin. Take a look at the following examples:

- Psalm 9:7–8, "But the Lord shall endure forever; He has prepared His throne for judgment. He shall judge the world in righteousness, and He shall administer judgment for the peoples in uprightness."

- Psalm 96:13, "For He is coming to judge the earth. He shall judge the world with righteousness and the peoples with His truth."

- Ecclesiastes 3:17, "I said in my heart, 'God shall judge the righteous and the wicked; for there is a time for every purpose and for every work.'"

- Ecclesiastes 11:9, "Rejoice, O young man in your youth, and let your heart cheer you in the days of your youth; walk in the ways of your heart, and in the sight of your eyes; but know that for all these God will bring you into judgment."

- Ecclesiastes 12:14, "For God will bring every work into judgment, including every secret thing, whether good or evil."

- Ezekiel 18:20, "The soul who sins shall die."

- Amos 4:12, "Therefore thus will I do to you, O Israel; because I will do this to you, prepare to meet your God, O Israel."

- Matthew 3:12, "His winnowing fan is in His hand, and He will thoroughly clean out His threshing floor, and gather His wheat into the barn; but He will burn up the chaff with unquenchable fire."

- Matthew 13:30, "Let both grow together until the harvest, and at the time of harvest I will say to the reapers, 'First gather together the tares and bind them in bundles to burn them, but gather the wheat into my barn.'"

- Matthew 22:13, "Then the king said to the servants, 'Bind him hand and foot, take him away, and cast him into outer darkness; there shall be weeping and gnashing of teeth.'"

- Luke 12:2-5, "For there is nothing covered that will not be revealed, nor hidden that will not be known. Therefore whatever you have spoken in dark will be heard in the light, and what you have spoken in the ear in inner rooms will be proclaimed on the housetops. And I say to you, My friends, do not be afraid of those who kill the body, and after that have no more that they can. But I will show you whom you shall fear: Fear Him who, after He has killed, has power to cast into hell; yes, I say to you, fear Him!"

- Acts 10:42, "And He commanded us to preach to the people, and to testify that it is He who was ordained by God to be Judge of the living and the dead."

- Acts 17:31, "Because He has appointed a day on which He will judge the world in righteousness by the Man whom He has ordained. He has given assurance of this to all by raising Him from the dead."

- Acts 24:25, "Now as he (Paul) reasoned about righteousness, self-control, and the judgment to come, Felix was afraid and answered, 'Go away for now; when I have a convenient time I will call for you.'"

- 2 Thessalonians 1:7–8, "And give you who are troubled rest with us when the Lord Jesus is revealed from heaven with His mighty angels, in flaming fire taking vengeance on those who do not know God, and on those who do not obey the gospel of our Lord Jesus Christ."

- Hebrews 9:27, "And as it is appointed for men to die once, but after this the judgment."

- I Peter 4:5, "They will give an account to Him who is ready to judge the living and the dead."

- 2 Peter 2:9, "Then the Lord knows how to deliver the godly out of temptations and to reserve the unjust under punishment for the day of judgment."

- Revelation 20:11–12, 15 "Then I saw a great white throne and Him who sat on it, from whose face the earth and the heaven fled away. And there was found no place for them. And I saw the dead, small and great, standing before God, and the books were opened. And another book was opened, which is the Book of Life. And the dead were judge according to their works, by the things which were written in the books. And anyone not found written in the Book of Life was cast into the lake of fire."

Unfortunately, it seems as if our culture seeks to overemphasize God's love and grace to the point of compromising His righteousness and wrath. As a result of this imbalance, many Christians end up presenting to the world a distorted view of God. If we want to have a truly redemptive ministry, however, we must embrace the full truth of God's revelation and warn people about the way He sees unrighteousness. This is exactly what Zechariah did; this is also what we must do.

Zechariah's Sixth Vision: The Flying Scroll (Zech 5:1-4)

Zechariah 5 teaches us the inevitability of God's judgment, which is based upon God's Word. Read one more time the prophet's fifth vision in Zechariah 5:1-4.

> Then I turned and raised my eyes, and saw there a flying scroll. And he said to me, "What do you see?" So I answered, "I see a flying scroll. Its length is twenty cubits and its width ten cubits." Then he said to me, "This is the curse that goes out over the face of the whole earth: 'Every thief shall be expelled,' according to this side of the scroll; and, 'Every perjurer shall be expelled,' according to that side of it. I will send out the curse," says the LORD of hosts; "It shall enter the house of the thief and the house of the one who swears falsely by My name. It shall remain in the midst of his house and consume it, with its timber and stones."

In the first two chapters of Zechariah, God made it clear that He intends to put down all the enemies of Israel at some time in the future. Furthermore, those chapters also promise that Israel will one day become a nation of priests, as God originally intended them to be. At the same time, however, we also learned in the vision of Joshua and Satan that the nation of Israel must be cleansed through judgment before God's purposes are fulfilled. In the two visions of Zechariah

5, moreover, we read that God's future judgment will not be restricted to the nation of Israel. God will eventually judge every individual from every nation, tongue, and tribe—everyone who refused to trust in the Lord Jesus Christ.

The "flying scroll" in Zechariah 5:1-4 signifies judgment, and it represents the Word of God. We also read about this same incredible scroll in Ezekiel 2:8-10:

> But you, son of man, hear what I say to you. Do not be rebellious like that rebellious house; open your mouth and eat what I give you. Now when I looked, there was a hand stretched out to me; and behold, a scroll of a book was in it. Then He spread it before me; and there was writing on the inside and on the outside, and written on it were lamentations and mourning and woe.

Similar expressions are also found in Revelation 5:1-14 and 10:1-11.

The size of the scroll was fifteen by thirty feet, the same exact dimensions as the Holy Place in the Tabernacle (1 Kings 6:3) and Solomon's porch in the Temple, where the Law was proclaimed. That was also the place where the priest would come and worship God according to the Law.

The expressions "this side" and "that side" indicates that the Law was written on both sides of the scroll. This signifies the completeness of the coming judgment, which will be based on the totality of God's Word. It is with the totality of God's Word that fallen man stands condemned without the forgiveness that is in Jesus Christ. For instance, this is exactly what we find in Romans 2:1-8.

> Therefore you are inexcusable, O man, whoever you are who judge, for in whatever you judge another you condemn yourself; for you who judge practice the same things. But we know that the judgment of God is according to truth against those who practice such things. And do you think this, O man, you who judge those practicing such things, and doing the same,

that you will escape the judgment of God? Or do you despise the riches of His goodness, forbearance, and longsuffering, not knowing that the goodness of God leads you to repentance? But in accordance with your hardness and your impenitent heart you are treasuring up for yourself wrath in the day of wrath and revelation of the righteous judgment of God, who "will render to each one according to his deeds": eternal life to those who by patient continuance in doing good seek for glory, honor, and immortality; but to those who are self-seeking and do not obey the truth, but obey unrighteousness—indignation and wrath.

The expressions "every thief" and "every perjurer" (verse 4) are references to the third and eight commandments, symbolizing man's sin against other men and against God. They are representative of every sin that we commit and every action that breaks the Law of God. Because of these sins, God promised to send out His curse in Zechariah 5:4a. This clearly reveals the terrible, certain, and complete judgment of God that is coming to every non-believer. At the End Times, Christ will come and judge the lost; during His earthly kingdom righteousness will reign for a thousand years, and at the end of the Millennium the final judgment will occur.

Zechariah's Seventh Vision: The Woman in the Basket (Zechariah 5:5-11)

We find the prophet's seventh vision in the second half of Zechariah 5. Read it one more time.

> Then the angel who talked with me came out and said to me, "Lift your eyes now, and see what this is that goes forth." So I asked, "What is it?" And he said, "It is a basket that is going forth." He also said, "This is their resemblance throughout the earth: Here is a lead disc lifted up, and this is a woman sitting inside

the basket"; then he said, "This is Wickedness!" And he thrust her down into the basket, and threw the lead cover over its mouth. Then I raised my eyes and looked, and there were two women, coming with the wind in their wings; for they had wings like the wings of a stork, and they lifted up the basket between earth and heaven. So I said to the angel who talked with me, "Where are they carrying the basket?" And he said to me, "To build a house for it in the land of Shinar; when it is ready, the basket will be set there on its base"

In Zechariah's time, the basket (also called "ephah") was a measuring device, commonly used to measure grain. In this passage, the basket is full, confirming the sinfulness of the nations and the need for judgment. Dr. Wiersbe comments on these verses, "The ephah was a common measure in Israel, but no ephah would be large enough to house a person, so, like the huge scroll, this was a special ephah. The woman attempted to get out of the ephah, so a heavy lead cover was put on the ephah to keep her in. A talent of lead would weigh from seventy-five to one hundred pounds."

Therefore, this vision seems to refer to the economic wickedness that commonly characterizes man's corrupt society. In other words, it symbolizes a worldwide system that worships materialism and glorifies lust for money and possessions.

The woman who was in the basket also symbolized the embodiment of all kinds of sin, including religious ones (see Revelation 17 & 18). The term "wickedness" (Zechariah 5:8) actually means "feminine" in Hebrew, and it denotes moral, religious, and civil evil. The other two women we read about in verse 9 may refer to strong demons who deceive the world systems with the lust of materialism. They had wings like the wings of a stork, a bird that was considered unclean according to Leviticus 11:19. The land of Shinar, mentioned in 5:11, denotes the location of Babel (Babylon). This becomes especially significant in light of what we read in Revelation 17:3-5.

> So he carried me away in the Spirit into the wilderness. And I saw a woman sitting on a scarlet beast which was full of names of blasphemy, having seven heads and ten horns. The woman was arrayed in purple and scarlet, and adorned with gold and precious stones and pearls, having in her hand a golden cup full of abominations and the filthiness of her fornication. And on her forehead a name was written: MYSTERY, BABYLON THE GREAT, THE MOTHER OF HARLOTS AND OF THE ABOMINATIONS OF THE EARTH.

Together, all of these expressions describe the evil and ungodly world system in which we live—the same system that one day will be rendered guilty by the Lord Jesus Christ.

What about You?

One day a young man was drowning. He cried for help and a man passing by the water jumped in and saved the fellow from death. Several years later this same young man, who had walked far from the Lord, stole a car and was brought into court. He was greatly relieved, however, to see the man who had saved him from the watery grave sitting as the judge on the bench. "He will save me again, I am sure," he thought.

Much to his surprise, the trial came to an end and the judge gave him a "guilty" verdict. The young man said to the judge, "Oh, but you were the one who saved my life before." The judge promptly replied, "Young man, one day I was your savior, but now I am your judge. Your day of grace has come to an end."

I believe this brief story illustrates very well the dark reality of those who die without a true knowledge of the Lord Jesus Christ. Hebrews 9:27 clearly states that it is appointed for a man to die once, but after that he must face judgment.

Even though it is true that it is never too late to trust in Christ for salvation, it is equally true that upon one's death the final choice has already been made. If you are reading this and you have not come to the point of placing your full trust in the person and in work of Jesus Christ, I plead with you not to wait another second. Surrender to Him today. After all, you might not have another chance.

Discussion Questions

1. Leonardo da Vinci once stated that "He who does not punish evil commands it to be done." What did he mean by that? Do you tend to agree or disagree with this statement? Why?

2. This chapter contained several verses that mention God's future judgment on sin. Which one(s) especially caught your attention? Why?

3. Why do you think the biblical concepts of God's wrath and judgment are so unpopular these days? Why is it dangerous to try to change what the Bible teaches about God?

4. In your own words, describe Zechariah's 6th vision. What did he see? What was the scroll? What did it contain?

5. In your own words, describe Zechariah's 7th vision. What did he see? Who were the women? What did they symbolize?

6. If you died today and God asked you why He should forgive all your sins and spare you from judgment, what reason(s) would you give Him?

That's Not All

You can find sermon outlines and other extras in the "Sermonars" section at the back of the book. These pages may be freely reproduced, either from the book or from the accompanying CD-ROM for any devotional or ministry use.

Chapter Eight

The Millennial Temple and Its King

1 Then I turned and raised my eyes and looked, and behold, four chariots were coming from between two mountains, and the mountains were mountains of bronze. 2 With the first chariot were red horses, with the second chariot black horses, 3 with the third chariot white horses, and with the fourth chariot dappled horses–strong steeds. 4 Then I answered and said to the angel who talked with me, "What are these, my lord?" 5 And the angel answered and said to me, "These are four spirits of heaven, who go out from their station before the Lord of all the earth. 6 The one with the black horses is going to the north country, the white are going after them, and the dappled are going toward the south country." 7 Then the strong steeds went out, eager to go, that they might walk to and fro throughout the earth. And He said, "Go, walk to and fro throughout the earth." So they walked to and fro throughout the earth. 8 And He called to me, and spoke to me, saying, "See, those who go toward the north country have given rest to My Spirit in the north country." 9 Then the word of the LORD came to me, saying: 10 "Receive the gift from the captives–from Heldai, Tobijah, and Jedaiah, who have come from Babylon–and go the same

*day and enter the house of Josiah the son of Zephaniah. 11
Take the silver and gold, make an elaborate crown, and set
it on the head of Joshua the son of Jehozadak, the high priest.
12 Then speak to him, saying, 'Thus says the LORD of hosts,
saying:*

> *"Behold, the Man whose name is the BRANCH!*
> *From His place He shall branch out,*
> *And He shall build the temple of the LORD;*
> *13 Yes, He shall build the temple of the LORD.*
> *He shall bear the glory,*
> *And shall sit and rule on His throne;*
> *So He shall be a priest on His throne,*
> *And the counsel of peace shall be between them*
> *both.'"*

*14 "Now the elaborate crown shall be for a memorial in the
temple of the LORD for Helem, Tobijah, Jedaiah, and Hen
the son of Zephaniah. 15 Even those from afar shall come
and build the temple of the LORD. Then you shall know that
the LORD of hosts has sent Me to you. And this shall come to
pass if you diligently obey the voice of the LORD your God."*
(Zechariah 6:1-15)

God's Instrument of Judgment: Angels

With seven of Zechariah's eight visions behind us, we
now turn to the final one. We find Zechariah's eighth vision in Zechariah 6:1-8 above.

We cannot properly understand Zechariah's eighth vision without understanding who angels are and what role
they play in God's program. God's angels are prominently
mentioned from Genesis to Revelation: 108 times in the
Old Testament and 175 times in the New Testament. Among
other things, the Scriptures teach us that angels:

1. **Are powerful beings**: Psalm 103:20, "Bless the LORD,

you His angels, who excel in strength, who do His word, heeding the voice of His word."

2. **Are swift beings**: Matthew 26:53, "Or do you think that I cannot now pray to My Father, and He will provide Me with more than twelve legions of angels?"

3. **Have superior intelligence**: 2 Samuel 14:17, 20 "Your maidservant said, 'The word of my lord the king will now be comforting; for as the angel of God, so is my lord the king in discerning good and evil. And may the LORD your God be with you... To bring about this change of affairs your servant Joab has done this thing; but my lord is wise, according to the wisdom of the angel of God, to know everything that is in the earth.'"

4. **Are immutable beings**: Deuteronomy 33:2, "And he said: 'The LORD came from Sinai, and dawned on them from Seir; He shone forth from Mount Paran, and He came with ten thousands of saints; from His right hand came a fiery law for them.'"

5. **Guide and guard believers**: Psalm 91:11, "For He shall give His angels charge over you, to keep you in all your ways."

6. **Execute judgment at God's direction**: Psalm 103:20, "Bless the LORD, you His angels, who excel in strength, who do His word, heeding the voice of His word."

We can see very clearly in Zechariah 6:1-8 that the angels Zechariah saw were delivering messages of future judgment from God.

The Angelic Execution of Judgment

In ancient times, the "tanks" of that day were chariots with iron wheels. These chariots were not used for common transportation but for war. The four chariots, therefore, represent God's vehicles of divine judgment. It is clear that this final vision of Zechariah deals with God's judgment on the nations.

The four chariots Zechariah saw were pulled by very distinctive horses. The first team was red, the second black, the third white, and the fourth pale (or dappled). These four chariots went out from between two mountains of bronze that represent Mount Zion and the Mount of Olives, located in the Kidron Valley (also called "Valley of Jehoshaphat"). This seems to be in agreement with Joel 3 (especially verses 2 and 12), which points to a time when God will bring judgment over all the nations in the Valley of Jehoshaphat (which means "Jehovah will judge").

Therefore, it is very clear that God is going to judge all the nations in a valley located between Mount Zion and the Mount of Olives. We also see judgment located in this valley elsewhere in God's Word. Take a look at the following examples:

- Zechariah 14:4, "And in that day His feet will stand on the Mount of Olives, which faces Jerusalem on the east. And the Mount of Olives shall be split in two, from east to west, making a very large valley; half of the mountain shall move toward the north and half of it toward the south."

- Joel 3:2, "I will also gather all nations, and bring them down to the Valley of Jehoshaphat; and I will enter into judgment with them there on account of My people, My heritage Israel, whom they have scattered among the nations; they have also divided up My land."

It is also important to notice that Zechariah mentions "four spirits of heaven" in verse 5. These spirits represent angels God will use to bring judgment to sinful mankind in the final battle. They are in charge of the judgments that will come upon the Gentile nations, as we also see in the book of Revelation. For instance, the Apostle John wrote in Revelation 7:1, "After these things I saw four angels standing at the four corners of the earth, holding the four winds of the earth, that the wind should not blow on the earth, on the sea, or on any tree."

Color of Horses

The colors of the four groups of horses Zechariah saw are also very important. The first chariot was pulled by red horses, which represent widespread war and bloodshed. We also see a red horse in Revelation 6:4, "Another horse, fiery red, went out. And it was granted to the one who sat on it to take peace from the earth, and that people should kill one another; and there was given to him a great sword."

The second chariot (the North country) was pulled by black horses, representing the famine conditions that often characterize wars. This image also can be found in Revelation, in 6:5-6.

> When He opened the third seal, I heard the third living creature say, "Come and see." So I looked, and behold, a black horse, and he who sat on it had a pair of scales in his hand. And I heard a voice in the midst of the four living creatures saying, "A quart of wheat for a denarius, and three quarts of barley for a denarius; and do not harm the oil and the wine."

The third chariot (also in the North country) was pulled by white horses, which represent victory and conquest. The apostle John wrote about him in Revelation 6:1-2, "Now I saw when the Lamb opened one of the seals; and I heard one of the four living creatures saying with a voice like thunder, 'Come and see.' And I looked, and behold, a white horse. He who sat on it had a bow; and a crown was given to him, and he went out conquering and to conquer." The white horse of Revelation 6 is an imposter. He is the Antichrist, who will deceive the world by setting up a bogus covenant of peace at the beginning of the Tribulation.

The fourth chariot (the South country) was pulled by

dappled or gray horses, representing death and hell. We also read about these same horses in Revelation 6:7-8, "When He opened the fourth seal, I heard the voice of the fourth living creature saying, 'Come and see.' So I looked, and behold, a pale horse. And the name of him who sat on it was Death, and Hades followed with him. And power was given to them over a fourth of the earth, to kill with sword, with hunger, with death, and by the beasts of the earth."

The judgment of the nations, which will be carried out by these four chariots, will take place at the end of the seven-year Tribulation, when the Lord will judge those who stand against Him.

Jesus Crowned King & Priest

The Lord's plans for the future, however, do not include only judgment. Immediately after describing the judgment that is to come through the four chariots, Zechariah received a new word from the Lord. This time, he was given information about the future enthronement of Jesus Christ as the Ruler of God's people for all eternity. Zechariah wrote in Zechariah 6:11-12,

> Take the silver and gold, make an elaborate crown, and set it on the head of Joshua the son of Jehozadak, the high priest. Then speak to him, saying, 'Thus says the LORD of hosts, saying: "Behold, the Man whose name is the BRANCH! From His place He shall branch out, and He shall build the temple of the LORD."'

The crowning of Joshua the high priest was representative of the future coronation of the Lord Jesus Christ, who is our High Priest today. The sequence of this crowning is simply fascinating. After the vision that depicts the judgment of God upon His people and upon all the Gentile nations of the world, we have the Second Coming of Christ and His crowning as King of Kings and Lord of Lords. With that in mind, Zechariah 6:9-15 teaches us at least eight important truths about Jesus Christ:

1. The term "The Branch," found in verse 12, is a Messianic title for Jesus Christ. We also find these same words in Zechariah 3:8, "Hear, O Joshua, the high priest, you and your companions who sit before you, for they are a wondrous sign; for behold, I am bringing forth My Servant the BRANCH."

2. Zechariah 6:12b states that "from His place He shall branch out." This means that Jesus, the Messiah, would come from Israel, from His own people. Unfortunately, many of us today tend to forget that Jesus was a Jew.

3. Furthermore, Zechariah also wrote that the Messiah would one day build the new temple of the Lord (6:12–13).

4. "He shall bear the glory" (v. 13b). The Millennium will be the time when Christ is exalted on the earth.

5. "And shall sit and rule on His throne" (v. 13c). This means that Jesus' rule is not figurative, but literal. He is our King, and in the future He will reign over all the nations as He sits on David's throne.

6. "So He shall be a priest on His throne" (v. 13d). Jesus is both King and High Priest. This means that He not only rules over us, but He also represents us before God the Father. In the Millennium, there will be no such thing as separation between church and state, between that which is secular and that which is sacred.

7. "Even those from afar shall come and build the temple of the Lord" (v. 15a). This means that saints from all ethnic groups (Jews and Gentiles alike) will be in the Millennial Kingdom because of Jesus' redemption. We see this very clearly in Isaiah 2:2, "Now it shall come to pass in the latter days that the mountain of the LORD's house shall be established on the top of

the mountains, and shall be exalted above the hills; and all nations shall flow to it."

8. "Then you shall know that the Lord of Hosts has sent Me to you" (15b). This implies that Jesus Himself was the One who spoke to Zechariah in this passage.

Our Participation is Conditional

Zechariah 6 ends with a very important warning to each one of us. The prophet wrote in Zechariah 6:15c, "And this shall come to pass if you diligently obey the voice of the Lord your God." This verse is a great reminder that before blessing there is always obedience. The elaborate crown in Zerubbabel's temple was a reminder that God would send Jesus, His Messiah, to die on our behalf. But we must respond to Jesus' death on the cross by faith if we want to be included in God's family. It is not enough to know that Jesus died on the cross in order for us to be saved. We must turn to Him in faith and accept His free gift. There is no way around it. Have you ever made this important decision in your life?

Discussion Questions

1. Who are angels? What are they like? How do they serve God?

2. Think of the ways in which our society portrays angels. Do they reflect the biblical descriptions of angels?

3. Some believe that angels should be worshipped. Why is this type of thinking unbiblical? What verses can you use to support your answer?

4. What did the four chariots that Zechariah saw represent? What did each of the four different groups of horses symbolize?

5. In your own words, explain what Zechariah taught about Jesus in Zechariah 6:9–15.

6. What is the warning we find in Zechariah 6:15c? How does it apply to your life?

That's Not All

You can find sermon outlines and other extras in the "Sermonars" section at the back of the book. These pages may be freely reproduced, either from the book or from the accompanying CD-ROM for any devotional or ministry use.

Mr. Z and Jesus

Chapter Nine

Rituals vs. Obedience

1 Now in the fourth year of King Darius it came to pass that the word of the LORD came to Zechariah, on the fourth day of the ninth month, Chislev, 2 when the people sent Sherezer, with Regem-Melech and his men, to the house of God, to pray before the LORD, 3 and to ask the priests who were in the house of the LORD of hosts, and the prophets, saying, "Should I weep in the fifth month and fast as I have done for so many years?" 4 Then the word of the LORD of hosts came to me, saying, 5 "Say to all the people of the land, and to the priests: 'When you fasted and mourned in the fifth and seventh months during those seventy years, did you really fast for Me—for Me? 6 When you eat and when you drink, do you not eat and drink for yourselves? 7 Should you not have obeyed the words which the LORD proclaimed through the former prophets when Jerusalem and the cities around it were inhabited and prosperous, and the South and the Lowland were inhabited?'" 8 Then the word of the LORD came to Zechariah, saying, 9 "Thus says the LORD of hosts:

> *'Execute true justice,*
> *Show mercy and compassion*
> *Everyone to his brother.*
> *10 Do not oppress the widow or the fatherless,*

The alien or the poor.
Let none of you plan evil in his heart
Against his brother.'

11 "But they refused to heed, shrugged their shoulders,
and stopped their ears so that they could not hear. 12
Yes, they made their hearts like flint, refusing to hear the
law and the words which the LORD *of hosts had sent by*
His Spirit through the former prophets. Thus great wrath
came from the LORD *of hosts. 13 Therefore it happened,*
that just as He proclaimed and they would not hear, so
they called out and I would not listen," says the LORD *of*
hosts. 14 "But I scattered them with a whirlwind among
all the nations which they had not known. Thus the land
became desolate after them, so that no one passed through
or returned; for they made the pleasant land desolate."
8:1 Again the word of the LORD *of hosts came, saying, 2*
"Thus says the LORD *of hosts:*

> *'I am zealous for Zion with great zeal;*
> *With great fervor I am zealous for her.'*
> *3 "Thus says the* LORD:
> *'I will return to Zion,*
> *And dwell in the midst of Jerusalem.*
> *Jerusalem shall be called the City of Truth,*
> *The Mountain of the* LORD *of hosts,*
> *The Holy Mountain.'*

4 "Thus says the LORD *of hosts:*

> *'Old men and old women shall again sit*
> *In the streets of Jerusalem,*
> *Each one with his staff in his hand*
> *Because of great age.*
> *5 The streets of the city*
> *Shall be full of boys and girls*
> *Playing in its streets.'*

6 *"Thus says the* LORD *of hosts:*

> *'If it is marvelous in the eyes of the remnant of this*
> *people in these days,*
> *Will it also be marvelous in My eyes?'*
> *Says the* LORD *of hosts.*

7 *"Thus says the* LORD *of hosts:*

> *'Behold, I will save My people from the land of the*
> *east*
> *And from the land of the west;*
> *8 I will bring them back,*
> *And they shall dwell in the midst of Jerusalem.*
> *They shall be My people*
> *And I will be their God,*
> *In truth and righteousness.'*

9 *"Thus says the* LORD *of hosts:*

> *'Let your hands be strong,*
> *You who have been hearing in these days*
> *These words by the mouth of the prophets,*
> *Who spoke in the day the foundation was laid*
> *For the house of the* LORD *of hosts,*
> *That the temple might be built.*
> *10 For before these days*
> *There were no wages for man nor any hire for beast;*
> *There was no peace from the enemy for whoever went*
> *out or came in;*
> *For I set all men, everyone, against his neighbor.*

11 *But now I will not treat the remnant of this people as*
in the former days,' says the LORD *of hosts.*

> *12 'For the seed shall be prosperous,*
> *The vine shall give its fruit,*

The ground shall give her increase,
And the heavens shall give their dew—
I will cause the remnant of this people
To possess all these.
13 And it shall come to pass
That just as you were a curse among the nations,
O house of Judah and house of Israel,
So I will save you, and you shall be a blessing.
Do not fear,
Let your hands be strong.'

14 "For thus says the LORD of hosts:

Just as I determined to punish you
When your fathers provoked Me to wrath,'
Says the LORD of hosts,
'And I would not relent,
15 So again in these days
I am determined to do good
To Jerusalem and to the house of Judah.
Do not fear.
16 These are the things you shall do:
Speak each man the truth to his neighbor;
Give judgment in your gates for truth, justice, and
peace;
17 Let none of you think evil in your heart against
your neighbor;
And do not love a false oath.
For all these are things that I hate,'

Says the LORD."

18 Then the word of the LORD of hosts came to me, saying,
19 "Thus says the LORD of hosts:

The fast of the fourth month,
The fast of the fifth,

> *The fast of the seventh,*
> *And the fast of the tenth,*
> *Shall be joy and gladness and cheerful feasts*
> *For the house of Judah.*
> *Therefore love truth and peace.'*

20 *"Thus says the LORD of hosts:*

> *'Peoples shall yet come,*
> *Inhabitants of many cities;*
> *21 The inhabitants of one city shall go to another,*
> *saying,*
> *"Let us continue to go and pray before the LORD,*
> *And seek the LORD of hosts.*
> *I myself will go also."*
> *22 Yes, many peoples and strong nations*
> *Shall come to seek the LORD of hosts in Jerusalem,*
> *And to pray before the LORD.'*

23 *"Thus says the LORD of hosts: 'In those days ten men from every language of the nations shall grasp the sleeve of a Jewish man, saying, "Let us go with you, for we have heard that God is with you."'" (Zechariah 7:1-8:23)*

As we read through the book of Zechariah, it is easy to forget that Zechariah did not receive God's entire message overnight. The prophet first received God's word during the second year of Darius (Zechariah 1:1). In Zechariah 7:1-3, however, we read that the word of the Lord came to Zechariah again in the fourth year of King Darius.

> Now in the fourth year of King Darius it came to pass that the word of the LORD came to Zechariah, on the fourth day of the ninth month, Chislev, when the people sent Sherezer, with Regem-Melech and his men, to the house of God, to pray before the LORD, and to ask the priests who were in the house of the LORD of hosts, and the prophets, saying, "Should I

97

weep in the fifth month and fast as I have done for so many years?"(Zechariah 7:1-3)

Rituals: Right or Wrong?

Almost two years had elapsed between chapters 1 and 7, and several good things had started to happen during that time. Through the Spirit-empowered ministries of Haggai and Zechariah, the people started to rebuild the Temple of the Lord in Jerusalem. The city, at the same time, was beginning to take on new life. Homes were being built, God was moving, and the scars of the invasion and destruction by Nebuchadnezzar were slowly being erased and removed.

Nevertheless, many Jews continued to live in bondage to empty rituals instead of experiencing a renewed relationship with the Lord. Because the nation of Israel as a whole did not embrace God's Word, they chose to focus on certain religious ceremonies, prayers, and recitations that aimed to make the people feel religious while lacking a true relationship with the Lord. These religious rituals were solemn acts devoid of substance because they ultimately sought to replace God's Word in the lives of the people.

In Zechariah 7:3, however, we read that a delegation from Bethel wanted to know if they should continue the ritual of fasting and crying, observed during the exile, now that the Temple was being rebuilt. Some of those leaders, it seems, had finally realized that those empty rituals might not needed after all. In Zechariah 8:19, for instance, we read that the Jews followed at least four main rituals throughout the year:

- They fasted on the fourth month, the day when the city walls were breached (2 Kings 25:3-4; Jer 39:2).

- They fasted on the fifth month, when the house of God was destroyed by fire (2 Kings 25:8-10).

- They fasted on the seventh month, the anniversary of

the assassination of Gedaliah, the son of Ahikam (2 Kings 25:25; Jer 41:2).

- They fasted on the tenth month, which was when Nebuchadnezzar laid siege to Jerusalem (2 Kings 25:1; Ezek 24:2).

It was now sixty-eight years later, the Temple was almost rebuilt, and the question was, "Are these ritualistic fasts necessary?" The Lord's reply through the prophet Zechariah must have pierced their hearts. Read carefully Zechariah 7:4-7.

> Then the word of the LORD of hosts came to me, saying, "Say to all the people of the land, and to the priests: 'When you fasted and mourned in the fifth and seventh months during those seventy years, did you really fast for Me—for Me? When you eat and when you drink, do you not eat and drink for yourselves? Should you not have obeyed the words which the LORD proclaimed through the former prophets when Jerusalem and the cities around it were inhabited and prosperous, and the South and the Lowland were inhabited?'"

God's answer implied that their rituals would have been legitimate and pure had their motives been legitimate and pure. In other words, had the people observed these rituals because of the Lord, not because of themselves, they would have met with God's approval. They did not receive God's approval, however, since their "godly" acts were devoid of God. These rituals were empty and self-centered. God was not a part of them. Therefore, their rituals were impure. In order to rescue the people from empty rituals, God spoke to them in Zechariah 7:8-14,

> Then the word of the LORD came to Zechariah, saying, "Thus says the LORD of hosts: 'Execute true justice, show mercy and compassion everyone to his brother. Do not oppress the widow or the fatherless, the alien or

the poor. Let none of you plan evil in his heart against his brother.' But they refused to heed, shrugged their shoulders, and stopped their ears so that they could not hear. Yes, they made their hearts like flint, refusing to hear the law and the words which the LORD of hosts had sent by His Spirit through the former prophets. Thus great wrath came from the LORD of hosts. Therefore it happened, that just as He proclaimed and they would not hear, so they called out and I would not listen," says the LORD of hosts. "But I scattered them with a whirlwind among all the nations which they had not known. Thus the land became desolate after them, so that no one passed through or returned; for they made the pleasant land desolate."

The people's rituals were no replacement for obedience in their lives. On the exterior, the lives of these people appeared to be characterized by seemingly impressive religious acts, but their hearts did not line up with God's will. Their rituals gave them false spiritual assurance, when in fact God rejected their empty works and was trying to redirect them back to true spirituality. The Lord was calling the people to forsake their legalism and to pursue the authentic worship of God in their lives.

Sadly, we too can easily fall into the trap of finding false assurance in rituals and religion. It can be very easy for us to develop our own Christian rituals while our hearts are cold and distant from God. These rituals might be good things—attending church services or teaching a class—but if the Lord is not in the center of the activity, then the ritual is empty. In order to avoid this trap, we must walk in the Spirit, die to ourselves, abide in Christ, and let Him live through us. Read carefully the following key biblical truths about living vibrant Christian lives:

- Galatians 5:16-18, "I say then: Walk in the Spirit, and you shall not fulfill the lust of the flesh. For the flesh lusts against the Spirit, and the Spirit against the flesh;

and these are contrary to one another, so that you do not do the things that you wish. But if you are led by the Spirit, you are not under the law."

- Galatians 2:20, "I have been crucified with Christ; it is no longer I who live, but Christ lives in me; and the life which I now live in the flesh I live by faith in the Son of God, who loved me and gave Himself for me."

- John 15:5, "I am the vine, you are the branches. He who abides in Me, and I in him, bears much fruit; for without Me you can do nothing."

If you are in bondage to rituals, you can find freedom in your relationship with the Lord. Confess your empty rituals to the Lord and ask him to cleanse you (1 John 1:9). Authentic Christianity is not about empty rituals and religion, but about a true relationship with our Creator through the Lord Jesus Christ. God wants you to rest on His grace, not on your own works!

Israel's Restoration & Kingdom

In Zechariah 8 we find God's promise that His people will not always struggle with empty rituals. There will be a day when we will be free from empty religion and when we will enjoy a genuine relationship with the Lord that is constantly satisfying to us and pleasing to Him. Consider the following key promises we find in Zechariah 8:1-23.

1. **God will punish Israel's enemies**: Zechariah 8:1-2, "Again the word of the LORD of hosts came, saying, 'Thus says the LORD of hosts: "I am zealous for Zion with great zeal; with great fervor I am zealous for her."'" The word "zealous" indicates a state of mind that seeks to preserve and protect. God will not let our enemies triumph over us. God is zealous for Israel and for His church. He is also zealous for you.

2. **The presence of God will be in the midst of Israel**

in the Millennial Kingdom: Zechariah 8:3, "Thus says the LORD: 'I will return to Zion, and dwell in the midst of Jerusalem. Jerusalem shall be called the City of Truth, the Mountain of the LORD of hosts, the Holy Mountain.'"

3. **God's peace will characterize the Millennial Kingdom**: Zechariah 8:4-5, "Thus says the LORD of hosts: 'Old men and old women shall again sit in the streets of Jerusalem, each one with his staff in his hand because of great age. The streets of the city shall be full of boys and girls playing in its streets.'"

4. **God's power will cause the Millennial Kingdom to happen**: Zechariah 8:6, "Thus says the LORD of hosts: 'If it is marvelous in the eyes of the remnant of this people in these days, will it also be marvelous in My eyes?' says the LORD of hosts." The word "marvelous" in this verse also means "impossible." God will accomplish the impossible because of His great power.

5. **God will regather His people, Israel, and the Millennial Kingdom will be based in Jerusalem**: Zechariah 8:7-8, "Thus says the LORD of hosts: 'Behold, I will save My people from the land of the east and from the land of the west; I will bring them back, and they shall dwell in the midst of Jerusalem. They shall be My people and I will be their God, in truth and righteousness.'"

6. **God's blessing of prosperity will characterize the Millennial Kingdom**: Zechariah 8:9-13,

> Thus says the LORD of hosts: "Let your hands be strong, you who have been hearing in these days these words by the mouth of the prophets, who spoke in the day the foundation was laid for the house of the LORD of hosts, that the temple might be built. For before these days there were no wages for man nor any hire for

beast; there was no peace from the enemy for whoever went out or came in; for I set all men, everyone, against his neighbor. But now I will not treat the remnant of this people as in the former days," says the LORD of hosts. "For the seed shall be prosperous, the vine shall give its fruit, the ground shall give her increase, and the heavens shall give their dew—I will cause the remnant of this people to possess all these. And it shall come to pass that just as you were a curse among the nations, O house of Judah and house of Israel, so I will save you, and you shall be a blessing. Do not fear, let your hands be strong."

7. **God will restore Israel and she will be redeemed**: Zechariah 8:14-15, "For thus says the LORD of hosts: 'Just as I determined to punish you when your fathers provoked Me to wrath,' says the LORD of hosts, 'And I would not relent, so again in these days I am determined to do good to Jerusalem and to the house of Judah. Do not fear.'"

In the final section of chapter 8, Zechariah went on to describe in more detail what the Millennial Kingdom would be like. First, it will be a time of perfect pleasure. We see this in Zechariah 8:19b, "[It] shall be joy and gladness and cheerful feasts for the house of Judah. Therefore love truth and peace." Second, it will also be a time when God's people will have perfect communion with God, as seen in Zechariah 8:21, "The inhabitants of one city shall go to another, saying, 'Let us continue to go and pray before the LORD, and seek the LORD of hosts. I myself will go also." Third, the Millennial Kingdom will also be a time when God's people will have perfect harmony with one another, as seen in Zechariah 8:22, "Yes, many peoples and strong nations shall come to seek the LORD of hosts in Jerusalem, and to pray before the LORD. 'Thus says the LORD of hosts: "In those days ten men from every language of the nations shall grasp the sleeve of a Jewish man, saying, 'Let us go with you, for we have heard that God is with you.'"""

Like the Jews in Zechariah's time, we may struggle with empty rituals in our relationship with God. But the time will come when we will enjoy perfect communion with God and with one another, when we will experience true intimacy in all of our relationships. Until then, may we grow in our relationship with God and learn how to relate to Him in spirit and in truth, not in empty rituals.

Discussion Questions

1. What are some common rituals Christians today can practice even without noticing?

2. Why can religious rituals be such a temptation in our walk with the Lord? What makes them so enticing?

3. What rituals and legalistic practices can be especially tempting to you? Why?

4. What rituals or legalistic practices do you see in your church?

5. What is the difference between religion and relationship?

6. How does God want you to live in order to avoid rituals in your relationship with Him?

7. What strikes you about the Millennial Kingdom? What makes you really anticipate that time when Christ will reign on earth?

That's Not All

You can find sermon outlines and other extras in the "Sermonars" section at the back of the book. These pages may be freely reproduced, either from the book or from the accompanying CD-ROM for ministry use.

Chapter Ten

Alexander the Great in Zechariah?

1 The burden of the word of the LORD
Against the land of Hadrach,
And Damascus its resting place
(For the eyes of men
And all the tribes of Israel
Are on the LORD);
2 Also against Hamath, which borders on it,
 And against Tyre and Sidon, though they are very
wise.
3 For Tyre built herself a tower,
Heaped up silver like the dust,
And gold like the mire of the streets.
4 Behold, the Lord will cast her out;
He will destroy her power in the sea,
And she will be devoured by fire.
5 Ashkelon shall see it and fear;
Gaza also shall be very sorrowful;
And Ekron, for He dried up her expectation.
The king shall perish from Gaza,
And Ashkelon shall not be inhabited.
6 "A mixed race shall settle in Ashdod,
And I will cut off the pride of the Philistines.

7 I will take away the blood from his mouth,
And the abominations from between his teeth.
But he who remains, even he shall be for our God,
And shall be like a leader in Judah,
And Ekron like a Jebusite. (Zechariah 9:1-7)

In Zechariah's second vision (Zechariah 1:18-21), the prophet saw four horns, or nations, that would scatter Judah, Israel, and Jerusalem. With the help of history and the biblical record, we were able in chapter 3 to identify those four Gentile powers who have ruled over Israel as Babylon, Medo-Persia, Greece, and Rome. At the time of Zechariah's ministry, the Jews were under the rule of the Medo-Persian Empire. According to Ezra 1:1-11, Cyrus, King of Persia, had issued a special degree that allowed the Jews in captivity to return to Jerusalem so that they could rebuild their temple and their city. The Medo-Persian Empire ruled over Israel and over other nations until it was defeated by the Greeks and their fearless commander, Alexander the Great.

When God Uses the Ungodly: Zechariah 9:1-7

Zechariah 9:1-7, which was written hundreds of years before Alexander the Great was ever born, presents the Greeks' battle plan, even listing certain specific cities Alexander would destroy centuries later. Take a look:

> The burden of the word of the LORD against the land of Hadrach, and Damascus its resting place (for the eyes of men and all the tribes of Israel are on the LORD); also against Hamath, which borders on it, and against Tyre and Sidon, though they are very wise. For Tyre built herself a tower, heaped up silver like the dust, and gold like the mire of the streets. Behold, the LORD will cast her out; He will destroy her power in the sea, and she will be devoured by fire. Ashkelon shall see it and fear; Gaza also shall be very sorrowful;

and Ekron, for He dried up her expectation. The king shall perish from Gaza, and Ashkelon shall not be inhabited. A mixed race shall settle in Ashdod, and I will cut off the pride of the Philistines. I will take away the blood from his mouth, and the abominations from between his teeth. But he who remains, even he shall be for our God, and shall be like a leader in Judah, and Ekron like a Jebusite.

Not surprisingly, liberal critics of the Bible have unfoundedly tried to deny the historicity of this portion of Zechariah's book, arguing that it must have been written after the facts took place, not before. The evidence, however, clearly indicates that the book of Zechariah in its entirety was written centuries before these events ever happened. Charles Feinberg comments:

> The testimony of the oldest translation of the Old Testament (which is in Greek) and the compilers of the Jewish canon are in favor of the genuineness of these chapters. The arguments of the liberals are untenable and can be refuted. We can rest assured that the Spirit of God used one author for all fourteen chapters... In verses 1 to 8 of chapter 9, the campaign of Alexander the Great is sketched. His successes are recounted in verses 1-7, and verse 8 notes the deliverance of Jerusalem. After the Battle of Issus, Alexander quickly conquered Damascus, Sidon, Tyre (after seven months it was burned), Gaza, Ashkelon, Ashdod, and Ekron. The course of his victories in 332 BC was from northern Syria south by the valley of the Orontes River to Damascus, then along the Phoenician and Philistine Coast.[1]

Besides the fact that Zechariah predicted Alexander the Great's conquest centuries in advance, it is also amazing the fact that God used a very ungodly man to accomplish His purposes. That is how great our God is. Nathan Stone and J. Vernon McGee comment:

The scene described in 9:1-8 is the course of the invasion and conquest by Alexander the Great and the beginning of the Grecian world empire ... It is quite remarkable indeed that in all this Jerusalem should have been spared. The Jewish historian Josephus sees this as the result of a dream Alexander had. Whether this was so or not, verse 8 plainly declares that it was the Lord's will to spare the city and He caused the enemy to bypass Jerusalem. So God makes His enemies carry out His purposes.[2]

Alexander the Great was unwittingly God's instrument of judgment. His forces subjugated "the land of Hadrach," taking key towns, Damascus and Hamath. Damascus was the capital of Syria and still is today. Also, it continues to cause Israel a great deal of difficulty. The cities mentioned in verses 1-7 trace the march of Alexander's great army down into the Promised Land. It is history now, but when it was written, it was prophecy. Its literal fulfillment makes it one of the most remarkable accounts we find in the Word of God. This is so disturbing to the liberal theologian that he attempts to move the timing of the writing of Zechariah up to the time of Alexander the Great![3]

There are, then, at least three main lessons we should learn from the discussion above. First, God is sovereign. He is the One who is ultimately in control over our lives and over the entire world. Second, God uses the just and the unjust to accomplish His purposes. We clearly see this in the way He used Alexander the Great to carry out Zechariah's prophecies. Third, no person or influence can ever stop God's plan. Whatever God decrees comes to fruition. Always!

Alexander's Trail of Destruction

Born in 356 BC in Pella, Macedonia, Alexander the Great

conquered the world with a speed matched by no one else, before or since! He was the son of Philip II of Macedonia, and he was taught by Aristotle as a boy. Very early Alexander showed military brilliance, helping to win a major battle at the age of 18. He succeeded his assassinated father in 336 BC and assumed the title "King of Macedon."

After ascending to the throne, Alexander left Europe and crossed into Asia Minor (modern day Turkey), taking city after city. Since he had an army of only 50,000 men, he could not leave any soldiers behind to hold his conquests. For this reason he destroyed every city the army conquered so as to avoid being attacked by them in the future. In fact, several of the cities mentioned in Zechariah 9 were so obliterated by Alexander's army that there is literally nothing left of them!

Zechariah presents Alexander's march in chapter 9 of his book. In verse 1, we read about God's judgment on Syria through the Greeks under the command of Alexander the Great. Both cities mentioned in this verse, Hadrach and Damascus, were located in Syria. In fact, Damascus was the capital of that nation. In verses 2-4 we read about the doom of Phoenicia. Zechariah wrote,

> Also against Hamath, which borders on it, and against Tyre and Sidon, though they are very wise. For Tyre built herself a tower, heaped up silver like the dust, and gold like the mire of the streets. Behold, the LORD will cast her out; He will destroy her power in the sea, and she will be devoured by fire.

Both Tyre and Sidon were famous Phoenician cities located in what is now southern Lebanon. A couple of centuries before Alexander arrived on the scene, Tyre had been conquered by the Babylonians. As a result, they moved their city from the mainland to an island a half mile offshore. Although small, the island seemed impenetrable. The new Tyre was built on a fortified rock, having a 150-foot wall around the entire island. Because of their offshore location and with the unsurpassed Phoenician navy to defend them, the people of Tyre believed they were invincible. Zechariah, however, prophesized Tyre's destruction by fire (similar prophecies can also be found in Ezekiel 26:4-12; 27:27; 28:20-24).

Every detail in Zechariah 9:2-4 was accomplished by Alexander the Great. During his campaign in Palestine he requested supplies from Tyre. When they refused to assist him, his army took the rubble that was left from the ancient city of Tyre, threw it into the sea to build a half-mile causeway, marched out to the island fortress, and defeated the city with the assistance of the navies of surrounding nations. Alexander did in seven months what the Assyrian king could not do in five years and what Nebuchadnezzar could not do in thirteen years! Today there is nothing left of Tyre.

In Zechariah 9:5-7, the prophet went on to describe Alexander's conquest of Philistia.

> Ashkelon shall see it and fear; Gaza also shall be very sorrowful; and Ekron, for He dried up her expectation. The king shall perish from Gaza, and Ashkelon shall not be inhabited. A mixed race shall settle in Ashdod, and I will cut off the pride of the Philistines. I will take away the blood from his mouth, and the abominations from between his teeth. But he who remains, even he shall be for our God, and shall be like a leader in Judah, and Ekron like a Jebusite.

Moving south Alexander next came to Philistia. By then the Philistines were terrified. They had watched Alexander wipe out the Medo-Persian army in the battle of Issus, sweep with lightning swiftness over Syria to the east, and then advance on Phoenicia in the south, conquering the impregnable fortress of Tyre. Alexander's defeat of Gaza is recorded in detail by first-century Greek historian Arrian in *The Campaigns of Alexander*. Because Gaza resisted him for five months, he refused to give this city the semi-independence he allowed other cities he conquered. Once again, Feinberg comments, "Special mention is made by a contemporary of

Alexander that the king of Gaza was brought alive to the conqueror after the city was taken; the satrap, or petty 'king' of the city, was bound to a chariot and dragged around the city to his death. Thus did the city lose its independence."[4]

Jerusalem Protected from Alexander

In the midst of Alexander's destruction, however, we also find God's grace and promise of redemption. First, in Zechariah 9:7 we read about God's millennial promise. It states, "I will take away the blood from his mouth, and the abominations from between his teeth. But he who remains, even he shall be for our God, and shall be like a leader in Judah, and Ekron like a Jebusite." This seemingly obscure verse promises future restoration for all the nations. In the Millennial kingdom, there will be a remnant from all nations who will enjoy a perfect kingdom under the rule of Christ.

Second, Zechariah also mentioned how the Lord protected Jerusalem, His Holy City, from Alexander the Great. Zechariah 9:8 reads, "I will camp around My house because of the army, because of him who passes by and him who returns. No more shall an oppressor pass through them, for now I have seen with My eyes." The pronoun "I" at the beginning of the verse signals the fact that it was God who spoke through Zechariah. Just as God was to be a "wall of fire" around Jerusalem (2:5), so here He promised, hundreds of years in advance, to camp around His house, which refers to the Jewish temple that had been rebuilt under Zerubbabel.

A fascinating story of Jerusalem's marvelous preservation of this occasion is told by Flavius Josephus (Antiquities, XI, 317-319). It reads:

> And Alexander, coming to Syria, took Damascus, became master of Sidon and besieged Tyre; from there he dispatched a letter to the high priest of the Jews, requesting him to send him assistance and supply his

army with provisions and give him gifts which they had formerly sent as tribute to Darius... But the high priest replied to the bearers of the letter that he had given his oath to Darius not to take up arms against him, and said that he would never violate this oath so long as Darius remained alive. When Alexander heard this, he was roused with anger, and while deciding not to leave Tyre, which was on the point of being taken, threatened that when he had brought it to terms he would march against the high priest of the Jews and through him teach all men what people it was to whom they must keep their oaths, and for this reason continuing the siege with greater effort, he took Tyre.

When the high priest Jaddus heard this, he was in an agony of fear, not knowing how he could meet the Macedonians, whose king was angered by his former disobedience. He therefore ordered the people to make supplication, and offering sacrifice to God together with them, besought Him to shield the nation and deliver them from the dangers that were hanging over them ... But, when he had gone to sleep after the sacrifice, God spoke oracularly to him in his sleep, telling him to take courage and adorn the city with wreaths and open the gates and to meet them, and that the people should be in white garments, and he himself with the priests in robes prescribed by the law, and that they should not look to suffer any harm, for God was watching over them. And when he understood that [Alexander] was not far from the city [Jerusalem] he went out in procession, with the priests and the multitude of citizens... When Alexander... saw the multitude at a distance, in white garments, while the priests stood clothed in fine linen, and the high priest in purple and scarlet clothing, with his mitre on his head having the golden plate on which the name of God was engraved, Alexander approached by himself, and adored that name, and first saluted the high priest. The Jews also did all together, with one voice, salute Alexander, and surround him.[5]

Alexander then entered Jerusalem and worshiped God in the temple. The story continues in Josephus' writings that Alexander the Great said he had seen this very scene in a dream before coming to Jerusalem and that his anger was replaced with an awe of God. He said that it even gave him courage to fight against the Persian nation and to conquer all of her cities! Another tradition says that not only did the high priest approach him arrayed in priestly garments, but that he also brought along the book of Daniel and showed Alexander the prophecy concerning him in the book! This so moved him that he went into the city and offered sacrifices and worshiped. Whatever the details, the bottom line is that Alexander did not destroy Jerusalem just as Zechariah 9:8 had predicted centuries in advance.

Israel's Coming Deliverer

In the second half of chapter 9, Zechariah moved from destruction to blessing, describing Israel's coming King and Deliverer.

> Rejoice greatly, O daughter of Zion! Shout, O daughter of Jerusalem! Behold, your King is coming to you; He is just and having salvation, lowly and riding on a donkey, a colt, the foal of a donkey. I will cut off the chariot from Ephraim and the horse from Jerusalem; the battle bow shall be cut off. He shall speak peace to the nations; His dominion shall be "from sea to sea, and from the river to the ends of the earth." As for you also, because of the blood of your covenant, I will set your prisoners free from the waterless pit. Return to the stronghold, you prisoners of hope. Even today I declare that I will restore double to you. For I have

bent Judah, My bow, fitted the bow with Ephraim, and raised up your sons, O Zion, against your sons, O Greece, and made you like the sword of a mighty man. Then the LORD will be seen over them, and His arrow will go forth like lightning. The Lord GOD will blow the trumpet, and go with whirlwinds from the south. The LORD of hosts will defend them; they shall devour and subdue with slingstones. They shall drink and roar as if with wine; they shall be filled with blood like basins, like the corners of the altar. The LORD their God will save them in that day, as the flock of His people. For they shall be like the jewels of a crown, lifted like a banner over His land—for how great is its goodness and how great its beauty! Grain shall make the young men thrive, and new wine the young women (Zechariah 9:9-17).

Zechariah 9:9 is undoubtedly one of the most popular verses of the entire book, since it was quoted in the New Testament in the Gospels of Matthew and John. Matthew 21:1-5, for instance, reads:

Now when they drew near Jerusalem, and came to Bethphage, at the Mount of Olives, then Jesus sent two disciples, saying to them, "Go into the village opposite you, and immediately you will find a donkey tied, and a colt with her. Loose them and bring them to Me. And if anyone says anything to you, you shall say, 'The Lord has need of them,' and immediately he will send them." All this was done that it might be fulfilled which was spoken by the prophet, saying: "Tell the daughter of Zion, 'Behold, your King is coming to you, lowly, and sitting on a donkey, a colt, the foal of a donkey.'"

Zechariah 9:9 refers to Jesus' first coming, when He entered Jerusalem as the Prince of Peace riding on an animal of peace. The next verse, however, refers to the Second Coming, when Jesus will return as God's Messiah, ready to judge the nations and to establish His Millennial Kingdom. Zechariah 9:10 reads, "I will cut off the chariot from Ephraim and the horse from Jerusalem; the battle bow shall be cut off. He shall speak peace to the nations; His dominion shall be from sea to sea, and from the River to the ends of the earth."

The Blood of the Covenant

Zechariah 9:11 is another key verse in that passage. It states, "As for you also, because of the blood of your covenant, I will set your prisoners free from the waterless pit." Because of the previous references to Jesus as Israel's King and Deliverer, we know that the blood mentioned in verse 11 is not the blood of those animals the Jews used to sacrifice in the Old Testament times. Rather, the "blood of the covenant" is a reference to Jesus' own blood, which he shed on the cross in order to inaugurate God's New Covenant, thus offering true forgiveness to all who come to Him by faith. Those who are sprinkled by that blood turn from prisoners to free citizens of God's Kingdom. As Jesus Himself stated in John 8:36, "If the Son sets you free, you will be free indeed." Have you experienced that type of freedom that only the Lamb of God can give?

Discussion Questions

1. Why have liberal critics of the Bible tried to attack Zechariah 9? What is so important about this chapter?

2. Who was Alexander the Great? How did this famous historical figure fit within God's plans?

3. What does Zechariah prophesy about the fate of Tyre? What did befall Tyre when Alexander attacked?

4. How did God protect Jerusalem from Alexander and his army? What does that teach you about God's character?

5. After having read Zechariah 9, what verse(s) stood out to you? Why?

6. How do you personally relate to Zechariah 9:11? In what ways have you experienced true freedom through the blood of the covenant?

That's Not All

You can find sermon outlines and other extras in the "Sermonars" section at the back of the book. These pages may be freely reproduced, either from the book or from the accompanying CD-ROM for any devotional or ministry use.

Chapter Eleven

The Time of the Latter Rain: What Does It Mean?

1 Ask the LORD for rain
In the time of the latter rain.
The LORD will make flashing clouds;
He will give them showers of rain,
Grass in the field for everyone.
2 For the idols speak delusion;
The diviners envision lies,
And tell false dreams;
They comfort in vain.
Therefore the people wend their way like sheep;
They are in trouble because there is no shepherd.
3 "My anger is kindled against the shepherds,
And I will punish the goatherds.
For the LORD of hosts will visit His flock,
The house of Judah,
And will make them as His royal horse in the battle.
4 From him comes the cornerstone,
From him the tent peg,
From him the battle bow,
From him every ruler together.
5 They shall be like mighty men,
Who tread down their enemies

In the mire of the streets in the battle.
They shall fight because the LORD is with them,
And the riders on horses shall be put to shame.
6 " I will strengthen the house of Judah,
And I will save the house of Joseph.
I will bring them back,
Because I have mercy on them.
They shall be as though I had not cast them aside;
For I am the LORD their God,
And I will hear them.
7 Those of Ephraim shall be like a mighty man,
And their heart shall rejoice as if with wine.
Yes, their children shall see it and be glad;
Their heart shall rejoice in the LORD.
8 I will whistle for them and gather them,
For I will redeem them;
And they shall increase as they once increased.
9 " I will sow them among the peoples,
And they shall remember Me in far countries;
They shall live, together with their children,
And they shall return.
10 I will also bring them back from the land of
Egypt,
And gather them from Assyria.
I will bring them into the land of
Gilead and Lebanon,
Until no more room is found for them.
11 He shall pass through the sea with affliction,
And strike the waves of the sea:
All the depths of the River shall dry up.
Then the pride of Assyria shall be brought down,
And the scepter of Egypt shall depart.
12 " So I will strengthen them in the LORD,
And they shall walk up and down in His name,"
Says the LORD. (Zechariah 10:1-12)

Dr. Walter Wilson, a great pastor and Christian leader

in the Kansas City area, was once praying with a missionary friend for a car that was greatly needed for the missionary's work in Africa. The missionary prayed, "O God, you know how badly I need a car for my work. Do, Lord, send me a car. Any kind of an old, ramshackle car will do!"

The wise Dr. Wilson promptly interrupted that missionary's prayer and stated, "Stop praying that way, brother! God is not in the junk business!"

What Kind of God Do We Serve?

Very sadly, there are many believers today who mistakenly believe that God is in the junk business. These Christians tend to have a very limited view of God's goodness, believing that (1) God usually gives His children second-hand blessings, and (2) that humility is the same as poverty. To them, being successful or having material possessions is a sign of carnality and sinfulness. Such perspectives, however, are not biblical. Whereas it is true that God does not necessarily want every Christian to be financially wealthy, it is also true that God is delighted to give His children whatever they need in abundance and that His gifts are always good and perfect (James 1:16). Therefore, deprivation is not necessarily a sign of spirituality. In fact, I believe that many times our needs as God's children go unmet simply because we lack the faith to believe that God wants to provide for us. As a result, we end up not praying as we should. Zechariah 10, however, teaches us that God wants to bless us with His perfect gifts. It is up to us to trust in His character and to turn to Him for what we need. If we call upon the Lord, he will answer us. He will answer our needs, but he will not do so according to our sinful ways but according to His perfect way. With that in mind, remember Zechariah's words in Zechariah 10:1-12.

Ask the Lord for Rain: Zechariah 10:1

Technically, Zechariah 10:1 belongs to chapter 9, since it continues the description of the prosperous conditions that will prevail during the Millennial Kingdom of Jesus Christ on this earth. Thus far in his book, Zechariah has already given us some important details about what heaven will be like. In his vision, Zechariah saw animals in the Kingdom, children playing in the streets, God's people living in perfect fellowship with one another and with Him, and plenty of "heavenly" grass and rain to ensure the abundance of "heavenly" crops and beautiful "heavenly" trees.

Zechariah's own condition, however, was quite different. At the time of his vision, the Jews were struggling to stay alive, as they fought against their enemies and against their own limited natural resources. They were not only trying to rebuild the Temple in spite of much opposition, but they were also suffering hardship as a result of successive years of drought. Through the centuries, God had taught Israel to trust Him for the rain they needed for their existence. He also told them to expect rains to be withheld if they were disobedient (which was often the case).

In my opinion, Zechariah 10:1 is simply striking because of what it reveals about God's heart. The Message paraphrases this verse this way, "Pray for rain—it's time for the spring rain—to God, the rainmaker, spring thunderstorm maker, maker of grain and barley." With these words, God was inviting his people, through the prophet, to ask Him for what they needed. God used the metaphor of sending life-giving rain during the Millennium to remind the Jews (and us) that He is a God who delights in caring for us and giving us what we need. Sadly, however, many Christians do not ask the Lord for all their needs. This is exactly what James had in mind when he wrote in James 4:2, "You lust and do not have. You murder and covet and cannot obtain. You fight and war. Yet you do not have because you do not ask."

Zechariah's prophecy promises literal rain in the kingdom that is to come, but it also promises a spiritual rain of blessings when we relate to God as we should. We can find a similar passage in Hosea 6:1-3, which states, "Come, and let us return to the LORD; for He has torn, but He will heal us; He has stricken, but He will bind us up. After two days He will revive us; on the third day He will raise us up, that we may live in His sight. Let us know, let us pursue the knowledge of the LORD. His going forth is established as the morning; He will come to us like the rain, like the latter and former rain to the earth."[1]

When interpreted figuratively, rain is a symbol of spiritual refreshment and is often used to symbolize the outpouring of the Holy Spirit (cf. Joel 2:28). By telling the people to ask for rain, God was actually reminding them that His plan on their behalf is not one of destruction but of salvation. We see this repeatedly throughout the Scriptures, especially in passages like the following:

- Isaiah 59:20-21, "'The Redeemer will come to Zion, and to those who turn from transgression in Jacob,' says the LORD. 'As for Me,' says the LORD, 'this is My covenant with them: My Spirit who is upon you, and My words which I have put in your mouth, shall not depart from your mouth, nor from the mouth of your descendants, nor from the mouth of your descendants' descendants,' says the LORD, 'from this time and forevermore.'"

- Jeremiah 29:10-11, "For thus says the LORD: After seventy years are completed at Babylon, I will visit you and perform My good word toward you, and cause you to return to this place. For I know the thoughts that I think toward you, says the LORD, thoughts of peace and not of evil, to give you a future and a hope."

- Romans 11:1, "I say then, has God cast away His people? Certainly not! For I also am an Israelite, of the seed of Abraham, of the tribe of Benjamin."

- Romans 11:26-27, "And so all Israel will be saved, as

it is written: 'The Deliverer will come out of Zion, and He will turn away ungodliness from Jacob; for this is My covenant with them, when I take away their sins.'"

In the same way that God plans to save His people and refresh their lives with the outpouring of His blessings, He also wants to accomplish the same amazing work in our lives today. If God were telling you to ask Him for rain, what would that mean in your own life? What blessing do you need from Him? How can His Holy Spirit refresh your soul?

Teraphim and False Shepherds: Zechariah 10:2-3

If, on the one hand, God wants to bless us with refreshing rain, on the other hand the idols we often turn to end up leaving us empty and disappointed. This is precisely what we read about in the next two verses.

> For the idols speak delusion; the diviners envision lies, and tell false dreams; they comfort in vain. Therefore the people wend their way like sheep; they are in trouble because there is no shepherd. My anger is kindled against the shepherds, and I will punish the goatherds. For the LORD of hosts will visit His flock, the house of Judah, and will make them as His royal horse in the battle (Zechariah 10:2-3).

The Teraphim were household idols. They were images that people often turned to whenever life got out of control. Feinberg comments, "The teraphim were household gods used for the purpose of divination, probably in the form of human beings. They were like the household gods of the Romans (See Genesis 31:19, 30). They were kept at shrines (Judges 17:5) and in private homes (1 Samuel 19:13, 16)."[2]

Sadly, Christians tend to commit the same sin of idolatry as the Israelites. Surely our idols have changed, but the principles remain the same. Whenever we turn to anything other than God to meet our deepest needs and to give us meaning in life, we are guilty of the sin of idolatry. Likewise, false shepherds were a problem to Israel just as they are to the church today. One does not need to look very hard among churches today before encountering false teachers whose so-called "ministries" only take people further away from God's truth. However, these false shepherds will not be allowed to lead people astray forever. In fact, Scriptures do tell us that God has a special punishment reserved for them (cf. Zechariah 10:3)! For instance, Ezekiel 34:6–10, states:

> My sheep wandered through all the mountains, and on every high hill; yes, My flock was scattered over the whole face of the earth, and no one was seeking or searching for them. Therefore, you shepherds, hear the word of the LORD: "as I live," says the Lord GOD, "surely because My flock became a prey, and My flock became food for every beast of the field, because there was no shepherd, nor did My shepherds search for My flock, but the shepherds fed themselves and did not feed My flock"—therefore, O shepherds, hear the word of the LORD! Thus says the Lord GOD: "Behold, I am against the shepherds, and I will require My flock at their hand; I will cause them to cease feeding the sheep, and the shepherds shall feed themselves no more; for I will deliver My flock from their mouths, that they may no longer be food for them."

The Cornerstone Jesus: Zechariah 10:4

Even though false gods and false shepherds are a real threat to God's people even today, all hope is not lost. We have God's assurance that He will never leave behind those who are His. This is exactly what we read about in Zechariah 10:4, which states, "From him comes the cornerstone, from him the tent peg, from him the battle bow, from him every ruler together." The one Zechariah wrote about in this verse is none other than Jesus Christ Himself. The prophet was reminding the people that the Messiah is coming and that, when He does, He will transform God's people from defenseless sheep into strong war horses (Zechariah 10:3c). In other words, through the ministry of the Messiah we will be transformed and finally become what God wants us to be.

Zechariah 10:4 gives us three key pieces of information about Jesus:

1. **He is the Cornerstone.** As such, Jesus Christ is the foundation of our faith and the foundation of God's work in us. Without Jesus, no one can have a relationship with God. It is through Him and Him alone that we can know who God is and what He has done to truly forgive our iniquities. That is why all who believe in Jesus stand on a solid foundation and are never disappointed. Read carefully the following key verses:

   - Isaiah 28:16, "Therefore thus says the Lord GOD: 'Behold, I lay in Zion a stone for a foundation, a tried stone, a precious cornerstone, a sure foundation; whoever believes will not act hastily.'"

   - Romans 9:33, "As it is written: 'Behold, I lay in Zion a stumbling stone and rock of offense, and whoever believes on Him will not be put to shame.'"

   - Ephesians 2:20, "Having been built on the foundation of the apostles and prophets, Jesus Christ Himself being the chief cornerstone."

2. **He is the Nail (or tent peg).** It could be said that the tent peg is to the tent what the cornerstone is to a building. An Old Assyrian inscription of Irishum suggests that a peg was driven into the wall of a temple as a symbol of its completion. In that case, the founda-

tion stone marked the beginning of the project, while the peg marked the end of it. Both terms came to be used metaphorically as that which is foundational (as in Isa 22:23 and Ezra 9:8).[3] This means that all the glory of the Kingdom rests on Jesus. He is our foundation. Without Him, we have nothing good left.

3. **Jesus is the Battle Bow**. Like the previous terms, this expression emphasizes the strong, stable, victorious, and trustworthy nature of Messiah's rule. More specifically, here we have a picture of the Messiah when He returns to planet earth at the end of the Tribulation. Whereas in His first coming Jesus came as the Lamb of God, in His second return He will come back as the Lion from the Tribe of Judah. At that time, He will judge the nations once and for all and unite His people so that they can spend eternity in His holy presence. Notice the other details Zechariah described about the Tribulation in Zechariah 10:5-8.

"They shall be like mighty men, who tread down their enemies in the mire of the streets in the battle. They shall fight because the LORD is with them, and the riders on horses shall be put to shame. I will strengthen the house of Judah, and I will save the house of Joseph. I will bring them back, because I have mercy on them. They shall be as though I had not cast them aside; for I am the LORD their God, and I will hear them. Those of Ephraim shall be like a mighty man, and their heart shall rejoice as if with wine. Yes, their children shall see it and be glad; their heart shall rejoice in the LORD. I will whistle for them and gather them, for I will redeem them; and they shall increase as they once increased."

Before the Messiah can establish His Kingdom, He must first deliver and restore Israel. He will strengthen them, save them, bring them back, have mercy on them, and hear them. The best thing about this entire process is that we are not excluded from God's grace. He will also do all of these things on our behalf. When God whistles for Israel's victory during the tumult of the Tribulation, those who are in Christ will most definitely be on the winning side.

Displacement again for Israel? Zechariah 10:9

But before God's people can enjoy the promises of the Millennium, they must go through God's process of refinement. This means that they must be molded, through trials and tribulations, into the kind of people God wants them to be. This is why Zechariah 10:9 reads, "I will sow them among the peoples, and they shall remember Me in far countries; they shall live, together with their children, and they shall return." This verse is especially significant when we keep in mind that the Jews who were alive in Zechariah's time had already returned from an exile. This verse, therefore, implies that there will be a future time when Israel will be once again displaced from the Promised Land.

The Permanent Regathering: Zechariah 10:10-12

God's prophecy, however, does not end with promises of destruction or isolation. Rather, God wants to once again comfort His people through the prophet as we can clearly see in Zechariah 10:10-12. Take a look:

> I will also bring them back from the land of Egypt, and gather them from Assyria. I will bring them into the land of Gilead and Lebanon, until no more room is found for them. He shall pass through the sea with affliction, and strike the waves of the sea: all the depths of the River shall dry up. Then the pride of Assyria shall be brought down, and the scepter of Egypt shall depart. So I will strengthen them in the LORD, and they shall walk up and down in His name," says the LORD.

Full of confidence in God's constant love for us, the Apostle Paul once wrote in Philippians 1:6, "Being confident of this very thing, that He who has begun a good work in you will complete it until the day of Jesus Christ." God will never give up on His people. This means that He will never give up on you. The real question, then, is: Have you given up on Him? Or do you still believe in Him enough to raise your voice to heaven and ask Him for His refreshing rain to fall upon your heart? It is never too late to turn to God—never too late.

Discussion Questions

1. What does Zechariah 10 reveal to us about God's heart? What is He like? What is His attitude toward us?

2. What does it mean to "ask the Lord for rain" (verse 1)? What did this mean to the Jews and how can we still do that today?

3. What are idols? What kind of idols are you tempted to have in your own life? Where do you go for "refreshing rain"?

4. Explain in your own words what Zechariah 10:4 teaches us about Jesus Christ.

5. What is the significance of Christ as the cornerstone, the tent peg, and the battle bow?

6. We have God's promise that He will never give up on those who are His. However, how can we "give up" on Him? What would that look like in your own life?

That's Not All

You can find sermon outlines and other extras in the "Sermonars" section at the back of the book. These pages may be freely reproduced, either from the book or from the accompanying CD-ROM for any devotional or ministry use.

Chapter Twelve

Thirty Pieces of Silver in Zechariah?

1 Open your doors, O Lebanon,
That fire may devour your cedars.
2 Wail, O cypress, for the cedar has fallen,
Because the mighty trees are ruined.
Wail, O oaks of Bashan,
For the thick forest has come down.
3 There is the sound of wailing shepherds!
For their glory is in ruins.
There is the sound of roaring lions!
For the pride of the Jordan is in ruins.

4 Thus says the LORD my God, "Feed the flock for slaughter,
5 whose owners slaughter them and feel no guilt; those who
sell them say, 'Blessed be the LORD, for I am rich'; and their
shepherds do not pity them. 6 For I will no longer pity the
inhabitants of the land," says the LORD. "But indeed I will
give everyone into his neighbor's hand and into the hand of
his king. They shall attack the land, and I will not deliver
them from their hand."

7 So I fed the flock for slaughter, in particular the poor of
the flock. I took for myself two staffs: the one I called Beauty,
and the other I called Bonds; and I fed the flock. 8 I dis-

missed the three shepherds in one month. My soul loathed them, and their soul also abhorred me. 9 Then I said, "I will not feed you. Let what is dying die, and what is perishing perish. Let those that are left eat each other's flesh." 10 And I took my staff, Beauty, and cut it in two, that I might break the covenant which I had made with all the peoples. 11 So it was broken on that day. Thus the poor of the flock, who were watching me, knew that it was the word of the LORD. 12 Then I said to them, "If it is agreeable to you, give me my wages; and if not, refrain." So they weighed out for my wages thirty pieces of silver.

13 And the LORD said to me, "Throw it to the potter"—that princely price they set on me. So I took the thirty pieces of silver and threw them into the house of the LORD for the potter. 14 Then I cut in two my other staff, Bonds, that I might break the brotherhood between Judah and Israel.

15 And the LORD said to me, "Next, take for yourself the implements of a foolish shepherd. 16 For indeed I will raise up a shepherd in the land who will not care for those who are cut off, nor seek the young, nor heal those that are broken, nor feed those that still stand. But he will eat the flesh of the fat and tear their hooves in pieces.

> *17 " Woe to the worthless shepherd,*
> *Who leaves the flock!*
> *A sword shall be against his arm*
> *And against his right eye;*
> *His arm shall completely wither,*
> *And his right eye shall be totally blinded."*

(Zechariah 11:1-17)

The Tragic Result of Rejecting Jesus

By now I hope you have noticed a common pattern that Zechariah uses to communicate his prophecy to us. All throughout the book the prophet's message alternates between hope and judgment, life and death, blessings and curses. This is, in fact, a common pattern of basically all prophetic material in the Bible. God's revelation to us always seems to include promises of both hope and doom. To those who repent from their sins and turn to God there is always forgiveness and redemption. To those who refuse to repent from their rebellion, however, there is always judgment and death.

In Zechariah 10—a chapter of hope—God reveals exciting prophetic material about the coming Kingdom and about the Messiah who would come to set His people free. In Zechariah 11—a chapter of judgment—He goes back to the themes of doom and judgment upon those who persist in their rejection of God. Feinberg writes about Zechariah 11, "The chapter is undoubtedly the darkest of Israel's history . . . . The context of the rest of the chapter is determining and points unmistakably to the judgment which resulted from the rejection of the Shepherd of Israel, that destruction which overtook the land and people in AD 70."[1] With that in mind, reflect upon Zechariah 11 (above) before we take a closer look at its teachings.

Two main themes should stand out as we read Zechariah 11. First we notice the contrast between the two shepherds mentioned in this passage: the Good Shepherd and the foolish shepherd. McGee writes, "This chapter presents the Good Shepherd of His people, the Good Shepherd who will give His life for the sheep. Then another shepherd is presented, the foolish shepherd, who will come much later. He pictures the Antichrist, the one who will shear the sheep and kill them for food."[2] Jesus Himself also spoke about the contrast between Himself (the Good Shepherd) and false shepherds. He said:

> The thief does not come except to steal, and to kill, and to destroy. I have come that they may have life, and that they may have it more abundantly. I am the good shepherd. The good shepherd gives His life for the sheep. But a hireling, he who is not the shepherd,

one who does not own the sheep, sees the wolf coming and leaves the sheep and flees; and the wolf catches the sheep and scatters them. The hireling flees because he is a hireling and does not care about the sheep. I am the good shepherd; and I know My sheep, and am known by My own. (John 10:10-14)

The second major theme we pick up from this chapter is that of sure judgment to those who reject Christ, the Good Shepherd sent by God to lay down His life on our behalf. As we read the record of Jesus' ministry in the gospels, it is clear to see how this prophecy was fulfilled: Jesus came to die for His own people, but they rejected Him and will suffer condemnation as a result of that. Take a look:

- John 1:10-11, "He was in the world, and the world was made through Him, and the world did not know Him. He came to His own, and His own did not receive Him."

- John 3:36, "He who believes in the Son has everlasting life; and he who does not believe the Son shall not see life, but the wrath of God abides on him."

- John 5:37-40, "[Jesus said:] And the Father Himself, who sent Me, has testified of Me. You have neither heard His voice at any time, nor seen His form. But you do not have His word abiding in you, because whom He sent, Him you do not believe. You search the Scriptures, for in them you think you have eternal life; and these are they which testify of Me. But you are not willing to come to Me that you may have life."

Israel's Tragic Invasion: Zechariah 11:1-3

It is always a tragedy when an individual or, in the case of this chapter, an entire nation rejects Jesus Christ. In the case of the Jews, such rejection meant—among other things—

the tragic invasion of their land. Zechariah 11:1-3 reads:

> Open your doors, O Lebanon, that fire may devour
> your cedars. Wail, O cypress, for the cedar has fallen,
> because the mighty trees are ruined. Wail, O oaks of
> Bashan, for the thick forest has come down. There
> is the sound of wailing shepherds! For their glory is
> in ruins. There is the sound of roaring lions! For the
> pride of the Jordan is in ruins.

It is very clear that these first three verses describe an invasion on the land of Israel. Three different locations are identified: Lebanon (north of Israel); Bashan (south of Israel); and Jordan. If we take these words literally (as we should), we have in these verses an all-encompassing picture of judgment on the land, a judgment that extends from north to south. The judgment described is exactly what happened to Israel in AD 70 when the Romans invaded Israel and ruthlessly attacked Jerusalem. At that time, over one million Jews were killed.

Zechariah 11:1 reveals that there would be a scattering of the people after the time of Zechariah. This is exactly what happened. The Romans used the same method as Alexander the Great to invade the land of Israel. They came down from the north, through Lebanon, and successfully took over the land without much opposition. In verses 2 and 3, therefore, Zechariah described the advance of a conqueror (who we now know to be the Roman Emperor Titus) who came down to attack Israel.

Most scholars believe that verse 2 is a figurative reference to the Jewish Temple. The cedar of Lebanon was a famous wood at the time. Not surprisingly, that is the very same type of wood used in Solomon's Temple. Thus, Zechariah was prophesying not only that Israel would be invaded but that their precious Temple would also be destroyed. Jesus too prophesied the same thing. Take a look:

- Matthew 23:37-39, "O Jerusalem, Jerusalem, the one
  who kills the prophets and stones those who are sent

to her! How often I wanted to gather your children together, as a hen gathers her chicks under her wings, but you were not willing! See! Your house is left to you desolate; for I say to you, you shall see Me no more till you say, 'Blessed is He who comes in the name of the LORD!'"

- Matthew 24:1-2, "Then Jesus went out and departed from the temple, and His disciples came up to show Him the buildings of the temple. And Jesus said to them, 'Do you not see all these things? Assuredly, I say to you, not one stone shall be left here upon another, that shall not be thrown down.'"

Because of such great destruction, Zechariah also wrote about wailing shepherds in verse 3. These are the false shepherds who gave God's people the wrong message. They were the hypocritical, religious leaders who rejected Jesus as God's Son and Messiah and who, consequently, lead the entire nation astray.

Feed the Flock for Slaughter: Zechariah 11:4-6

The bulk of this passage, verses 4-14, give us the details of the Messiah's rejection, which was the reason for such desolation to be visited upon the land. In these verses, God the Father (verse 4, "The Lord my God") used the prophet as an actor playing the part of a shepherd. Through this device, Zechariah represented the true Shepherd, Jesus Christ, and the rejection He encountered. In the vision, Zechariah performed the actions to be performed years later by the Messiah. The Messiah, Zechariah suggested, was to be a shepherd and feed the flock (Israel), whose destiny was slaughter at the hands of the Roman army. Furthermore, Zechariah portrayed a shepherd leading his flock to death because that is precisely what Israel's false shepherds did when they rejected the Christ. It was because of their rebellion that God promised that the land would be attacked and subdued (verse 6).

The Ministry of the True Shepherd: Zechariah 11:7-11

At the center of Zechariah 11 is a powerful description of the ministry of the true Shepherd. Zechariah 11:7-8 states,

> So I fed the flock for slaughter, in particular the poor of the flock. I took for myself two staffs: the one I called Beauty, and the other I called Bonds; and I fed the flock. I dismissed the three shepherds in one month. My soul loathed them, and their soul also abhorred me.

Verse 7 starts out by informing us that the true Shepherd would feed the flock, in particular the poor, even though they were destined for slaughter. That is precisely what we see Jesus do in the gospels.

During Jesus' ministry, it was the poor who gravitated to Him, heard Him, and followed Him. Because they were so needy, they were well aware that they needed Jesus to take care of them. Out of their worldly poverty, therefore, came a deep sense of poverty of spirit. This is what Jesus referred to in Matthew 5:3-5, "Blessed are the poor in spirit, for theirs is the kingdom of heaven. Blessed are those who mourn, for they shall be comforted. Blessed are the meek, for they shall inherit the earth."

As it was the custom among the shepherds of Old Testament times, two staffs are mentioned in verse 7. Shepherds of that day carried two staffs: one to protect the flock against wild beasts and the other to help rescue the sheep when they went to difficult places. In this specific passage, "Beauty" refers to God's favor on our behalf, while "Bonds" refers to the unity we share with our Good Shepherd. Therefore, Jesus stands in contrast against the "loathsome three shepherds" (verse 8), a probable reference to the priests, elders, and scribes of Israel who hated and rejected Him.

It was because of them that the flock would perish and despair to the point of "eating each other's flesh" (verse 9).

Not surprisingly, this is exactly what happened when the Romans surrounded Jerusalem in AD 70. Some of the survivors were so desperate for food that they practiced cannibalism as a way of staying alive. God's providential care for Israel was set aside because of her sin. This is why the staff Favor was broken in verse 10. When that happened, the people were on their own, without a Shepherd to shield them. As mentioned before, tragic things do happen when people reject God's Anointed! When we disobey God, we might be placing ourselves in a position that is outside of God's protection for us.

Thirty Pieces of Silver: Zechariah 11:12-14

In verses 12-14 Zechariah was called on to portray another prophetic role, that of a foolish shepherd. The Hebrew word translated "foolish" in verse 15 suggests a person who is a coarse, hardened fool. This shepherd would have no concern for the flock and its needs. Instead, he would be interested only in his own gluttony. Instead of defending the flock, the foolish shepherd would destroy it. The breaking of the staff Bonds in verse 14 was a declarative statement that the nation of Israel would be broken when the Romans invaded Jerusalem in AD 70.

It is in this context that we read Zechariah's amazing reference to "thirty pieces of silver" in verses 12-13. If you recall it, this is the very same amount of money Judas received from Israel's false shepherds for his betrayal of Christ. In other words, this passage is an exact prediction of Matthew 27:3-10. Thirty pieces of silver was the price of a slave that had been injured by an ox. By selling Jesus for thirty pieces of silver, Judas was in fact declaring to the entire world his low view of Christ. How about you? How much is Jesus Christ worth to you?

The Evil Shepherd to Come: Zechariah 11:15-17

This dark chapter ends with an equally somber reference to the ultimate enemy who is yet to come and to lead people away from God one last time. In Zechariah 11:15-17 he is described as the false and foolish shepherd. He is the worthless shepherd who rightfully deserves the condemnation pronounced upon him. The reference to the arm indicates his strength, while the eye symbolizes his intelligence. In the New Testament, this same shepherd is described as the Antichrist (cf. 1 John 4:3), the one who will deceive the nations and persecute God's children at the time of the Great Tribulation. Paul wrote about him in 2 Thessalonians 2:7-12.

> For the mystery of lawlessness is already at work; only He who now restrains will do so until He is taken out of the way. And then the lawless one will be revealed, whom the Lord will consume with the breath of His mouth and destroy with the brightness of His coming. The coming of the lawless one is according to the working of Satan, with all power, signs, and lying wonders, and with all unrighteous deception among those who perish, because they did not receive the love of the truth, that they might be saved. And for this reason God will send them strong delusion, that they should believe the lie, that they all may be condemned who did not believe the truth but had pleasure in unrighteousness.

Praise be to God that we do not have to be led by a false shepherd. God has sent us His very Son, Jesus Christ, our Good Shepherd. Jesus once stated in John 10:14, "I am the good shepherd; and I know My sheep, and am known by My own." Do you know Jesus? I am not asking you about knowing facts about Jesus, but about truly knowing Him personally, as your Good Shepherd, your Savior, your Lord, and your King. Do you know Him?

Discussion Questions

1. In your own words, compare and contrast the Good Shepherd and the false shepherds. Who are they? How are they different? What effects do they have on the flocks they lead?

2. What were the two staffs that an Old Testament-era shepherd carried? What is their significance to this chapter? To our own time?

3. How did Jesus' own people treat Him? How do people today still do the same? How do you treat Jesus with your own life?

4. What roles did Zechariah portray in this chapter? What or whom did he symbolize? What was he trying to communicate to the people?

5. Why do you think that it might be easier for the "poor" to turn to Christ for salvation? In what ways are you "poor"?

6. What can you learn about God as our Shepherd and Jesus as our Good Shepherd in Psalm 23 and John 10:1-18, respectively?

That's Not All

You can find sermon outlines and other extras in the "Sermonars" section at the back of the book. These pages may be freely reproduced, either from the book or from the accompanying CD-ROM for any devotional or ministry use.

Chapter Thirteen

The Deceit of the Antichrist

15 And the LORD said to me, "Next, take for yourself the implements of a foolish shepherd. 16 For indeed I will raise up a shepherd in the land who will not care for those who are cut off, nor seek the young, nor heal those that are broken, nor feed those that still stand. But he will eat the flesh of the fat and tear their hooves in pieces.

17 " Woe to the worthless shepherd,
Who leaves the flock!
A sword shall be against his arm
And against his right eye;
His arm shall completely wither,
And his right eye shall be totally blinded."
(Zechariah 11:15-17)

The Deceitful Character of the Antichrist

The Antichrist is such an important figure in both Old and New Testaments that I find it important to take a closer look at Zechariah's final three verses in chapter 11, since they give us important information about this pivotal figure. Because Israel rejected the True Shepherd, they will tragically receive the false shepherd, the Antichrist. Notice in the verses above how Zechariah mentions him.

And the LORD said to me, "Next, take for yourself the implements of a foolish shepherd. For indeed I will raise up a shepherd in the land who will not care for those who are cut off, nor seek the young, nor heal those that are broken, nor feed those that still stand. But he will eat the flesh of the fat and tear their hooves in pieces. Woe to the worthless shepherd, who leaves the flock! A sword shall be against his arm and against his right eye; His arm shall completely wither, and his right eye shall be totally blinded (Zech 11:15-17)."

The Apostle John once wrote in 1 John 2:18, "Little children, it is the last hour; and as you have heard that the Antichrist is coming, even now many antichrists have come, by which we know that it is the last hour." According to this verse, several antichrists have already come, but the Antichrist who will lead sinful mankind against God is yet to come. Throughout the ages, however, people of faith have tried very hard to identify the Antichrist with a living historical figure. The list is, indeed, quite long. Muhammad was seen as the Antichrist in the Middle Ages, Saladin at the time of the Crusades, the Grand Sultan of the Ottoman Turks when they threatened the gates of Vienna, and Napoleon in the aftermath of the French Revolution. Martin Luther, along with other famous religious figures such as Calvin, Zwingli, Tyndale, and John Knox, denounced the pope (or, more precisely, the papacy) as the Antichrist. The Roman emperors Nero and Caligula, Lenin, Stalin, Hitler, Mussolini, Roosevelt, Kennedy, Henry Kissinger, Ayatollah Khomeini, Sadam Hussein, and even Osama bin Laden have also been mistakenly named the Antichrist. But instead of trying to identify the Antichrist based on our own conjectures, it is a much better idea to let God's Word identify him for us.

According to Zechariah 11:15, the Antichrist is the foolish shepherd. Baron comments on this specific verse:

But who is meant by this foolish or wicked shepherd?

Jewish commentators interpret it as Herod; some Christian interpreters apply it to "all the evil native Jewish rulers collectively," who, subsequent to the rejection of Christ, oppressed and devoured the flock. Others again identify him with the imperial Roman power. But the full and final fulfillment of this solemn prophecy will take place in the final phase of the development of the fourth great world power (i.e., the Roman), when amid the ten horns, or kingdoms, there shall come up 'a little horn' who shall be master of them all.[1]

Scholar Homer Heater also wrote about the Antichrist in this particular context:

This shepherd is obviously some very wicked person who will seek to destroy the people of Israel. Many people in history would fit that description, but a coming wicked ruler fits it in a horrifying way. Revelation 13 speaks of a "beast" coming up from the sea who will rule most of the world through Satan's power. This person is called "the Antichrist" because he is against all that Christ stands for and puts himself in the place of Christ. He will be active during the Great Tribulation. The nation of Israel, having rejected the true shepherd, will have to face the wicked one.[2]

Nathan Stone adds the following:

Verses 15-18 are full of awful omen. Since Israel rejects the true Shepherd, an evil shepherd will be raised up whom they will receive (John 5:43). He will exploit and cruelly treat them (Ezek 34:2-4). This will find its full manifestation in the future man of lawlessness (2 Thess 2). But he will be judged (v. 17), in the arm and the eye, emblems of his power and perception.[3]

The first trait that stands out about the Antichrist in Zechariah 11:15 is his foolishness. The Hebrew word translated "foolish" is a synonym for "wicked," which adequately describes the Antichrist's overall intentions and actions. We see this very clearly in verse 16,

> For indeed I will raise up a shepherd in the land who will not care for those who are cut off, nor seek the young, nor heal those that are broken, nor feed those that still stand. But he will eat the flesh of the fat and tear their hooves in pieces.

Furthermore, the various names used to describe the Antichrist throughout the Scriptures also tend to convey the evil that characterizes his being. Take a look at the following examples:

- The bloody and deceitful man (Ps 5:6)
- The wicked one (Ps 10:2-4)
- The enemy (Ps 55:3)
- The adversary (Ps 74:8-10)
- The violent man (Ps 140:1)
- The spoiler (Isa 16:4-5; Jer 6:26)
- The vile person (Dan 11:21)
- The man of sin (2 Thess 2:8)
- The son of perdition (2 Thess 2:3)
- The lawless one (2 Thess 2:8)
- The abomination of desolation (Matt 24:15)

In spite of the Antichrist's great power and evil, it is important to keep in mind that he will not operate outside of God's control. Rather, Zechariah 1:16 reminds us that he functions within God's sovereign plan. God is the One who will raise up the Antichrist. This does not mean that God is responsible for the Antichrist's evil. Instead, it indicates that God allows the Antichrist to take an important role in His dealings with sinful mankind. When the time is right,

God will allow the Antichrist to come in order to inflict unparalleled misery during the Tribulation period. Many will die and experience a horrendous fate because of him.

The Condemnation of the Antichrist

J. Vernon McGee writes about the Antichrist:

> The false shepherd, the Antichrist, will actually be the one who brings in the Great Tribulation in all its fury. In the first part of the Tribulation Israel will be deceived into thinking that Antichrist is their Good Shepherd, but by the time they discover his real character, he will be the world dictator, and the armies of the world will come against Jerusalem.[4]

The time will come, however, when the Antichrist shall face God's judgment. His wickedness will not endure forever. Once his purpose is fulfilled, God will see to it that the Antichrist is properly condemned for his evil. We see this truth clearly in Zechariah 11:17, "Woe to the worthless shepherd, who leaves the flock! A sword shall be against his arm and against his right eye; his arm shall completely wither, and his right eye shall be totally blinded."

The opening word "woe" indicates a curse. The Hebrew word actually denotes trouble. At the appointed hour, God will remove the power of the Antichrist. His might (the arm) and craftiness (eye) will be taken away from him once and for all.

Fascinating Facts about the Antichrist

Because the Antichrist is such a prominent figure in biblical prophecy, it is very important for Christians today to have a proper understanding of what the Bible teaches about him. Consider, therefore, the following nine important scriptural truths about the Antichrist:

1. **The Holy Spirit hinders the Antichrist at present**. It is only after the Rapture that the Antichrist will be revealed and his sinister works begin. We know this because of what Paul wrote in 2 Thessalonians 2:6-8, "And now you know what is restraining, that he may be revealed in his own time. For the mystery of lawlessness is already at work; only He who now restrains will do so until He is taken out of the way. And then the lawless one will be revealed, whom the Lord will consume with the breath of His mouth and destroy with the brightness of His coming."

   According to these verses, there will come a day when the restraining ministry of the Holy Spirit will end (at the Rapture of the church). It is at that time that the Antichrist will be given permission to commence his seven-year reign of terror (at the Tribulation).

2. **The Antichrist will rise from the Roman Empire, the very nation that destroyed Jerusalem in AD 70**. According to Daniel 2:40-43, there will be a revival of the Roman Empire that will encompass much of the territory of the old Roman Empire. Out of that revived Roman Empire (which we believe to be the European Union) will rise a great leader who will hold power like nothing the world has ever seen before! The Antichrist will make an alliance with Israel against the Russian-Arab alliance (described in Ezekiel 38) that will come against them. Following the Antichrist's alliance with Israel, armies from the north, south, and east will fight against the Antichrist and his Western confederacy, but he will defeat them (Daniel 11:40-45). At this point, after becoming Israel's protector and defeating the world powers, he will commit the abomination of desolation (that is, he will consecrate the Temple and declare himself God).

3. **The Antichrist will be the head of a union of ten nations: the European Confederacy**. The book of

Daniel tells of the Tribulation period, which will pre-
cede the Messiah's kingdom. Daniel wrote that the
Antichrist will rule a great kingdom largely composed
of the territory that constituted the Roman Empire
(Daniel 7:7, 8). Some of the countries of Europe will
form a confederacy, and the Antichrist will rule over
them. Daniel indicates that the European Union will
be made up of ten nations. We read about this super
world power in various biblical passages, such as:

> Revelation 13:1, "Then I stood on the sand of
> the sea. And I saw a beast rising up out of the
> sea, having seven heads and ten horns, and on
> his horns ten crowns, and on his heads a blas-
> phemous name."

> Revelation 17:12-13, "The ten horns which you
> saw are ten kings who have received no king-
> dom as yet, but they receive authority for one
> hour as kings with the beast. These are of one
> mind, and they will give their power and au-
> thority to the beast."

> Daniel 11:40-43, "At the time of the end the
> king of the South shall attack him; and the
> king of the North shall come against him like
> a whirlwind, with chariots, horsemen, and with
> many ships; and he shall enter the countries,
> overwhelm them, and pass through. He [the
> Antichrist] shall also enter the Glorious Land,
> and many countries shall be overthrown; but
> these shall escape from his hand: Edom, Moab,
> and the prominent people of Ammon. He shall
> stretch out his hand against the countries, and
> the land of Egypt shall not escape. He shall
> have power over the treasures of gold and silver,
> and over all the precious things of Egypt; also
> the Libyans and Ethiopians shall follow at his
> heels."

4. **In his rise to worldwide power, the Antichrist will have destroyed three rulers.** We read about this in Daniel 7:24, "The ten horns are ten kings who shall arise from this kingdom. And another shall rise after them; he shall be different from the first ones, and shall subdue three kings." This probably refers to the fact that at the beginning of the Tribulation, the Antichrist will pretend to be on Israel's side and protect it against three enemy nations. It is only after this initial war that the Antichrist will reveal his true intentions. Daniel 11:36 tells us what will happen then, "Then the king [the Antichrist] shall do according to his own will: he shall exalt and magnify himself above every god, shall speak blasphemies against the God of gods, and shall prosper till the wrath has been accomplished; for what has been determined shall be done."

5. **The Antichrist will exude charm, intelligence, oration, persuasiveness, and unparalleled political and commercial skills.** This is a reason why people will fall for him so easily. In many ways, he will have all the traits of what our corrupted world system considers to be perfect. Daniel writes about this impressive figure:

> Daniel 7:20, "And the ten horns that were on its head, and the other horn which came up, before which three fell, namely, that horn which had eyes and a mouth which spoke pompous words, whose appearance was greater than his fellows."

> Daniel 8:23, "And in the latter time of their kingdom, when the transgressors have reached their fullness, a king shall arise, having fierce features, who understands sinister schemes."

> Daniel 8:25, "Through his cunning he shall

cause deceit to prosper under his rule; and he shall exalt himself in his heart. He shall destroy many in their prosperity. He shall even rise against the Prince of princes; but he shall be broken without human means."

6. **In his ascent to power, the Antichrist will survive an assassination attempt.** We see this in Revelation 13:3, "And I saw one of his heads as if it had been mortally wounded, and his deadly wound was healed. And all the world marveled and followed the beast." The Antichrist will be allowed to come back to life because Satan will empower him and try to mimic the resurrection of God's slain Son, Jesus Christ.

7. **In the middle of the Tribulation, the Antichrist will break the covenant with the Jews and proclaim himself as god.** Daniel 9:27 states, "Then he shall confirm a covenant with many for one week [i.e., seven years]; But in the middle of the week he shall bring an end to sacrifice and offering. And on the wing of abominations shall be one who makes desolate, even until the consummation, which is determined, is poured out on the desolate." Furthermore, Daniel 11:36–37 reads, "Then the king shall do according to his own will: he shall exalt and magnify himself above every god, shall speak blasphemies against the God of gods, and shall prosper till the wrath has been accomplished; for what has been determined shall be done. He shall regard neither the God of his fathers nor the desire of women, nor regard any god; for he shall exalt himself above them all."

8. **The Antichrist will be energized by Satan and deception will be characteristic of him.** The only reasons why the Antichrist will be such an impressive figure are because of God's temporary permission and Satan's supernatural enablement. In fact, Satan will try to use the Antichrist to fulfill his desire of taking

over God's rightful position as Creator and Ruler of all. Take a look:

> Revelation 13:4, "So they worshiped the dragon who gave authority to the beast; and they worshiped the beast, saying, "Who is like the beast? Who is able to make war with him?"

> 2 Thessalonians 2:9-12, "The coming of the lawless one is according to the working of Satan, with all power, signs, and lying wonders, and with all unrighteous deception among those who perish, because they did not receive the love of the truth, that they might be saved. And for this reason God will send them strong delusion, that they should believe the lie, that they all may be condemned who did not believe the truth but had pleasure in unrighteousness."

9. **At Jesus Christ's Second Coming, the Antichrist will be destroyed**. This means that the fulfillment of Satan's dream will be short-lived. God will judge both Satan and the Antichrist at the right time. The Apostle John wrote in Revelation 19:19-20,

> And I saw the beast, the kings of the earth, and their armies, gathered together to make war against Him who sat on the horse and against His army. Then the beast was captured, and with him the false prophet who worked signs in his presence, by which he deceived those who received the mark of the beast and those who worshiped his image. These two were cast alive into the lake of fire burning with brimstone.

The Antichrist will indeed be an impressive and wicked figure. However, there will never be a time when he truly matches the power and the greatness of our God. John once wrote in 1 John 4:4, "You are of God, little children, and have overcome them, because He who is in you is greater than he who is in the world." Our confidence in the future is not based on our own efforts but on the person and the work of Jesus Christ and on the Holy Spirit who dwells in us.

Discussion Questions

1. Who are some of the historical figures that have been incorrectly identified as the Antichrist? What essential error led to these identifications?

2. If someone asked you to describe the person of the Antichrist, what would you say? Make a list of all you can think of.

3. What are some names used in the Scriptures to describe the Antichrist? What do they reveal about his character?

4. Why is it important to remember that the Antichrist will never operate outside of God's control?

5. What role does the Holy Spirit play in relation to the Antichrist? Why is this significant?

6. What does Satan want to accomplish through the Antichrist? Why?

7. This chapter contained several Bible references. Which one(s) especially caught your attention? Why?

That's Not All

You can find sermon outlines and other extras in the "Sermonars" section at the back of the book. These pages may be freely reproduced, either from the book or from the accompanying CD-ROM for any devotional or ministry use.

Chapter Fourteen

The Coming War against Jerusalem

1 The burden of the word of the LORD against Israel. Thus says the LORD, who stretches out the heavens, lays the foundation of the earth, and forms the spirit of man within him: 2 "Behold, I will make Jerusalem a cup of drunkenness to all the surrounding peoples, when they lay siege against Judah and Jerusalem. 3 And it shall happen in that day that I will make Jerusalem a very heavy stone for all peoples; all who would heave it away will surely be cut in pieces, though all nations of the earth are gathered against it. 4 In that day," says the LORD, "I will strike every horse with confusion, and its rider with madness; I will open My eyes on the house of Judah, and will strike every horse of the peoples with blindness. 5 And the governors of Judah shall say in their heart, 'The inhabitants of Jerusalem are my strength in the LORD of hosts, their God.' 6 In that day I will make the governors of Judah like a firepan in the woodpile, and like a fiery torch in the sheaves; they shall devour all the surrounding peoples on the right hand and on the left, but Jerusalem shall be inhabited again in her own place—Jerusalem.

7 "The LORD will save the tents of Judah first, so that the glory of the house of David and the glory of the inhabitants

*of Jerusalem shall not become greater than that of Judah. 8
In that day the LORD will defend the inhabitants of Jerusalem; the one who is feeble among them in that day shall be
like David, and the house of David shall be like God, like
the Angel of the LORD before them. 9 It shall be in that day
that I will seek to destroy all the nations that come against
Jerusalem.*

*10 "And I will pour on the house of David and on the in-
habitants of Jerusalem the Spirit of grace and supplication;
then they will look on Me whom they pierced. Yes, they will
mourn for Him as one mourns for his only son, and grieve
for Him as one grieves for a firstborn. 11 In that day there
shall be a great mourning in Jerusalem, like the mourning
at Hadad Rimmon in the plain of Megiddo. 12 And the
land shall mourn, every family by itself: the family of the
house of David by itself, and their wives by themselves; the
family of the house of Nathan by itself, and their wives by
themselves; 13 the family of the house of Levi by itself, and
their wives by themselves; the family of Shimei by itself, and
their wives by themselves; 14 all the families that remain,
every family by itself, and their wives by themselves. (Zech
12:1-14)*

In 1984, President Ronald Reagan was questioned by re-
porter Marvin Kalb about his view on the End Times. President Reagan's was both succinct and profound. He said,
"We must plan according to Armageddon." In his mind, the
time is drawing near when God will fulfill all the prophecies of the Bible that are still unfulfilled. If this was true
over twenty years ago in 1984, how much more today! Not
surprisingly, people today are becoming increasingly interested in apocalyptic information. Take, for instance, the *Left
Behind* series, which by now has sold over 60,000,000 copies,
out-selling famous authors such as Stephen King and John
Grisham. A *Time*/CNN poll found that more than one-third
of Americans say they are paying more attention to how
the news might relate to the end of the world and that they

have talked about what the Bible has to say on the subject. According to the same poll, fifty-nine percent of Americans say they believe the events in Revelation are going to come true some day.[1]

Five Amazing Facts about Chapters 12-14

As we continue our journey through Zechariah's prophetic material, it is imperative for us to understand how this present section fits within the overall outline of the book. Take a look:

- Zechariah 1-8 covers events that happened during Zechariah's time, attributing to them prophetic implications.

- Zechariah 9-14 presents very clearly the prophetic picture of End Time events. This section is subdivided in two parts:

  o Zechariah 9-11 speaks of Christ's First Coming.

  o Zechariah 12-14, the present section under study, speaks of Christ's Second Coming, which is yet to happen!

Therefore, we are about the take a look at one of the most exciting sections in the entire book of Zechariah. Chapters 12-14 comprise the final portion of the book, where the prophet laid out for us key End Times events that will affect every single person alive at the time they happen. Zechariah 12:1a sets the tone for what is to come. It introduces the idea of the "burden of the word of the LORD against Israel." One of the focus points of all End Times events is God's burden against Israel's rebellion and His desire to bring them back unto Himself. With that in mind, we can make five basic statements about the content of this final section in Zechariah's book:

- **Israel will be the focal point of the world at the Second Coming of Christ.** This is why Jerusalem is mentioned ten times in chapter 12 alone.

- **The final battle, Armageddon (Rev 16:16), will be a major military build-up from the four corners of the globe,** which will come together against Israel (Daniel 11:36–45).

- **The Second Coming of Christ will bring an end to the worst battle mankind will ever know** (Rev 19:11–21).

- **One of the key terms explored in these chapters is that of "The Day of the Lord."** This expression refers to the period of time that begins with the Great Tribulation and continues until the end of the final judgment, which will happen after the Millennium (take a look at the illustrations below). The phrase "in that day" is cited fourteen times in Zechariah 12-14 alone. This is a clear reference to the terrible Day of the Lord. Other key facts about The Day of the Lord include the following:

  o It is mentioned directly at least eighteen times in Zechariah alone.

  o It is the overall theme of the book of Joel.

  o As mentioned above, it is not a twenty-four-hour period of time.

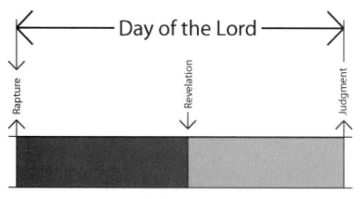

o It will begin with the Rapture of the church. (1 Thessalonians 5:2, "For you yourselves know perfectly that the day of the Lord so comes as a thief in the night.")

- God will fulfill His plan for Israel through the Great Tribulation, which will culminate with spiritual salvation and victory for God's chosen people. We see this very clearly in Daniel 12:1, "At that time Michael shall stand up, the great prince who stands watch over the sons of your people; and there shall be a time of trouble, such as never was since there was a nation, even to that time. And at that time your people shall be delivered, every one who is found written in the book."

Jerusalem Will Be...: Zechariah 12:2-4

Before God's elect can be saved, however, they will have to go through an unparalleled time of widespread destruction as never seen before. Zechariah 12:2-4 reads:

> "Behold, I will make Jerusalem a cup of drunkenness to all the surrounding peoples, when they lay siege against Judah and Jerusalem. And it shall happen in that day that I will make Jerusalem a very heavy stone for all peoples; all who would heave it away will surely be cut in pieces, though all nations of the earth are gathered against it. In that day," says the LORD, "I will strike every horse with confusion, and its rider with madness; I will open My eyes on the house of Judah, and will strike every horse of the peoples with blindness."

God promised that He will make Jerusalem a "cup of drunkenness," which refers to a large basin that everyone can drink from. This means that attacking nations will be like a drunkard who cannot walk a straight line and who cannot be satisfied, continually going to Israel for more destruction. Raymond Saxe comments on these verses as follows:

> The thought is this: Jerusalem and Judah will both become a cup or goblet which causes intoxication. This will result in staggering. Like men greedy with their drink from a glass of wine and ending up hopelessly drunk, so will God make those nations which besiege Jerusalem! They will reel in their attempt to overthrow the city.[2]

John Phillips adds these words:

> The final target of God-hate on this planet will be the Jew and Jerusalem. As the nations of the last days work on getting rid of the last lingering reminders of the Judeo-Christian ethic, they will concentrate their efforts on Jerusalem. The Jews will refuse to surrender their city and will defend it with fanatical zeal. The nations will be so obsessed with Jerusalem that they will be like drunkards who tarry too long at the cup.[3]

God also promised in verse 3 that He will make Jerusalem a "heavy stone." This sports figure of speech refers to a heavy stone used in weightlifting contests. In colloquial language, it is almost as if God will give a hernia to any nation that tries to gain victory over Israel. The language is very clear: there is no hope whatsoever for those who set themselves against the purpose of God. They will be "cut into pieces." This reaches back all the way to Genesis 12:3, where God promised Abraham, "I will bless those who bless you, and I will curse him who curses you; and in you all the families of the earth shall be blessed." The prophet Isaiah also wrote on the same lines in Isaiah 54:17, "'No weapon formed against you shall prosper, and every tongue which rises against you in judgment you shall condemn. This is the heritage of the servants of the LORD, and their righteousness is from Me,' says the LORD."

The Invading Armies: Zechariah 12:4-14

Zechariah's prophecy is not a fairy tale. A day is indeed coming when the entire world (or what is left of it) will attack the nation of Israel and lose. The prophet went on to describe those events in Zechariah 12:4-6.

> "In that day," says the LORD, "I will strike every horse with confusion, and its rider with madness; I will open My eyes on the house of Judah, and will strike every horse of the peoples with blindness. And the governors of Judah shall say in their heart, 'The inhabitants of Jerusalem are my strength in the LORD of hosts, their God.' In that day I will make the governors of Judah like a firepan in the woodpile, and like a fiery torch in the sheaves; they shall devour all the surrounding peoples on the right hand and on the left, but Jerusalem shall be inhabited again in her own place—Jerusalem."

Even though Jerusalem will be extremely vulnerable at that time, the Lord promised that the city would withstand the attacks of its fierce enemies. Based on other biblical passages, we know that Israel's enemies during the Tribulation will be many and powerful. As a matter of fact, there will be four armies at Armageddon:

- The army from the west (Daniel 7:7-8, 24; Revelation 17:12-14), which probably refers to the European Confederacy, the revived Roman Empire that will be made up of ten nations and that will be led by the Antichrist.

- The army from the north (Ezekiel 38:1-6, 14-16), which would be most likely comprised of Russia and her allies (i.e., Persia, Cush, Put, Gomer, and Togermah—ancient names of modern Arab states).

- The army from the south (Daniel 11:40-44), which would be Egypt and her Arab allies.

- The army from the east (Revelation 9:13-16; 16:12-16), which will have as many as 200,000,000 soldiers.

There is no doubt about it: God will send invaders like never before to attack Israel. Nevertheless, the Lord has also promised that He will not allow His holy nation to be destroyed. He will miraculously preserve His people and bring them to a renewed relationship with Him. Once again, Phillips comments, "Humanly speaking, there will be no reason for the world dictator, with vast military resources at his command, not to be able to conquer the troublesome city. But the besiegers will be up against God Himself. No matter what strategies they employ or what armies they summon, they will be incapacitated by God's direct intervention."[4]

Zechariah continued his prophecy in verses 7-14.

> The LORD will save the tents of Judah first, so that the glory of the house of David and the glory of the inhabitants of Jerusalem shall not become greater than that of Judah. In that day the LORD will defend the inhabitants of Jerusalem; the one who is feeble among them in that day shall be like David, and the house of David shall be like God, like the Angel of the LORD before them. It shall be in that day that I will seek to destroy all the nations that come against Jerusalem. And I will pour on the house of David and on the inhabitants of Jerusalem the Spirit of grace and supplication; then they will look on Me whom they pierced. Yes, they will mourn for Him as one mourns for his only son, and grieve for Him as one grieves for a firstborn. In that day there shall be a great mourning in Jerusalem, like the mourning at Hadad Rimmon in the plain of Megiddo. And the land shall mourn, every family by itself: the family of the house of David by itself, and their wives by themselves; the family of the house of Nathan by itself, and their wives by themselves; the family of the house of Levi by itself, and their wives by themselves; the family of Shimei by

itself, and their wives by themselves; all the families that remain, every family by itself, and their wives by themselves.

These verses tell us that in the midst of the battle the Lord will keep His eyes on Israel for the sake of their protection (Zechariah 12:4b, "I will open my eyes on the house of Judah..."). When that happens, Jews outside of Jerusalem will be protected and reminded of God's covenant to them (Zechariah 12:5, "And the governors of Judah shall say in their heart, 'The inhabitants of Jerusalem are my strength in the LORD of hosts, their God.'"). Then God will supernaturally empower Israel to defeat her enemies. Both the land and the people outside of Jerusalem will be protected, ensuring eventual victory for the city. In her most difficult hour, Israel will be infused with the strength of Jesus the Conqueror. When Israel's eyes finally focus on God, she will see God incarnate, Jesus the Messiah. They will finally realize that their Messiah is the God-Man they had pierced on the cross thousands of years earlier. Such realization will change their lives forever!

Discussion Questions

1. Why do you think people today tend to be so interested in the End Times? What makes this such an interesting subject?

2. What overall plan of the book of Zechariah is presented in this chapter?

3. How does Zechariah 12-14 fit within this overall outline of the book?

4. In your own words, explain the five basic statements we can make about this final section of Zechariah's prophecy (chapters 12-14).

5. Answer the reporters' questions (who, what, where, when, why, how) about the battle of Armageddon.

6. What is "The Day of the Lord"? Where else in Scripture do we find this day referred to?

That's Not All

You can find sermon outlines and other extras in the "Sermonars" section at the back of the book. These pages may be freely reproduced, either from the book or from the accompanying CD-ROM for any devotional or ministry use.

Chapter Fifteen

When Israel Views the Pierced One

10 *"And I will pour on the house of David and on the inhabitants of Jerusalem the Spirit of grace and supplication; then they will look on Me whom they pierced. Yes, they will mourn for Him as one mourns for his only son, and grieve for Him as one grieves for a firstborn. 11 In that day there shall be a great mourning in Jerusalem, like the mourning at Hadad Rimmon in the plain of Megiddo. 12 And the land shall mourn, every family by itself: the family of the house of David by itself, and their wives by themselves; the family of the house of Nathan by itself, and their wives by themselves; 13 the family of the house of Levi by itself, and their wives by themselves; the family of Shimei by itself, and their wives by themselves; 14 all the families that remain, every family by itself, and their wives by themselves.*

13:1 *"In that day a fountain shall be opened for the house of David and for the inhabitants of Jerusalem, for sin and for uncleanness.*

2 *"It shall be in that day,"* says the LORD of hosts, *"that I will cut off the names of the idols from the land, and they*

shall no longer be remembered. I will also cause the prophets and the unclean spirit to depart from the land. 3 It shall come to pass that if anyone still prophesies, then his father and mother who begot him will say to him, 'You shall not live, because you have spoken lies in the name of the LORD.' And his father and mother who begot him shall thrust him through when he prophesies.

4 "And it shall be in that day that every prophet will be ashamed of his vision when he prophesies; they will not wear a robe of coarse hair to deceive. 5 But he will say, 'I am no prophet, I am a farmer; for a man taught me to keep cattle from my youth.' 6 And one will say to him, 'What are these wounds between your arms?' Then he will answer, 'Those with which I was wounded in the house of my friends.' (Zechariah 12:10-13:6)

There are two "burdens" that dominate the final six chapters of Zechariah:

- The first burden covers Zechariah 9-11 (Zech 9:1, "The burden of the word of the LORD against the land of Hadrach, and Damascus its resting place (for the eyes of men and all the tribes of Israel are on the LORD)."

- The second burden covers Zechariah 12-14 (Zech 12:1, "The burden of the word of the LORD against Israel. Thus says the LORD, who stretches out the heavens, lays the foundation of the earth, and forms the spirit of man within him.").

Both of these burdens converge on the culmination of God's marvelous plan of grace for his chosen people, Israel.

God's Plan to Redeem Israel

According to Zechariah 12, God will destroy the enemy

Gentile nations as they descend on Jerusalem in a last attempt to overtake it. In the midst of the battle of all battles—Armageddon—God will pour out His Holy Spirit on every Jew in Israel. That same Spirit will cause Israel to turn to God with humility. The Jews will come under the most intense conviction as their eyes are opened at last to behold Jesus Christ for whom He is, the "One whom they have pierced" (Zechariah 12:10). We also see this in Revelation 1:7, "Behold, He is coming with clouds, and every eye will see Him, even they who pierced Him. And all the tribes of the earth will mourn because of Him. Even so, Amen." Suddenly the Jews will realize that the Savior is that same man they once crucified on a hill just outside of the city Jerusalem thousands of years ago. When that realization dawns upon them, their shock and grief will know no bounds.

Ultimately, however, God's purpose is not simply to sadden His people, but to use that conviction to draw them back unto Himself. Their mourning is one that will lead to true repentance. The Jewish nation will become aware of their responsibility for the death of the Messiah, even though all sinful humanity is guilty of Jesus' death. Therefore, the final portion of Zechariah, chapters 12-14, teaches us that God will ultimately save and cleanse Israel. His purpose will be accomplished. Even though it has been thousands of years since Jesus' death, God's plans have not changed, and they will never change. The Scriptures make it clear that God is a forgiving God who wants to cleanse and forgive His people. Take a look:

- Micah 7:18-19, "Who is a God like You, pardoning iniquity and passing over the transgression of the remnant of His heritage? He does not retain His anger forever, because He delights in mercy. He will again have compassion on us, and will subdue our iniquities. You will cast all our sins into the depths of the sea."

- Psalm 103:12, "As far as the east is from the west, so

far has He removed our transgressions from us."

• Psalm 130:4, "But there is forgiveness with You, That You may be feared."

• Jeremiah 31:34, "No more shall every man teach his neighbor, and every man his brother, saying, 'Know the LORD,' for they all shall know Me, from the least of them to the greatest of them, says the LORD. For I will forgive their iniquity, and their sin I will remember no more."

• 2 Peter 3:8-10, "But, beloved, do not forget this one thing, that with the Lord one day is as a thousand years, and a thousand years as one day. The Lord is not slack concerning His promise, as some count slackness, but is longsuffering toward us, not willing that any should perish but that all should come to repentance. But the day of the Lord will come as a thief in the night, in which the heavens will pass away with a great noise, and the elements will melt with fervent heat; both the earth and the works that are in it will be burned up."

Israel's Day of Salvation and Cleansing

Feinberg writes with insight about the final portion of Zechariah 12 (verses 10-14), "In the remainder of Zechariah 12, the prophet sets forth, as nowhere else in Scripture with such vividness and power, the conversion of Israel to the Lord. Nothing in Israel's past history can be interpreted as the fulfillment of this passage."[1] In other words, the content of these verses looks to the future for its fulfillment. Let's take at this key section one more time:

> And I will pour on the house of David and on the inhabitants of Jerusalem the Spirit of grace and supplication; then they will look on Me whom they pierced. Yes, they will mourn for Him as one mourns for his

only son, and grieve for Him as one grieves for a first-born. In that day there shall be a great mourning in Jerusalem, like the mourning at Hadad Rimmon in the plain of Megiddo. And the land shall mourn, every family by itself: the family of the house of David by itself, and their wives by themselves; the family of the house of Nathan by itself, and their wives by themselves; the family of the house of Levi by itself, and their wives by themselves; the family of Shimei by itself, and their wives by themselves; all the families that remain, every family by itself, and their wives by themselves.

Commenting on verse 10, Feinberg once again writes powerfully:

The great grief is spoken of as the most intense kind of sorrow, like that for an only son. This is especially forceful, because childlessness was considered a curse and dishonor. Their hearts will be smitten with grief like that for the firstborn in the home, a peculiar sorrow to loving parents. The mourning has been compared to the greatest private sorrow; now it is likened to the most intense public grief exhibited in Israel.[2]

God used an interesting comparison in verse 11 to help Zechariah's Jewish audience better understand the immensity of their future grief (" In that day there shall be a great mourning in Jerusalem, like the mourning at Hadad Rimmon in the plain of Megiddo"). The future mourning of Israel over her Messiah is likened to the weeping on the day when godly King Josiah, the last hope of the fading Judean nation, was slain by the Egyptians at Hadad Rimmon, traditionally identified as a village in the plain of Megiddo (cf. 2 Chronicles 35:20–27). Thus the greatness of the mourning at this final outpouring of the Holy Spirit can be compared only to the weeping of a most extreme individual (Zech. ariah 12:10) and to a corporate (v. 11) catastrophes of the nation.[3]

The mourning described in verses 12-14 truly describes Israel's day of repentance, forgiveness, and mourning over their sins. David, Levi, Nathan, and Shimei represent kingly and priestly lines. This means that everyone will be included in the process of turning back to God—from the leaders and their families to the lowest servants. We find this same promise in Hosea 3:4-5,

> For the children of Israel shall abide many days without king or prince, without sacrifice or sacred pillar, without ephod or teraphim. Afterward the children of Israel shall return and seek the LORD their God and David their king. They shall fear the LORD and His goodness in the latter days.

When Revival Comes to Israel

Israel's mourning will not be in vain. An unparalleled spiritual revival will happen at that time according to Zechariah 13:1-6. Verse 1 states, "In that day a fountain shall be opened for the house of David and for the inhabitants of Jerusalem, for sin and for uncleanness." The phrase "in that day" refers to the Day of the Lord, when Christ finally returns and Israel is saved. "The house of David and the inhabitants of Jerusalem" implies that everyone in Israel—every single one of the twelve tribes—will return to their God. God promises that a "fountain" will open to cleanse the people from filthiness. As a matter of fact, the Hebrew indicates that this fountain will be open forever, implying that those same people will never become unclean again. Their revival will never end.

Zechariah also makes it clear that this cleansing fountain will be for "sin" and "uncleanness." The word "sin" refers to that which misses the mark or goes the wrong way. "Uncleanness" identifies something that must be shunned and avoided at all costs. God promises that He will cleanse us from both, since they are problems we cannot solve on our own. Only God can deliver us from the pollution of sin. We find a similar idea in Ezekiel 36:24-25, "For I will take you from among the nations, gather you out of all countries, and bring you into your own land. Then I will sprinkle clean water on you, and you shall be clean; I will cleanse you from all your filthiness and from all your idols."

Israel Cleansed of False Prophets

God also promised that He will cleanse the people from the pollution of idolatry and from the wrong teaching of false prophets. We read in Zechariah 13:2, "'It shall be in that day,' says the LORD of hosts, 'that I will cut off the names of the idols from the land, and they shall no longer be remembered. I will also cause the prophets and the unclean spirit to depart from the land.'" This is especially significant for the nation of Israel, since through the centuries they have been plagued by two main besetting sins: idolatry and false prophets. Take a look:

- Psalm 96:5, "For all the gods of the peoples are idols, but the LORD made the heavens."

- Psalm 106:36, "They served their idols, which became a snare to them."

- Psalm 115:4, "Their idols are silver and gold, the work of men's hands."

- Hosea 2:17, "For I will take from her mouth the names of the Baals, and they shall be remembered by their name no more."

- Deuteronomy 18:20, "But the prophet who presumes to speak a word in My name, which I have not commanded him to speak, or who speaks in the name of other gods, that prophet shall die. And if you say in your heart, 'How shall we know the word which the LORD has not spoken?'—when a prophet speaks in the name of the LORD, if the thing does not happen or come to pass, that is the thing which the LORD has not spoken; the prophet has spoken it presumptuously; you shall not be afraid of him.'"

• Jeremiah 8:10-11, "Therefore I will give their wives to others, and their fields to those who will inherit them; because from the least even to the greatest everyone is given to covetousness; from the prophet even to the priest everyone deals falsely. For they have healed the hurt of the daughter of My people slightly, saying, 'Peace, peace!' When there is no peace."

• Jeremiah 14:14-15, "And the LORD said to me, 'The prophets prophesy lies in My name. I have not sent them, commanded them, nor spoken to them; they prophesy to you a false vision, divination, a worthless thing, and the deceit of their heart. Therefore thus says the LORD concerning the prophets who prophesy in My name, whom I did not send, and who say, 'Sword and famine shall not be in this land'—By sword and famine those prophets shall be consumed!'"

Phillips comments on the specific usage of "idols" in Zechariah 13:2. He writes:

Zechariah did not name the idols, but we know that one of them will be the blasphemous image of the antichrist, which the false prophet (a Jew) will place in the rebuilt temple in Jerusalem (Revelation 13). Perhaps the antichrist will consider it sound policy to set up other idols in Jerusalem, his religious capital—Shinto idols from Japan and images of Buddha, and the multitudinous gods of the Hindus, for example. As long as worship of his image is paramount, he may not care if other idols are worshiped too. Perhaps the antichrist will take sardonic satisfaction in establishing a pantheon of all the world's false gods to exacerbate Jewish monotheistic sensibilities. When the Lord comes, He will cleanse His beloved Jerusalem of all its images and put an end to all idolatry.[4]

The End of the Millennium

The prophet went on to describe in Zechariah 13:3-6 what will happen at the time when the prophets will be judged for their ungodly leadership. He wrote:

> It shall come to pass that if anyone still prophesies, then his father and mother who begot him will say to him, "You shall not live, because you have spoken lies in the name of the LORD." And his father and mother who begot him shall thrust him through when he prophesies. And it shall be in that day that every prophet will be ashamed of his vision when he prophesies; they will not wear a robe of coarse hair to deceive. But he will say, "I am no prophet, I am a farmer; for a man taught me to keep cattle from my youth." And one will say to him, "What are these wounds between your arms?" Then he will answer, "Those with which I was wounded in the house of my friends."

Commentators are divided about whether or not these verses contain a reference to Jesus (verse 6, "What are these wounds between your arms?"). John MacArthur, Charles Feinberg, J. Carl Laney, Paul L. Redditt, and Homer Heater, for instance, believe that this is not a prophecy about Jesus Christ. Others like J. Vernon McGee and John Phillips, however, believe that these verses do speak of Christ and the pierced Messiah. Phillips writes once again:

> Or perhaps the focus is on the later years of the millennium. Countless millions of children, grandchildren, and great-grandchildren will be born; all these will know nothing of war, woe, pestilence, famine, and injustice. They will make annual pilgrimages to Jerusalem to see the wonders of the capital, to catch a

glimpse of the King, and to see the heavenly Jerusalem above (in stationary orbit over the earthly Jerusalem) shining like a diamond in the sky. In spite of these ideal conditions and in spite of the ease with which a person born in the millennium can be born again, an ever increasing number of people will remain unregenerate. We know from Revelation 20:7–10 that at the end of the millennium Satan will be released from his prison to fan these flames into a universal conflagration. It may be that the prophecy in Zechariah 13:2b–5 refers to the first tentative sparks of a final outbreak of rebellion.[5]

Whether these verses refer to the false prophets living in the End Times or to the final rebellion that will happen at the end of the Millennium, the bottom line is that our God holds the future in His hands. He has established the end from the beginning, and nothing or no one can ever change His plans of make Him change His mind. In that we should find great comfort!

Discussion Questions

1. What would you say to someone who believes that God has given up on the nation of Israel? Is this type of thinking truly biblical? Why or why not?

2. Do the passages cited in this chapter help us to understand the prevalence of anti-Semitism that has been witnessed throughout the centuries?

3. What will be the reaction of the people when their eyes are opened and they behold the one whom they had pierced (Zech 12:10)? What is significant about this?

4. What is the significance of the fountain mentioned in Zechariah 13:1? Why is the fountain described as "open forever"?

5. Take some time to read the following verses one more time: Micah 7:18–19; Psalm 103:12; 130:4. Our God is a God of forgiveness. What does that mean? What difference does this truth make in the way you see your past and plan for the future?

6. In your own words, explain how studying this passage from the book of Zechariah should strengthen your hope for the future and your view of God.

That's Not All

You can find sermon outlines and other extras in the "Sermonars" section at the back of the book. These pages may be freely reproduced, either from the book or from the accompanying CD-ROM for any devotional or ministry use.

Chapter Sixteen

When & Where Jesus Quoted Zechariah

7 *"Awake, O sword, against My Shepherd,*
Against the Man who is My Companion,"
Says the LORD of hosts.
"Strike the Shepherd,
And the sheep will be scattered;
Then I will turn My hand against the little ones.
8 And it shall come to pass in all the land,"
Says the LORD,
"That two-thirds in it shall be cut off and die,
But one-third shall be left in it:
9 I will bring the one-third through the fire,
Will refine them as silver is refined,
And test them as gold is tested.
They will call on My name,
And I will answer them.
I will say, 'This is My people';
And each one will say, 'The LORD is my God.'"

(Zechariah 13:7-9)

Jesus Quoted Zechariah in Matthew 26:31

God sends trials in the lives of those He loves. He does that not because He wants us to suffer but because He knows that our difficulties can refine us and mold us into the kind of people He wants us to be. This was true of God's own Son, Jesus Christ; this is also true of us today. When reading through the gospels, it is easy to see that Jesus approached His own suffering from God's perspective. The Messiah was so "in tune" with the Father that He continually acknowledged the fact that whatever happened to Him was within God's perfect plans. Such confidence allowed Jesus to completely surrender Himself to the care of His Father—even as He was about to be beaten, humiliated, and crucified.

Shortly before He was arrested by His enemies, Jesus told the disciples in Matthew 26:31, "All of you will be made to stumble because of Me this night, for it is written: 'I will strike the Shepherd, and the sheep of the flock will be scattered.'" This statement by Jesus shows us His reliance on the Father's plans because these same words had been spoken by the Father Himself through the prophet Zechariah centuries before Jesus' ministry on earth. By quoting the prophet's words, Jesus was in fact embracing God's plans and declaring His willingness to experience whatever God had planned for Him. Take a look at Zechariah's words in Zechariah 13:7-9.

> "Awake, o sword, against My Shepherd, against the Man who is My Companion," says the LORD of hosts. "Strike the Shepherd, and the sheep will be scattered; then I will turn My hand against the little ones. And it shall come to pass in all the land," says the LORD, "that two-thirds in it shall be cut off and die, but one- third shall be left in it: I will bring the one-third through the fire, will refine them as silver is refined, and test them as gold is tested. They will call on My name, and I will answer them. I will say, 'This is My people'; and each one will say, 'The LORD is my God.'"

Seven Great Truths in Zechariah 13:7-9

There are at least seven key truths that should stand out to us from Zechariah 13:7-9:

1. **God was symbolically speaking to a sword, an instrument of death.** We see this in the opening words of verse 7 ("Awake, o sword, against My Shepherd..."). In the same way that God was going to use the sword in Jesus' life to show forth His grace and mercy to all who believe, He also wants to use trials in your life to help you experience Him in a way you have never experienced before. Therefore, it is important for you to ask yourself three important questions: (1) What is my "sword"?; (2) How have I reacted to this "sword" in my life?; (3) Am I truly willing to face this "sword" in order to know God more deeply?

2. **The sword was against God's Shepherd, Jesus Christ** (verse 7). There are at least two basic truths about suffering in this broken world. First, God never wastes our suffering; He always has a wonderful purpose for it, even when we cannot see it. Second, because of sin no one is exempt from suffering, not even the sinless Christ. In His sovereignty, God allowed the suffering and death of His Son to take place so that we could find forgiveness and redemption in Him. Take a look:

    - 2 Corinthians 5:21, "For He made Him who knew no sin to be sin for us, that we might become the righteousness of God in Him."

    - Isaiah 53:10, "Yet it pleased the LORD to bruise Him; He has put Him to grief. When You make His soul an offering for sin, He shall see His seed, He shall prolong His days, and the pleasure of the LORD shall prosper in His hand."

    - Acts 2:23, "Him [Jesus], being delivered by the

determined purpose and foreknowledge of God, you have taken by lawless hands, have crucified, and put to death."

Although you may be facing many trials today, never forget this important biblical truth: you have never suffered like Jesus Christ did on your behalf!

3. **We see a beautiful picture of the plurality of persons in the Godhead in Zechariah 13:7** ("'...against the Man who is My Companion,' says the Lord of Hosts."). The Hebrew word for "man" in this verse is a somewhat uncommon term, referring to a strong man, not an ordinary one. The word "Companion" refers to a close associate. It also conveys the thought of one united together to another by the possession of common nature, rights, and privileges.[1] In this verse, God identifies Jesus Christ as the mighty One who is closely united to the Father Himself. Therefore, this verse could read, "The Mighty Man [Jesus] who is co-equal with Me." McGee writes, "The Lord God is the speaker and Christ, the Messiah, is the person spoken of. The term, 'the man that is my fellow' would be better translated, 'the man my equal' or 'the man of my union.' This is an unmistakable Old Testament reference to the deity of Christ."[2] Even though the Holy Spirit is not mentioned in this specific verse, God's statement about the Shepherd (i.e., Christ) opens the door to the New Testament teaching of the Trinity of God (i.e., there are three persons within the Godhead, distinct but yet equal in essence).

4. **God promised that after the Shepherd was stricken, the sheep would scatter** (verse 7). This is exactly what happened after the crucifixion, when the Romans destroyed Jerusalem in AD 70 and the Jewish dispersion began.

5. **These verses also give us a vivid prediction of an unthinkable death toll that will happen during the Tribulation.** Zechariah 13:7d–8 states, "'Then I will turn My hand against the little ones. And it shall come to pass in all the land,' says the LORD, 'that two-thirds in it shall be cut off and die, but one- third shall be left in it.'" I believe the term "little ones" in this passage refers to three groups of people: the disciples of the first century who suffered persecution because of their faith; Jews in general who have been dispersed throughout the world; and the Jews who will be alive during the Tribulation. Therefore, Zechariah 13:7–9 probably will be completely fulfilled in Israel's dispersion in the Tribulation. At that time two-thirds of the Jewish nation will be struck down and perish, but the surviving remnant will be restored to their covenant relationship with the Lord.[3] Dr. Homer Heater comments:

> The fulfillment of this promise is the Tribulation, when Israel will undergo a time of trouble hitherto unknown (Matthew 24:21). Two-thirds will be cut off and die (13:8, the two-thirds probably should be taken as 'majority'), and one third will be left. Then the remaining third will be tested as silver and gold (13:9), and the results will be glorious. Israel will call on the name of the Lord, and He will answer her.[4]

6. **Thus this passage clearly reminds us that God sends trials to His people because He loves them.** God has promised that one-third of the people will be left to experience the time of the Tribulation (verse 8). But their suffering will not be in vain, since through it the Lord will refine them as silver and test them as God (verse 9). We find a similar promise in Revelation 7:13–14, "Then one of the elders answered, saying to me, 'Who are these arrayed in white robes, and where did they come from?' And I said to him, 'Sir, you

know.' So he said to me, 'These are the ones who come out of the great tribulation, and washed their robes and made them white in the blood of the Lamb.'"

Trials are an important part of God's blessings in this broken world where we live. The apostle Peter himself wrote about trials in 1 Peter 1:6, "In this you greatly rejoice, though now for a little while, if need be, you have been grieved by various trials, that the genuineness of your faith, being much more precious than gold that perishes, though it is tested by fire, may be found to praise, honor, and glory at the revelation of Jesus Christ." The Greek word translated "trial" in 1 Peter 1:6 denotes a process of testing for the purpose of displaying the quality of the thing or person being tested, much like God's reference to refining silver and testing gold in Zechariah 13:9. As you go through trials in your own life, embrace the following basic biblical truths:

- God allows trials to humble us (2 Corinthians 12:7–10).

- God uses trials to increase our spiritual values and to help us focus on eternity (John 16:33).

- God uses trials to prepare us to help the hurting (2 Corinthians 1:3–7).

- God uses trials to discipline us because of our sin (Hebrews 12:5–12).

- God uses trials to strengthen our spiritual character (James 1:2–4).

7. **Finally, Zechariah 13:7–9 also reminds us that trials do not last forever.** God will ultimately save Israel through the Second Coming of Christ (Zech 13:9b, "I will say, 'This is My people'; and each one will say, 'The Lord is my God.'"). Likewise, God wants to use the trials you face in your own life to bring you closer to Him. If you truly know Jesus Christ as your Savior

and King, the day will come when your trials will be over and you will be thankful for what they taught you about sin, about yourself, and about your God. Therefore, whatever you are going through right now, hang on and do not lose hope. God loves you. He cares for us. He even wants to use your difficulties for your own good. And He is powerful enough to do that. He is, indeed, that kind of God!

Discussion Questions

1. There is an African proverb that says, "Smooth seas do not make skillful sailors." What does this mean? How does this relate to what you have just read in this chapter? How does it relate to you?

2. What is the sword referred to in this chapter? Is there a sword in your life?

3. In what ways does God want to use trials in your life according to the following verses: 2 Cor 12:7-10; John 16:33; 2 Cor 1:3-7; Heb 12:5-12; James 1:2-4?

4. Looking back at your life, can you think of any examples of problems you faced that God used for your own good? Write down a couple of examples.

5. Who were some characters in the Bible whose trials turned to be for their own good? What happened to them? How did they face their trials? Why?

6. How did Jesus endure His own suffering, humiliation, and death? What allowed Him to have that type of response? How can you be more like Him?

That's Not All

You can find sermon outlines and other extras in the "Sermonars" section at the back of the book. These pages may be freely reproduced, either from the book or from the accompanying CD-ROM for any devotional or ministry use.

Chapter Seventeen

Our Thousand Year Reign: Why We Reject Amillennialism

1 Then I saw an angel coming down from heaven, having the key to the bottomless pit and a great chain in his hand. 2 He laid hold of the dragon, that serpent of old, who is the Devil and Satan, and bound him for a thousand years; 3 and he cast him into the bottomless pit, and shut him up, and set a seal on him, so that he should deceive the nations no more till the thousand years were finished. But after these things he must be released for a little while.

4 And I saw thrones, and they sat on them, and judgment was committed to them. Then I saw the souls of those who had been beheaded for their witness to Jesus and for the word of God, who had not worshiped the beast or his image, and had not received his mark on their foreheads or on their hands. And they lived and reigned with Christ for a thousand years. 5 But the rest of the dead did not live again until the thousand years were finished. This is the first resurrection. 6 Blessed and holy is he who has part in the first resurrection. Over such the second death has no power, but they shall be

*priests of God and of Christ, and shall reign with Him a
thousand years.*

*7 Now when the thousand years have expired, Satan will
be released from his prison 8 and will go out to deceive the
nations which are in the four corners of the earth, Gog and
Magog, to gather them together to battle, whose number is
as the sand of the sea. 9 They went up on the breadth of the
earth and surrounded the camp of the saints and the beloved
city. And fire came down from God out of heaven and devoured them. (Revelation 20:1-9)*

Understanding the Millennium

Few areas of Christian doctrine are as controversial in
our day and age as the eschatological teaching of the Millennium. Christian scholars and lay people alike tend to
disagree about the nature of the millennial kingdom we read
about in the Scriptures. Because this is such an important
topic, we must have a firm grasp on it before we can properly interpret and apply Zechariah's final chapter. So before we consider Zechariah 14, let us take a look at another
key passage that describes the millennial kingdom that is
to come. Led by the Holy Spirit, the Apostle John wrote in
Revelation 20:1-9:

Then I saw an angel coming down from heaven, having the key to the bottomless pit and a great chain in
his hand. He laid hold of the dragon, that serpent of
old, who is the Devil and Satan, and bound him for a
thousand years; and he cast him into the bottomless
pit, and shut him up, and set a seal on him, so that he
should deceive the nations no more till the thousand
years were finished. But after these things he must be
released for a little while. And I saw thrones, and they
sat on them, and judgment was committed to them.
Then I saw the souls of those who had been beheaded

for their witness to Jesus and for the word of God, who had not worshiped the beast or his image, and had not received his mark on their foreheads or on their hands. And they lived and reigned with Christ for a thousand years. But the rest of the dead did not live again until the thousand years were finished. This is the first resurrection. Blessed and holy is he who has part in the first resurrection. Over such the second death has no power, but they shall be priests of God and of Christ, and shall reign with Him a thousand years. Now when the thousand years have expired, Satan will be released from his prison and will go out to deceive the nations which are in the four corners of the earth, Gog and Magog, to gather them together to battle, whose number is as the sand of the sea. They went up on the breadth of the earth and surrounded the camp of the saints and the beloved city. And fire came down from God out of heaven and devoured them.

There are three primary views regarding Revelation 20:1–9 and the nature of the kingdom that is to come:

1. *Postmillennialism.* The prefix "post," which means "after in time," argues that Christ will return after the "thousand years" John wrote about in Revelation 20. By allegorizing the meaning of "a thousand years," they believe that man will usher in the kingdom by preaching the gospel to all nations and by bringing all humanity to a saving knowledge of Christ. According to this view, the world is progressively getting better as it becomes more Christianized. Eventually, the entire world will embrace Christianity and, at that time, Jesus will return (post, or after, the figurative millennium). This view, however, fails to interpret Scripture literally. It also goes completely against what we see in the world throughout history. Since the fall of mankind things in this world are progressively getting

worse, not better!

2. *Amillennialism*. This view, which is currently more popular than Postmillennialism, teaches that there will be no thousand-year reign of Christ on earth and no earthly kingdom of God. By allegorizing the Scriptures, amillennialists argue that the New Testament church inherits all of the spiritual promises and prophecies of Old Testament Israel. Therefore, key Old Testament promises God made to the nation of Israel (not to the church!) in the Old Testament (including Zechariah 14) are no longer seen as valid promises according to this position.

3. *Premillennialism*. Based on a literal, historical, and grammatical interpretation of the Bible, Premillennialism holds that Christ will literally and bodily return to earth before the beginning of a literal, thousand-year kingdom. Premillennialists argue that the Old Testament prophecies God made concerning a literal kingdom await a future fulfillment. They believe that God's prophecies should not be improperly spiritualized or allegorized, since that would compromise the Lord's very character. Just as prophecies concerning Christ's First Coming were fulfilled literally, so will the prophecies of Jesus' Second Coming also be fulfilled literally. Thus they argue that John's six references to a kingdom that will last "a thousand years" in Revelation 20:1-9 should be taken literally!

Why the Millennium & Israel?

Church fathers Clement of Rome (40-100); Ignatius (50-115); Polycarp (70-167); Justin Martyr (100-168); Irenaeus (140-202); and Tertullian (150-220) all embraced Premillennialism. It was not until the fourth century, with the rise of the Roman Catholic Church (which viewed herself as God's instrument to usher in the promised glory), that

Premillennialism faded. Like the church fathers mentioned above, however, many today still hold to Premillennialism for several biblical reasons, including the following:

1. God's unconditional covenant with Abraham. God promised Abraham that his seed (the nation of Israel) would become a mighty nation and that some day they would own the Promised Land forever (Genesis 12:1-3; 13:14-17; 15:5; 17:7; 22:17-18). Because the nation of Israel has never fully occupied the land God promised them, this promise still awaits literal fulfillment, which will happen at the Millennium.

2. God's unconditional covenant with David, which includes a threefold promise: an everlasting throne (2 Samuel 23:5; 2 Chronicles 13:5); an everlasting kingdom, and an everlasting king (2 Samuel 7:12-13). As it is the case with the Abrahamic covenant, the Davidic covenant also awaits literal fulfillment in the millennial kingdom.

3. God's covenant with Israel to possess the land in the Palestinian covenant. This too will be fulfilled in the millennial kingdom (Isaiah 11:11,12; 65:9, Ezekiel 16:60-63; 36:28-29, 39:28; Hosea 1:10-2:1; Micah 2:12; Zechariah 10:6).

4. God's promise of a new covenant, a time when God will give His people a new heart, the filling of the Spirit at all times, and complete forgiveness of sin (Jer 31-32; Rom 11:26-29). Once again, this will be fulfilled in the millennial kingdom.

Therefore, a literal millennial kingdom is necessary for God to fulfill the promises He made to His people in the Old Testament. If there is no literal kingdom, there is also no literal fulfillment of God's promises.

Names of the Millennium

Scriptures use different names to describe the Millennium. Take a look at the following examples:

1. "The world to come." Hebrews 2:5, "For He has not put the world to come, of which we speak, in subjection to angels."

2. "The kingdom of heaven." Matthew 5:10, "Blessed are those who are persecuted for righteousness' sake, for theirs is the kingdom of heaven."

3. "The kingdom of God." Mark 1:14, "Now after John was put in prison, Jesus came to Galilee, preaching the gospel of the kingdom of God."

4. "The last day." John 6:40, ""And this is the will of Him who sent Me, that everyone who sees the Son and believes in Him may have everlasting life; and I will raise him up at the last day."

5. "The regeneration." Matthew 19:28, "So Jesus said to them, 'Assuredly I say to you, that in the regeneration, when the Son of Man sits on the throne of His glory, you who have followed Me will also sit on twelve thrones, judging the twelve tribes of Israel.'"

In spite of these different names (and many more!) used to described the millennial kingdom, the bottom line is that all of these terms refer to the same period of time when Jesus Christ will reign on earth for a thousand years. It is during the Millennium that Christ will fulfill God's promises to the nation of Israel and reverse the curse of sin on God's creation.

The Location of the Millennium

Even though the millennial kingdom will encompass the whole earth, its center will be in Israel, more specifically in the city of Jerusalem. Read carefully the prophet's words in Isaiah 2:2-4.

> Now it shall come to pass in the latter days that the mountain of the LORD's house shall be established on the top of the mountains, and shall be exalted above the hills; and all nations shall flow to it. Many people shall come and say, "Come, and let us go up to the mountain of the LORD, to the house of the God of Jacob; He will teach us His ways, and we shall walk in His paths." For out of Zion shall go forth the law, and the word of the LORD from Jerusalem. He shall judge between the nations, and rebuke many people; they shall beat their swords into plowshares, and their spears into pruning hooks; nation shall not lift up sword against nation, neither shall they learn war anymore."

Israel is sometimes called "the navel of the earth." It binds together Asia, Europe, and Africa, where the majority of mankind lives. Israel's capital, the holy city of Jerusalem, will be the center of the Millennium on earth (Jeremiah 31:6; Micah 4:1; Zechariah 2:10-11). As such, it will become the center of worship of the king, Jesus Christ (Jerermiah 30:16-21; 31:6, 23; Joel 3:17; Zechariah 8:8, 20-23), and it will endure forever (Isaiah 9:7; 33:20-21; 60:15; Joel 3:19-21; Zechariah 8:4). Not surprisingly, Zechariah himself wrote in 14:10, "All the land shall be turned into a plain from Geba to Rimmon south of Jerusalem. Jerusalem shall be raised up and inhabited in her place from Benjamin's Gate to the place of the First Gate and the Corner Gate, and from the Tower of Hananeel to the king's winepresses."

The Purpose of the Millennium

There are four main purposes for Christ's millennial kingdom. The first is to fulfill God's unconditional covenants (Abrahamic, Palestinian, Davidic, and New covenants), as mentioned above. The other three reasons are the following:

1. To reward believers for their obedience and faithfulness to God:

   - Psalm 58:11, "So that men will say, 'Surely there is a reward for the righteous; surely He is God who judges in the earth.'"

   - Proverbs 11:18, "The wicked man does deceptive work, but he who sows righteousness will have a sure reward."

   - Matthew 16:27, "For the Son of Man will come in the glory of His Father with His angels, and then He will reward each according to His works."

   - Matthew 25:34. "Then the King will say to those on His right hand, 'Come, you blessed of My Father, inherit the kingdom prepared for you from the foundation of the world.'"

2. To fulfill Jesus' model prayer as seen in Luke 11:2, "So He said to them, 'When you pray, say: Our Father in heaven, hallowed be Your name. Your kingdom come. Your will be done on earth as it is in heaven.'"

3. To redeem the physical creation that has been corrupted by the pollution of sin. Paul wrote in Romans 8:19-22,

   > For the earnest expectation of the creation eagerly waits for the revealing of the sons of God. For the creation was subjected to futility, not willingly, but because of Him who subjected it in hope; because the creation itself also will be delivered from the bondage of corruption into the glorious liberty of the children of God. For we know that the whole creation groans and la-

bors with birth pangs together until now.

If there is no literal millennial kingdom, none of these four purposes can be fulfilled as the Scriptures predict.

The Glory of the Millennial Kingdom

We see many intricacies of our world today and marvel, even though our world is cursed by sin. In this millennial kingdom, however, that curse will be forever removed and we will be able to experience God's glory like never before. We get a glimpse of what the Millennium will be like in verses like Daniel 7:27, which states, "Then the kingdom and dominion, and the greatness of the kingdoms under the whole heaven, shall be given to the people, the saints of the Most High. His kingdom is an everlasting kingdom, and all dominions shall serve and obey Him." Among other blessings we will enjoy in the Millennium are the following:

- There will be perfect peace (Isaiah 2:4; 9:4-7; 11:6-9; 32:17-18; 33:5-6; 54:13; 55:12; 60:18; 65:25; 66:12; Ezekiel 28:26; 34:25, 28; Hosea 2:18; Micah 4:2-3; Zechariah 9:10).

- There will be perfect joy (Isaiah 9:3-4; 12:3-6; 14:7-8; 25:8-9; 30:29; 42:1, 10–12; 52:9; 60:15; 61:7, 10; 65:18-19; 66:10-14; Jeremiah 30:18-19; 31:13-14; Zephaniah 3:14-17; Zechariah 8:18-19; 10:6-7).

- There will be perfect holiness (Isaiah 1:26-27; 4:3-4; 29:18-23; 31:6-7; 35:8-9; 52:1; 60:21; 61:10; Jeremiah 31:23; Ezekiel 36:24-31; 37:23-24; 43:7-12; 45:1; Joel 3:21; Zephaniah 3:11, 13; Zechariah 8:3; 13:1-2; 14:20-21).

- There will be perfect comfort (Isaiah 12:1-2; 29:22-23; 30:26; 40:1-2; 49:13; 51:3; 61:3-7; 66:13-14; Jeremiah 31:23-25; Zephaniah 3:18-20; Zechariah 9:11-12; Revelation 21:4).

- There will be perfect justice (Isaiah 9:7; 11:5; 32:16; 42:1-4; 65:21-23; Jeremiah 23:5; 31:23; 31:29-30).

- There will be full knowledge (Isaiah 11:1-2, 9; 41:19-20; 54:13; Habakkuk 2:14).

- There will be perfect instruction (Isaiah 2:2-3; 12:3-6; 25:9; 29:17-24; 30:20-21; 32:3-4; 49:10; 52:8; Jeremiah 3:14-15; 23:1-4; Micah 4:2).

- The curse will be totally removed (Isaiah 11:6-9; 35:9; 65:25). This means that there will be no more death and sickness will be completely eliminated (Isaiah 33:24; Jeremiah 30:17; Ezekiel 34:16).

- There will be total protection (Isaiah 41:8-14; 62:8-9; Jeremiah 32:27; 23:6; Ezekiel 34:27; Joel 3:16-17; Amos 9:15; Zechariah 8:14-15; 9:8; 14:10-11).

- There will continue to be human reproduction. Children are specifically mentioned in Scripture in the millennial kingdom (Jeremiah 30:20; 31:29; Ezekiel 47:22; Zechariah 10:8). Some of these children who will be born during the Millennium will refuse to believe in Christ and rebel against Him at the end of a thousand years.

- There will be purposed labor. This means that you will have a job to do, that your job will be meaningful, and that you will enjoy doing it (Isaiah 62:8-9; 65:21-23; Jeremiah 31:5; Ezekiel 48:18-19).

- There will be an increase of light, since God will dwell among men and we will behold Christ's unveiled glory (Isaiah 4:5; 30:26; 60:19-20; Zechariah 2:5).

- There will unified worship of Jesus Christ. Idols will be a thing of the past (Isaiah 45:23; 52:1, 7-10; 66:17-23; Zechariah 13:2; 14:16; 8:23; 9:7; Zephaniah 3:9; Malachi 1:11; Revelation 5:9-14).

- There will be the full presence of God (Ezekiel 37:27-

28; Zechariah 2:2, 10-13; Revelation 21:3).

- There will be the fullness of the Holy Spirit (Isaiah 32:13-15; 41:1; 44:3; 59:19, 21; 61:1; Ezekiel 36:26-27; 37:14; 39:29; Joel 2:28-29; Ezekiel 11:19-20).

- There will be the privilege of reigning with Christ (Revelation 20:4-6). What we do for Christ in this life will influence what we do for Him in heaven.

The Close of the Millennium

Though the Millennium will wonderful, it will not last forever. Revelation 20:7-8 states, "Now when the thousand years have expired, Satan will be released from his prison and will go out to deceive the nations which are in the four corners of the earth, Gog and Magog, to gather them together to battle, whose number is as the sand of the sea." Incredibly, after a thousand years of Christ reigning on earth some will be deceived by Satan and rebel against the Lord. It is at that time that Satan and his followers will be judged and sent to hell for eternity. After that, God will usher in the New Heaven and New Earth, where we shall be with Him forever! John wrote about our eternal abode with God in Revelation 21:1-4.

Now I saw a new heaven and a new earth, for the first heaven and the first earth had passed away. Also there was no more sea. Then I, John, saw the holy city, New Jerusalem, coming down out of heaven from God, prepared as a bride adorned for her husband. And I heard a loud voice from heaven saying, "Behold, the tabernacle of God is with men, and He will dwell with them, and they shall be His people. God Himself will be with them and be their God. And God will wipe away every tear from their eyes; there shall be no more death, nor sorrow, nor crying. There shall be no more pain, for the former things have passed away."

Discussion Questions

1. In your own words, describe Postmillennialism, Amillennialism, and Premillennialism.

2. Why should we favor Premillennialism over the other two views? In other words, why is a literal millennial kingdom important?

3. What are the purposes of Christ's millennial kingdom?

4. What will the Millennium be like? Which characteristic of the Millennium is especially appealing to you as you consider your life right now?

5. What will happen at the end of the Millennium?

6. How should looking forward to the Millennium change the way you live your life today?

That's Not All

You can find sermon outlines and other extras in the "Sermonars" section at the back of the book. These pages may be freely reproduced, either from the book or from the accompanying CD-ROM for any devotional or ministry use.

Chapter Eighteen

What the World Will Be Like Someday

1 Behold, the day of the LORD is coming,
And your spoil will be divided in your midst.
2 For I will gather all the nations to battle against
Jerusalem;
The city shall be taken,
The houses rifled,
And the women ravished.
Half of the city shall go into captivity,
But the remnant of the people shall not be cut off
from the city.
3 Then the LORD will go forth
And fight against those nations,
As He fights in the day of battle.
4 And in that day His feet will stand on the Mount
of Olives,
Which faces Jerusalem on the east.
And the Mount of Olives shall be split in two,
From east to west,
Making a very large valley;
Half of the mountain shall move toward the north
And half of it toward the south.
5 Then you shall flee through My mountain valley,

For the mountain valley shall reach to Azal.
Yes, you shall flee
As you fled from the earthquake
In the days of Uzziah king of Judah.
Thus the LORD my God will come,
And all the saints with You.
6 It shall come to pass in that day
That there will be no light;
The lights will diminish.
7 It shall be one day
Which is known to the LORD—
Neither day nor night.
But at evening time it shall happen
That it will be light.
8 And in that day it shall be
That living waters shall flow from Jerusalem,
Half of them toward the eastern sea
And half of them toward the western sea;
In both summer and winter it shall occur.
9 And the LORD shall be King over all the earth.
In that day it shall be—
" The LORD is one,"
And His name one.

10 All the land shall be turned into a plain from Geba to Rimmon south of Jerusalem. Jerusalem shall be raised up and inhabited in her place from Benjamin's Gate to the place of the First Gate and the Corner Gate, and from the Tower of Hananel to the king's winepresses.

11 The people shall dwell in it;
And no longer shall there be utter destruction,
But Jerusalem shall be safely inhabited.

12 And this shall be the plague with which the LORD will strike all the people who fought against Jerusalem:

Their flesh shall dissolve while they stand on their feet,

Their eyes shall dissolve in their sockets,
And their tongues shall dissolve in their mouths.
13 It shall come to pass in that day
That a great panic from the LORD will be among
them.
Everyone will seize the hand of his neighbor,
And raise his hand against his neighbor's hand;
14 Judah also will fight at Jerusalem.
And the wealth of all the surrounding nations
Shall be gathered together:
Gold, silver, and apparel in great abundance.
15 Such also shall be the plague
On the horse and the mule,
On the camel and the donkey,
And on all the cattle that will be in those camps.
So shall this plague be.

*16 And it shall come to pass that everyone who is left of all
the nations which came against Jerusalem shall go up from
year to year to worship the King, the LORD of hosts, and to
keep the Feast of Tabernacles. 17 And it shall be that whichever of the families of the earth do not come up to Jerusalem
to worship the King, the LORD of hosts, on them there will
be no rain. 18 If the family of Egypt will not come up and
enter in, they shall have no rain; they shall receive the plague
with which the LORD strikes the nations who do not come up
to keep the Feast of Tabernacles. 19 This shall be the punishment of Egypt and the punishment of all the nations that do
not come up to keep the Feast of Tabernacles.*

*20 In that day "HOLINESS TO THE LORD" shall be en-
graved on the bells of the horses. The pots in the LORD's house
shall be like the bowls before the altar. 21 Yes, every pot in
Jerusalem and Judah shall be holiness to the LORD of hosts.
Everyone who sacrifices shall come and take them and cook
in them. In that day there shall no longer be a Canaanite in
the house of the LORD of hosts. (Zechariah 14:1-21)*

Longing to Go Home

U.S. astronaut Shannon Lucid desperately wanted to go home. She had spent six months on the Russian Mir space station, from March to September 1996. Her ride home was delayed six weeks by two hurricanes and assorted mechanical problems with the shuttle booster rockets, making her stay in space the longest of any American astronaut, man or woman. Nevertheless, she faced each setback with patient good cheer and a stiff upper lip. But as the days wore on, she knew where she would rather be. Eventually she admitted she wanted to return home to see her family, to feel the sun and wind on her face, and to do common things like checking out the new books published in the last six months. Prior to being picked up for her return to Earth by the space shuttle Atlantis, Shannon Lucid remarked, "You can rest assured I am not going to be on the wrong side of the hatch when they close it."[1]

Like Shannon Lucid, many of us we have been waiting a long time to go to our permanent spiritual home. Many of us are anxious to go see our families and loved ones who knew Christ and who are now enjoying God's very presence in heaven. On the final pages of the final book of C. S. Lewis' *The Chronicles of Narnia*, some of the children who have been to Narnia lament that they once again must return to their homeland—the Shadowlands. But Aslan (the lion who represents Jesus) has the best news of all for them. At one point he reassures them, saying, "You do not yet look so happy as I mean you to be." One of the series' main characters, a little girl named Lucy, replies in return, "We're so afraid of being sent away, Aslan. And you have sent us back into our own world so often." "No fear of that," said Aslan. "Have you not guessed?" Their hearts leaped and a wild hope rose within them. "There was a real railway accident," said Aslan softly. "Your father and mother and all of you are—as you used to call it in the Shadowlands—dead. The term is over; the holidays have begun. The dream has ended; this is morning!" Lewis described what happened next, closing the book with the following words:

> And as he (Aslan) spoke he no longer looked to them like a lion; but the things that began to happen after that were so great and beautiful that I cannot write them... All their lives in this world and all their adventures in Narnia had only been the cover and title page: now at last they were beginning Chapter One of the Great Story, which no one on earth has read: which goes on forever: in which every chapter is better than the one before.[2]

In his typical skillful manner, Lewis wanted us to understand that this present world, be it Earth or Narnia, is only a small (through important) fraction of our existence, and that life does not end with death. Rather, to those who know Christ death functions as the door through which we can enter a new reality: a perfect world where sin is nowhere and God's glory is everywhere.

Much like Lewis, Zechariah also closed his book with a description of what the world will be like someday. After writing about so many dark prophecies and promises of coming judgment to Israel and to the nations, Zechariah focused his attention on other the key events that will take place in the End Times. With that in mind, let us take a closer look at Zechariah's final chapter.

The Day of the Lord: Zechariah 14:1-2

The prophet opened the final chapter of his book by mentioning the Day of the Lord, an important event he had already mentioned elsewhere in his prophecy. He wrote, "Behold, the day of the LORD is coming, and your spoil will be divided in your midst. For I will gather all the nations to battle against Jerusalem; the city shall be taken, the houses rifled, and the women ravished. Half of the city shall go into captivity, but the remnant of the people shall not be cut off from the city (Zech 14:1-2)."

As mentioned previously, the Day of the Lord is a great and terrible day when, among other things, God will pour out His judgment on the nations for their rebellion against Him and against His Messiah. The prophet Joel also wrote about the Day of the Lord. Take a look:

- Joel 1:15, "Alas for the day! For the day of the LORD is at hand; it shall come as destruction from the Almighty."

- Joel 2:1–3, "Blow the trumpet in Zion, and sound an alarm in My holy mountain! Let all the inhabitants of the land tremble; for the day of the LORD is coming, for it is at hand: a day of darkness and gloominess, a day of clouds and thick darkness, like the morning clouds spread over the mountains. A people come, great and strong, the like of whom has never been; nor will there ever be any such after them, even for many successive generations. A fire devours before them, and behind them a flame burns; the land is like the Garden of Eden before them, and behind them a desolate wilderness; surely nothing shall escape them."

The Second Coming of Christ: Zechariah 14:3-5

The Day of the Lord, however, will include more than God's unprecedented judgment on the nations. On that day, the Lord Jesus Christ will also physically return to the earth as he promised He would in passages such as John 14:3 ("And if I go and prepare a place for you, I will come again and receive you to Myself; that where I am, there you may be also."). We find a similar promise in Acts 1:11, when the angels said to the disciples shortly after Jesus' ascension, "Men of Galilee, why do you stand gazing up into heaven? This same Jesus, who was taken up from you into heaven, will so come in like manner as you saw Him go into heaven." Zechariah also wrote about Jesus' Second Coming in 14:3-5.

Then the LORD will go forth and fight against those nations, as He fights in the day of battle. And in that day His feet will stand on the Mount of Olives, which faces Jerusalem on the east. And the Mount of Olives shall be split in two, from east to west, making a very large valley; half of the mountain shall move toward the north and half of it toward the south. Then you shall flee through My mountain valley, for the mountain valley shall reach to Azal. Yes, you shall flee as you fled from the earthquake in the days of Uzziah king of Judah. Thus the LORD my God will come, and all the saints with You.

Jesus will return at His Second Coming to the same location where He left after the resurrection: the Mount of Olives (cf. Acts 1:12, "Then they returned to Jerusalem from the mount called Olivet, which is near Jerusalem, a Sabbath day's journey.). John Phillips writes:

At the present time the Mount of Olives is at the center of a mile-long line of hills that dominate Jerusalem. The Mount of Olives stands 187 feet above Mount Zion, 245 feet above Mount Moriah, and 443 feet above Gethsemane. Located to the east of Jerusalem, toward the sunrise, the Mount of Olives is separated from the city by the narrow Kidron valley. On the other side of the mountain is the wilderness that runs down to the Dead Sea. The road to Bethany and the Jordan river run around the side of the mountain. The valley created by the coming convulsion will be a miraculous escape route for the desperate Jewish survivors in Jerusalem.

When Christ returns at the Second Coming, the Mount of Olive will split in two, a large new valley of escape will be created, and innumerable saints will return with Christ. This supports the view that the church will not endure the Tribulation, since believers will return with Christ to the earth at the Second Coming. Take a look:

- 1 Thessalonians 3:13, "So that He may establish your hearts blameless in holiness before our God and Father at the coming of our Lord Jesus Christ with all His saints."

- Colossians 3:4, "When Christ who is our life appears, then you also will appear with Him in glory."

- Jude 14, "Now Enoch, the seventh from Adam, prophesied about these men also, saying, 'Behold, the Lord comes with ten thousands of His saints.'"

- Revelation 19:19, "And I saw the beast, the kings of the earth, and their armies, gathered together to make war against Him who sat on the horse and against His army."

The Strangest Day: Zechariah 14:6-8

After mentioning Christ's Second Coming, Zechariah went on to describe what else will happen at that time. Read on:

> It shall come to pass in that day that there will be no light; the lights will diminish. It shall be one day which is known to the LORD—neither day nor night. But at evening time it shall happen that it will be light. And in that day it shall be that living waters shall flow from Jerusalem, half of them toward the eastern sea and half of them toward the western sea; in both summer and winter it shall occur (Zech 14:6-8).

Jesus' return as King of Kings and Lord of Lords will be so stupendous that nothing will be the same. A strange kind of darkness and light will characterize that moment. It will be like a day that is not day and a night that is not night. When Jesus returns the world will change, and all the focus will be on Him! Also at that moment, Jesus will punish His enemies. Zechariah 14:12-15 describes to us what will happen then:

And this shall be the plague with which the LORD will strike all the people who fought against Jerusalem: Their flesh shall dissolve while they stand on their feet, their eyes shall dissolve in their sockets, and their tongues shall dissolve in their mouths. It shall come to pass in that day that a great panic from the LORD will be among them. Everyone will seize the hand of his neighbor, and raise his hand against his neighbor's hand; Judah also will fight at Jerusalem. And the wealth of all the surrounding nations shall be gathered together: gold, silver, and apparel in great abundance. Such also shall be the plague on the horse and the mule, on the camel and the donkey, and on all the cattle that will be in those camps. So shall this plague be."

Jerusalem's New River: Zechariah 14:8

However, Jesus' Second Coming will not be characterized by the punishment of the wicked alone. As the giver and sustainer of life, Jesus will also bring with Him healing and restoration. Zechariah 14:8 states, "And in that day it shall be that living waters shall flow from Jerusalem, half of them toward the eastern sea and half of them toward the western sea; in both summer and winter it shall occur." This verse should catch our attention because of what Israel looks like today. In today's Jerusalem there is no river! But at the ushering in of the millennial kingdom, not only will there be a river in Jerusalem but even the Dead Sea will come alive! It will be alive with its banks lined with all kinds of trees for food, always fruit-bearing, and with fishermen on its shores (Ezekiel 47:8–12).

McGee and Stone comment on Zechariah 14:8, writing:

> In other words, this will be a spring that will gush up water, and I think it means literal water. Apparently, Jerusalem, which has been an inland city, will sud-

denly become a seagoing city, that is, a port town.[3]

As a result of the Lord's triumph several things follow: (1) Living waters flow from Jerusalem to the Dead Sea and to the Mediterranean (Joel 3:18; Ezek 47:1-12). This will have been caused by the earthquake which split the Mount of Olives. The water's flow will not be hindered by summer or winter. It is healing and life-giving in the physical sense. But it may also have a spiritual meaning, typifying fullness of spiritual blessing (Rev. 22:1).[4]

Therefore, Zechariah's mention of a river of living waters in Jerusalem should remind us of the fact that in heaven there will also be a river of water of life. Revelation 22:1-2 states, "And he showed me a pure river of water of life, clear as crystal, proceeding from the throne of God and of the Lamb. In the middle of its street, and on either side of the river, was the tree of life, which bore twelve fruits, each tree yielding its fruit every month. The leaves of the tree were for the healing of the nations."

The Millennial Kingdom: Zechariah 14:9-11

The end result of Jesus' Second Coming is not only the destruction of God's enemies but also the establishment of Christ's literal reign on earth. After Jesus returns He will be crowned as King over all the earth. Read on:

- Zechariah 14:9-11, "And the LORD shall be King over all the earth. In that day it shall be—'The LORD is one,' and His name one. All the land shall be turned into a plain from Geba to Rimmon south of Jerusalem. Jerusalem shall be raised up and inhabited in her place from Benjamin's Gate to the place of the First Gate and the Corner Gate, and from the Tower of Hananeel to the king's winepresses. The people shall dwell in it; and no longer shall there be utter destruction, but

Jerusalem shall be safely inhabited."

- Zechariah 14:20-21, "In that day 'HOLINESS TO THE LORD' shall be engraved on the bells of the horses. The pots in the LORD's house shall be like the bowls before the altar. Yes, every pot in Jerusalem and Judah shall be holiness to the LORD of hosts. Everyone who sacrifices shall come and take them and cook in them. In that day there shall no longer be a Canaanite in the house of the LORD of hosts."

- Zephaniah 3:9, ""For then I will restore to the peoples a pure language, that they all may call on the name of the LORD, to serve Him with one accord."

When Jesus returns, barriers will be destroyed! Language will no longer separate people from different nations. More importantly, sin will no longer separate us from each other or from God.

Worldwide Worship: Zechariah 14:16-21

Ultimately, there will be in God's Kingdom true worship and adoration of God. There will be hundreds of millions of redeemed people who will sing praises to God and who will enjoy true intimacy with the Triune God and with one another. Read carefully Zechariah's final words:

And it shall come to pass that everyone who is left of all the nations which came against Jerusalem shall go up from year to year to worship the King, the LORD of hosts, and to keep the Feast of Tabernacles. And it shall be that whichever of the families of the earth do not come up to Jerusalem to worship the King, the LORD of hosts, on them there will be no rain. If the family of Egypt will not come up and enter in, they shall have no rain; they shall receive the plague with which the LORD strikes the nations who do not come up to keep the Feast of Tabernacles. This shall be the punishment of Egypt and the punishment of all the nations that do not come up to keep the Feast of Tabernacles. In that day "HOLINESS TO THE LORD" shall be engraved on the bells of the horses. The pots in the LORD's house shall be like the bowls before the altar. Yes, every pot in Jerusalem and Judah shall be holiness to the LORD of hosts. Everyone who sacrifices shall come and take them and cook in them. In that day there shall no longer be a Canaanite in the house of the LORD of hosts.

Jesus Christ will come back some day to establish His kingdom on earth. On that day, He will punish the wicked and bless those who are His.

When astronaut Shannon Lucid finally returned home after six months in space, she said, "You can rest assured I am not going to be on the wrong side of the hatch when they close it." What about you? What side are you going to be on when Jesus returns? Are you sure your name is written on the Book of Life?

Discussion Questions

1. Read John 14:1–4 and 1 Corinthians 2:9. What are these verses saying about God's plans for our final destination in heaven?

2. What can those who know Christ anticipate as far as their eternal life in heaven is concerned?

3. Read Philippians 3:20-21. How would your life be truly different if you adopted Paul's mindset that your citizenship is in heaven? What is preventing you from doing that?

4. In your own words, describe Jesus' Second Coming. What will it be like? In what ways will it be like His First Coming? In what ways will it be different?

5. Take a few minutes to read out loud and to meditate on Revelation 21. What will heaven be like according to this amazing chapter?

6. What stands out to you from our study on the book of Zechariah? Why?

That's Not All

You can find sermon outlines and other extras in the "Sermonars" section at the back of the book. These pages may be freely reproduced, either from the book or from the accompanying CD-ROM for any devotional or ministry use.

The Sermonars

On the pages that follow, you will find a series of pages constituting Sermonars, the interactive sermon outlines that we provide at worship services so that our people can follow along with the sermon and leave with a very thorough overview of the material covered.

Regardless of how you use this book, you are invited to utilize the pages that follow in whatever manner meets your needs. How might you use them? These are a few of our ideas.

- You could duplicate our usage of them, reproducing the relevant pages for a church service so that worshippers can follow along through a sermon.

- You could use them in a small-group setting as a guide to discussion.

- To create a more involved setting, you could assign individuals or groups within the class the responsibility of answering various questions. Similarly, you could assign various scripture verses to individuals.

- In an individual study situation, you might employ the Sermonar as a sort of review and self-test. The ability to fill in the various blanks will measure your understanding of the material.

- You could imagine some usage of these pages that never crossed our minds.

Feel free to reproduce any or all of the following pages. Permission to use them in any setting is hereby granted provided that you do not drastically change the original intent of this volume.

the Thrilling Prophecies of
Mr. Z and Jesus

Jerusalem, the Jew, and You

The Panorama of the Prophetic in Zechariah

Message #1 in the series, Mr. Z. and Jesus

Bible Text: Zechariah 1:12-14

Message, 1:12 "Upon hearing this, the angel of the Lord prayed this prayer: 'O Lord of Heaven's Armies, for seventy years now you have been angry with Jerusalem and the towns of Judah. How long until You again show mercy to them?' 13)And the Lord spoke kind and comforting words to the angel who talked with me. 14)Then the angel said to me, 'Shout this message for all to hear. "This is what the Lord of Heaven's Armies says: My love for Jerusalem and Mount Zion is passionate and strong.""'

PROPHECY – A GOD WHO REMEMBERS

PROPHECY - specific [1]_____, some hundreds of years in advance, that have literally been fulfilled or point to a definite future time when they will come true.

"Zechariah, like Haggai, was a prophet to the remnant which returned after the 70 years. There is much of symbol in Zechariah, but these difficult passages are readily interpreted in the light of the whole body of related prophecy. The great Messianic passages are, upon comparison with the other prophecies of the kingdom perfectly clear. Both advents (comings) of Christ are in Zechariah's prophecy (9:9 with Mt. 21:1-11 and Zech. 14:3-4). More than Haggai or Malachi, Zechariah gives us the mind of God about the Gentiles world-powers surrounding the restored remnant."
-Rev. C. I. Scofield, D.D., The Scofield Study Bible, C, 1909 by Oxford University Press, Inc.

• With the exception of Isaiah there is more prophecy about [2]_____ in Zechariah than any other Old Testament book. More than any other minor prophet!

• Two scholars, Nestle and Aland, list [3]_____New Testament citations or allusions to Zechariah's book.

TIMETABLE

• The prophecy was written in [4]_____ B.C. Zechariah's ministry began two months after Haggai's (Haggai 1:1 and Zechariah 1:1). Their joint ministry resulted in the completion of the Jewish temple in 515 B.C.

P URPOSE/CONTEXT

• Zechariah is a book of [5]_____ for God's people (both present and future).

Zechariah 1:13 "And the Lord answered the angel who talked to me, with good and comforting words."

Zechariah 1:13 "Again proclaim, saying, 'Thus says the Lord of hosts: 'My cities shall again spread out through prosperity; the Lord will again comfort Zion, and will again choose Jerusalem.'"

• Zechariah words minister the practical and [6]_____!

Zechariah 1:12 "Then the Angel of the Lord answered and said, 'O Lord of hosts, how long will You not have mercy on Jerusalem and on the cities of Judah, against which You were angry these seventy years.'"

• [7]_____ is the main character of Zechariah – and He is seen comforting His people/Israel.

ZECHARIAH, THE PRIEST & PROPHET

Zechariah 1:1 "In the eighth month of the second year of Darius, the word of the Lord came to Zechariah, the son of Berechiah, the son of Iddo the prophet, saying."

• Zechariah means, "Jehovah [8]_____."

• He was a [9]_____ prophet working with the aged Haggai (4 months vs. a 3-year ministry).

Zechariah 2:4 "Who said to him, 'Run, speak to this young man, saying: 'Jerusalem shall be inhabited as towns without walls, because of the multitude of men and livestock in it.'"

• Zechariah was born in pagan Babylon, wrote his book in Palestine, and was [10]_____ _____ for his faith. (Josephus confirms this fact!)

Matthew 23:34-35 "Therefore, indeed, I send you prophets, wise men, and scribes: some of them you will kill and crucify, and some of them you will scourge in your synagogues and persecute from city to city; 35)that on you may come all the righteous blood shed on the earth, from the blood of righteous Abel to the blood of Zechariah, son of Berechiah, whom you murdered between the temple and the altar."

THE PANORAMA OF PROPHECY IN ZECHARIAH REGARDING JESUS CHRIST

1 Jesus as the [11]_____.

Zechariah 3:8 "Hear, O Joshua, the high priest, You and Your companions who sit before you, for they are a wondrous sign; for behold, I am bringing forth My Servant the BRANCH."

2 Jesus' entry in Jerusalem on a [12]_____.

Zechariah 9:9 "Rejoice greatly, O daughter of Zion! Shout, O daughter of Jerusalem! Behold, Your King is coming to you; He is just and having salvation, lowly and riding on a donkey, a colt, the foal of a donkey."

3 Jesus as God's smitten [13]_____ (desertion of Jesus' disciples at His torture/death).

> Zechariah 13:7 "Awake, O sword, against My Shepherd, against the Man who is My Companion', says the Lord of hosts. 'Strike the Shepherd, and the sheep will be scattered; then I will turn My hand against the little ones.'"

4 Judas' betrayal of Jesus for [14]_____ pieces of silver.

> Zechariah 11:12-13 "Then I said to them, 'If it is agreeable to you, give me my wages; and if not, refrain.' So they weighed out for my wages thirty pieces of silver. 13)And the Lord said to me, 'Throw it to the 'potter' - that princely price they set on me. So I took thirty pieces of silver and threw them into the house of the Lord for the potter."

5 Jesus' hands [15]_____ in His crucifixion death.

> Zechariah 12:10 "And I will pour on the house of David and on the inhabitants of Jerusalem the Spirit of grace and supplication; then they will look on Me whom they have pierced. Yes, they will mourn for Him as one mourns for his only son, and grieve for Him as one grieves for a firstborn."

6 The Jews, Christ's people, will be [16]_____.

> Zechariah 13:1 "In that day a fountain shall be opened for the house of David and for the inhabitants of Jerusalem, for sin and for uncleanness."
> Message, 12:10 "I, God, will begin by restoring the common households of Judah so that the glory of David's family and the leaders in Jerusalem won't overshadow the ordinary people in Jerusalem."

7 Jesus' [17]_____ by His own people, the Jews.

> Zechariah 13:6 "And one will say to him, 'What are these wounds between your arms?' Then he will answer, 'Those with which I was wounded in the house of my friends.'"

8 Jesus' Second Coming on the Mount of [18]_____.

> Zechariah 14:3-4 "Then the Lord will go forth and fight against those nations, as He fights in the day of battle. 4)And in that day His feet will stand on the Mount of Olives, which faces Jerusalem on the east. And the Mount of Olives shall be split in two, from east to west, making a very large valley; half of he mountain shall move toward the north and half of it toward the south."

MORE PROPHECY IN ZECHARIAH

9 The restoration and [19]_____ of Israel.

> Zechariah 8:8 "I will bring them back, and they shall dwell in the midst of Jerusalem. They shall be My people and I will be their God, in truth and righteousness."

> Zechariah 10:9 "I will sow them among the peoples, and they shall remember Me in far countries; they shall live, together with their children, and they shall return."

10 The evil reign of the [20]_____.

> Zechariah 11:16 "For indeed I will raise up a shepherd in the land who will not care for those who are cut off, nor seek the young, nor heal those that are broken, nor feed those that still stand. But he will eat the flesh of the fat and tear their hooves in pieces."

11 Jerusalem in the final [21]_____ of Armageddon.

> Zechariah 14:2 "For I will gather all the nations to battle against Jerusalem; the city shall be taken, the houses rifled, and the women ravished. Half of the city shall go into captivity, but the remnant of the people shall not be cut off from the city."

> Zechariah 12:3 "And it shall happen in that day that I will make Jerusalem a very heavy stone for all peoples; all who would heave it away will surely be cut in pieces, though all nations of the earth are gathered against it."

12 Two-thirds of [22]_____ to perish in the Tribulation.

> Zechariah 13:8 "And it shall come to pass in all the land, says the Lord, that two-thirds in it shall be cut off and die, but one-third shall be left in it."

13 [23]_____ will worship the Lord.

> Zechariah 14:16 "And it shall come to pass that everyone who is left of all the nations which came against Jerusalem shall go up from year to year to worship the King, the Lord of hosts, and to keep the Feast of Tabernacle."

14 Jesus will build His [24]_____ .

> Zechariah 6:13 "Yes, He shall build the temple of the Lord. He shall bear the glory, and shall sit and rule on His throne; so He shall be a priest on His throne, and the counsel of peace shall be between them both."

ZECHARIAH'S EIGHT NIGHT VISIONS

1 RIDER ON THE RED HORSE - 1:7-17

2 THE FOUR HORNS & FOUR CRAFTESMEN 1:18-21

3 MAN WITH THE MEASURING LINE - 2:1-13

4 THE CLOTHING OF JOSHUA THE HIGH PRIEST - 3:1-10

5 THE GOLDEN LAMPSTAND AND THE TWO OLIVE TREES - 4:1-14

6 THE FLYING SCROLL - 5:1-4

7 THE WOMAN IN THE EPHAH - 5:5-11

8 THE FOUR CHARIOTS - 6:1-8

ANSWERS

1. predictions 2. Jesus 3. 41 4. 520 5. comfort 6. prophetic 7. Jesus Christ 8. remember 9. young 10. murdered 11. BRANCH 12. colt 13. Shepherd 14. 30 15. pierced 16. saved 17. rejected 18. Olives 19. protection 20. antichrist 21. battle 22. Jews 23. Gentiles 24. temple

The Rider on the Red Horse

Message #2 in the series, Mr. Z. and Jesus

Bible Text: Jeremiah 29:10-14; Zechariah 1:1-14
COMFORT ONLY BY REPENTANCE – 1:1-6

Zechariah 1:2 "The Lord has been very angry with your fathers."

- [1] _____ brings the anger and judgment of God.

  Zechariah 1:3-4 "Therefore say to them, 'Thus says the Lord of hosts: 'Return to Me,' says the Lord of hosts. 4)Do not be like your fathers, to whom the former prophets preached, saying, 'Thus says the Lord of hosts: "Turn now from your evil ways and your evil deeds." But they did not hear nor heed Me,' says the Lord."

- There is no comfort from God unless we turn from [2] _____.

  Isaiah 59:1-2 "Behold, the Lord's hand is not shortened, that it cannot save; nor His ear heavy, that it cannot hear. 2)But your iniquities have separated you from your God; and your sins have hidden His face from you, so that He will not hear."

- [3] _____ the sins of your past; cancel the generational sins of your family!

  Zechariah 1:5-6 "Your fathers, where are they? And the prophets, do they live forever? 6)Yet, surely My words and My statues, which I command My servants the prophets, did they not overtake your fathers? So they returned and said: 'Just as the Lord of hosts determined to do to us, according to our ways and according to our deeds, so He has dealt with us.'"

- God's [4] _____ means He will both bless and curse depending upon obedience or disobedience!

  Jeremiah 25:7-9, 12 "Yet you have not listened to Me, says the Lord, that you might provoke Me to anger with the words of your hands to your own hurt. 8)Therefore thus says the Lord of hosts: 'Because you have not heard My words, 9)behold, I will send and take all the families of the north,' says the Lord, 'and Nebuchadnezzar the king of Babylon, My servant, and will bring them against this land, against its inhabitants, and against these nations all around, and will utterly destroy them, and make them an astonishment, a hissing, and perpetual desolations. 12)Then it will come to pass, when seventy years are completed, that

I will punish the king of Babylon and that nation, the land of the Chaldeans, for their iniquity, says the Lord; and I will make it a perpetual desolation."

- The [5]_____ years refers to the period of exile during which the temple lay in ruins (586-515B.C.).

- God's judgment is [6]_____!

    Isaiah 44:28 "Who says of Cyrus, 'He is My shepherd, and he shall perform all My pleasure, saying to Jerusalem, "You shall be built," and to the temple, "your foundation shall be laid."'"

    Isaiah 45:1 "Thus says the Lord to His anointed, to Cyrus, whose right hand I have held - to subdue nations before him and loose the armor of kings, to open before him the double doors, so that the gates will not be shut."

    Ezra 1:1-3 "Now in the first year of Cyrus king of Persia, that the word of the Lord by the mouth of Jeremiah might be fulfilled, the Lord stirred up the spirit of Cyrus king of Persia, so that he made a proclamation throughout all his kingdom, and also put in writing, saying, 2)Thus says Cyrus king of Persia: All the kingdoms of the earth the Lord God of heaven has given me. And He has commanded me to build Him a house at Jerusalem which is in Judah. 3)Who is among you of all His people? May his God be with him, and let him go up to Jerusalem which is in Judah, and build the house of the Lord God of Israel (He is God), which is in Jerusalem."

- 140 years before Cyrus issued the decree allowing the Israelites to return; Isaiah prophesied that a man named [7]_____ would issue such an order!

- God's promises are [8]_____!

COMFORT BY A CALL TO REPENTANCE – 1:1-6
COMFORT TO ISRAEL THROUGH VISIONS 1:7-6:15
COUNSEL REGARDING FASTS – 7:1-8:23
COMING EVENTS/JESUS' FIRST & SECOND COMING – 9:1-14:21

    Zechariah 1:7 "On the twenty-fourth day of the eleventh month, which is the month of Sebat, in the second year of Darius, the word of the Lord came to Zechariah the son of Berechiah, the son of Iddo the prophet."

- This vision was "the word of the Lord."

    Zechariah 1:8-9 "I saw by night, and behold, a man riding on a red horse, and it stood among the myrtle trees in the hollow; and behind him were horses: red, sorrel, and white the hollow. 9)Then I said, 'My lord, what are these? So the angel who talked with me said to me, "I will show you what they are."'"

- Vision = is an awareness of reality [9]_____ the human senses; extra physical sight - "I saw".

- Night Vision #1: The Divine Plan for Jerusalem/Israel.

WHAT DOES IT MEAN?

1 "A MAN" – who is it? [10] _____.

2 "RIDING ON A RED HORSE" – In Scripture the horse represents
[11] _____; color translation is "reddish brown."

3 "IT STOOD AMONG THE MYRTLE TREES IN THE HOLLOW" – most common bush in Israel; can grow to 8 feet; promised plant in the Millennium (Is. 49:19; 55:13). It represents [12] _____.

4 "AND BEHIND HIM WERE HORSES: RED, SORREL, AND WHITE" – angels keep a protective watch on Jerusalem/[13] _____. The white horse reminds us of ultimate [14] _____ for Israel!

WHAT DOES IT MEAN?

Zechariah 1:11 "So they answered the Angel of the Lord, who stood among the myrtle trees, and said, 'We have walked to and fro throughout the earth, and behold, all the earth is resting quietly.'"

Genesis 16:7, 9, 10, 11 (the Angel of the Lord), 13 "Then she called the name of the Lord who spoke to her, You-Are-the-God-Who-Sees; for she said, 'Have I also here seen Him sees me.'"

Exodus 3:2, 4 "And the Angel of the Lord appeared to him in a flame of fire from the midst of a bush. So he looked, and behold, the bush was burning with fire, but the bush was not consumed. 4)So when the Lord saw that he turned aside to look, God called to him from the midst of the bush and said, 'Moses, Moses.'"

WHAT NIGHT VISION #1 TEACHES US?

• Jesus is the [16] _____ and deliverer of Israel.

• Jesus intercedes for Israel.

• Jesus will [17] _____ Israel.

• What a beautiful parallel of Jesus' ministry to the church!

Psalm 34:7 "The angel of the Lord encamps all around those who fear Him, and delivers them."

Remember, Zechariah's prophecies have both a practical and [18] _____ meaning!

PRACTICALLY: Four years later the temple was built! 80 years later the walls were built!

PROPHETICALLY: During the Tribulation Jews will see the Messiah revealed as Savior and find Him to be their friend!

ANSWERS

1. Sin 2. sin 3. Break 4. promises 5. 70 6. sure 7. Cyrus 8. sure 9. beyond 10. Jesus Christ 11. war 12. Jerusalem 13. Israel 14. victory 16. protector 17. comfort 18. prophetic 19. revealed

215

The Times of the Gentiles
Message #3 in the series, Mr. Z. and Jesus

Bible Text: Zechariah 1:18-21, Luke 21:24

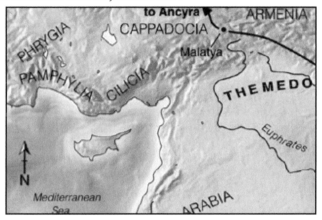

The Medo-Persian Empire

Ezra and Nehemiah

The Medo-Persian Empire included the lands of Media and Persia, much area shown on this map and more. The Jewish exiles were concentrated in the area around Nippur in the Babylonian province. The decree by King Cyrus that allowed the Israelites to return to their homeland and rebuild the Temple was discovered in the palace at Ecbatana.

> Zechariah 1:18-21 (The Message) "Then I looked up and saw four animal horns. 19)'What are these?' I asked the angel who was talking with me. He replied, 'These horns represent the nations that scattered Judah, Israel, and Jerusalem.' 20)Then the Lord showed me four blacksmiths. 21)'What are these men coming to do?' I asked. The angel replied, 'These four horns – these nations – scattered and humbled Judah. Now these blacksmiths have come to terrify those nations and throw them down and destroy them.'"

THE TIMES OF THE GENTILES

- The "Times of the Gentiles" (Luke 21:24) refers to the period of time in which **Jerusalem was/is ruled over by Gentiles nations.**
- The rule of the [1]_____ will end the "Times of the Gentiles" at the second coming of Jesus Christ. "In Luke 21:24 the Lord indicates that Jerusalem will continue in Gentile domination 'until the times of the Gentiles

be fulfilled.' Zechariah 12:2; 14:2-3 indicate that this will not be until the second advent, when the armies the of the Beast are destroyed by the Lord, as He is seen to do in Revelation 19:17-19." -*Things to Come* by J. Dwight Pentecost

FOUR HORNS 1:18-19

- In Zechariah chapter 1 "Horns" are symbols of power referring to both Gentile kings and [2]_____.

    Jeremiah 48:25 "The horn of Moab is cut off, and his arm is broken, says the Lord."

    Lamentations 2:3 "He has cut off in fierce anger every horn of Israel; he has drawn back His right hand from before the enemy. He has blazed against Jacob like a flaming fire devouring all around."

    Psalm 75:10 "All the horns of the wicked I will also cut off, but the horns of the righteous shall be exalted."

    Zechariah 1:19 "And I said to the angel who talked with men, 'What are these?' So he answered me, 'These are the horns that scattered Judah, Israel, and Jerusalem.'"

- "scattered" – past tense in our English translation is in the Hebrew perfect tense and refers to a completed action in the past, present, and [3]_____. Again, we see the prophetic element in Zechariah 1:19. "The Four Horns represent the Nations that had destroyed Judah and Israel. The Four Smiths ('carpenters') represent God's Destroyers of those nations. It was a figurative way of saying that prevailing World-Powers would be broken, and Judah again be exalted. God is on the throne, even when His people are temporarily vanquished." -*Halley's Bible Handbook* by Henry H. Halley.

- The horns are Gentile [4]_____ which afflicted and conquered Israel! "The concept of four horns (nations) reminds us of Daniel's visions of the image (Daniel 2) and the beasts (Daniel 7), both of which speaks of four empires: Babylon, Medo-Persia, Greece, and Rome. In 722, Assyria devastated the Northern Kingdom of Israel, but God raised up Babylon to defeat Assyria (Jer. 25:9; 27:6) and eventually take Judah in captivity in 586. Babylon did indeed oppress the Jews, but then God raised up Cyrus to conquer Babylon in 539 (Isa. 44:28; 45:1); and in 538, he permitted the Jews to return to their land. The Persians were conquered by the Greeks under Alexander the Great, and Greece was conquered by Rome" -The Bible Exposition Commentary/Prophets by Warren W. Wiersbe.

ISRAEL'S FOUR AFFLICTING GENTILE NATIONS:

1 [5]_____ Empire

2 Medo – [6]_____ Empire

3 Empire of [7]_____

4 [8]_____ Empire/Future revived Roman Empire

- These same four nations are cited by [9]_____ in his prophecy. History corroborates the accuracy of Scripture.

HORN & LITTLE HORNS IN DANIEL

    Daniel 7:21 "I was watching; and the same horn was making war against the saints, and prevailing against them."

- We see the [10]_____ aligned with the revived Roman Em-

218

pire making final war against Tribulation saints, Israel.

Daniel 7:24 "The ten horns are ten kings who shall arise from this kingdom. And another shall rise after them; he shall be different from the first ones, and he shall subdue three kings."

Daniel 2:31-34 "You, O king, were watching; and behold, a great image! This great image, whose splendor was excellent stood before you; and its form was awesome. 32)This image's head was of fine gold, its chest and arms of silver, its belly and thighs of bronze, 33)its legs of iron, its feet partly of iron and partly of clay. 34)You watched while a stone was cut out without hands, which struck the image on its feet or iron and clay, and broke them in pieces."

Daniel 2:36-41 "This the dream. Now we will tell the interpretation of it before the king. 37)You, O king, are a king of kings. For the God of heaven has given you a kingdom, power, strength, and glory; 38)and wherever the children of men dwell or the beasts of the field and the birds of heaven, He has given them into your hand, and has made you ruler over them all – you are this head of gold. 39)But after you shall arise another kingdom inferior to yours; then another, a third kingdom of bronze, which shall rule over all the earth. 40)And the fourth kingdom shall be as strong as iron, inasmuch as iron breaks in pieces and shatters everything; and like iron that crushes, that kingdom will break in pieces and crush all the others. 41)Whereas you saw the feet and toes, partly of potter's clay and partly of iron, the kingdom shall be divided; yet the strength of the iron shall be in it, just as you saw the iron mixed with ceramic clay."

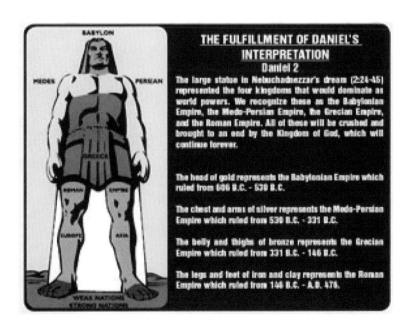

THE FULFILLMENT OF DANIEL'S INTERPRETATION
Daniel 2

The large statue in Nebuchadnezzar's dream (2:24-45) represented the four kingdoms that would dominate as world powers. We recognize these as the Babylonian Empire, the Medo-Persian Empire, the Grecian Empire, and the Roman Empire. All of these will be crushed and brought to an end by the Kingdom of God, which will continue forever.

The head of gold represents the Babylonian Empire which ruled from 606 B.C. - 539 B.C.

The chest and arms of silver represents the Medo-Persian Empire which ruled from 539 B.C. - 331 B.C.

The belly and thighs of bronze represents the Grecian Empire which ruled from 331 B.C. - 146 B.C.

The legs and feet of iron and clay represents the Roman Empire which ruled from 146 B.C. - A.D. 476.

Daniel 2:44 "And in the days of these kings the God of heaven will set up a kingdom which shall never be destroyed; and the kingdom shall not be left to other people; it shall break in pieces and consume all these kingdoms, and it shall stand forever."

- • At His second coming [11]_____ will set up His kingdom, defeat the Antichrist, and bring the "times of the Gentiles" to an end.

FOUR CRAFTSMEN – 1:20-21

Zechariah 1:20-21 "Then the Lord showed me four craftsmen. 21)And I said, 'What are these coming to do?' So he said, 'These are the horns that scattered Judah, so that no one could lift up his head; but the craftsmen are coming to terrify them, to cast out the horns of the nations that lifted up their horn against the land of Judah to scatter it.'"

"Next Zechariah saw four 'carpenters' (1:20) – that is, ironsmiths – and again he requested an explanation. The 'carpenters' symbolize those who would be raised up to 'fray [terrify]' the world powers responsible for terrifying the Jews through the centuries (1:21). In the vision the Jews were so maltreated 'that no man did lift up his head.' The Lord showed Zechariah that God has His own instruments for cutting even superpowers down to size. The repatriated Jews were living proof. The Babylonian empire, which had deported them, had collapsed like a house of cards. God eventually pulls down all nations that persecute or ill-treat the Jews." -*Exploring The Minor Prophets* by John Phillips, p. 275.

Possible suggestions of craftsmen :

- [12]_____ who defeated Babylon (Daniel 5).
- [13]_____ the Great, who defeated Persia.
- Various [14]_____ generals who subdued Greece.
- [15]_____ who destroyed the revived Roman Empire under Antichrist's reign.

Zechariah 1:13 "And the Lord answered the angel who talked to me, with good and comforting words."

Answers

15. Jesus Christ

8. Roman 9. Daniel 10. Antichrist 11. Jesus Christ 12. Cyrus 13. Alexander 14. Roman

1. Antichrist 2. nations 3. future 4. nations 5. Babylonian 6. Persia 7. Greece

220

A Wall of Fire : Discovering God's Protection
Message #4 in the series, Mr. Z and Jesus
Bible Text: Zechariah 2:1-13

ISAIAH'S STUNNING PROPHECIES

Isaiah 48:6, "You have heard; see all this. And will you not declare it? I have made you hear new things from this old time, even hidden things, and you did not know them."

- Paths in the [1]_____.

    Isaiah 43:15-16, "I am the Lord, your Holy One, the Creator of Israel, your King. 16)Thus says the Lord, who makes a way in the sea and a path through the mighty waters."

- The Earth is [2]_____.

    Isaiah 40:22, "It is He who sits above the circle of the earth, and its inhabitants are like grasshoppers, who stretches out the heavens like a curtain, and spreads them out like a tent to dwell in."

- [3]_____ warfare predicted.

    Isaiah 24:6, "Therefore the curse has devoured the earth and those who dwell in it are desolate. Therefore the inhabitants of the earth are burned, and few men are left."

- [4]_____ prophecy includes nuclear warfare.

    Zechariah 14:12, "And this shall be the plague with which the Lord will strike all the people who fought against Jerusalem: Their flesh shall dissolve while they stand on their feet, their eyes shall dissolve in their sockets, and their tongues shall dissolve in their mouths."

- Destruction of [5]_____.

    Isaiah 23:1, "The burden against Tyre. Wail, you ships of Tarshish! For it is laid waste, so that there is no house, no harbor; from the land of Cyprus it is revealed to them."

- Jewish Babylonian captivity and return.

    CAPTIVITY: Isaiah 39:6, "'Behold, the days are coming when all that is in your house, and what your fathers have accumulated until this day, shall be carried to Babylon; nothing shall be left,' says the Lord."

    PERSIAN KING CYRUS' DECREE TO RETURN: Isaiah 44:28, "Who says of Cyrus, 'He is My shepherd, and he shall perform all My pleasure,' saying to Jerusalem, 'You shall be built,' and to the temple, 'Your foundation shall be laid.'"

BABYLON'S DESTRUCTION BY PERSIA: Isaiah 13:19-20, "And Babylon, the glory of kingdoms, the beauty of Chaldeans' pride, will be as when God overthrew Sodom and Gomorrah. 20)It will never be inhabited, nor will it be settled from generation to generation; nor will the Arabian pitch tents there, nor will the shepherds make their sheepfolds there."

- Numerous prophecies about [6]_____.

    Isaiah 7:14, "Therefore the Lord Himself will give you a sign: Behold, the virgin shall conceive and bear a Son, and shall call His name Immanuel." (cf. 9:6; 53:1-12)

- Rebirth of the nation Israel in [7]_____ day.

    Isaiah 66:8, "Who has heard such a thing? Who has seen such things? Shall the earth be made to give birth in one day? Or shall a nation be born at once? For as soon as Zion was in labor, she gave birth to her children." [Note: On May 14, 1948, when Britain ended the Palestine mandate, the Jews in Israel proclaimed themselves an independent nation IN ONE DAY - exactly what Isaiah predicted 2,500 years before!]

    Isaiah 11:11-12, "It shall come to pass in that day that the Lord shall set His hand again the second time to recover the remnant of His people who are left, from Assyria an Egypt, from Pathros and Cush, from Elam and Shinar, from Hamath and the islands of the sea. 12)He will set up a banner for the nations, and will assemble the outcasts of Israel, and gather together the dispersed of Judah from the four corners of the earth."

JERUSALEM: God's Eternal City - 2:1-4

- The Lord has chosen [8]_____ as His eternal city.

    Psalm 132:13-14, "For the Lord has chosen Zion; He has desired it for His dwelling place: 14)This is My resting place forever; here I will dwell, for I have desired it." Psalm 137:4-6, "How shall we sing the Lord's song in a foreign land? 5)If I forget you, O Jerusalem, let my right hand forget it skill! 6)If I do not remember you, let my tongue cling to the roof of my mouth - if I do not exalt Jerusalem above my chief joy." Psalm 48:2-3, "Beautiful in elevation, the joy of the whole earth, is Mount Zion on the sides of the north, the city of the great King. 3)God is in her palaces; He is known as her refuge." Psalm 102:13, 16, "You will arise and have mercy on Zion; for the time to favor her, yes, the set time has come. 16)For the Lord shall build up Zion; He shall appear in His glory." Daniel 9:26, "And after sixty-two weeks Messiah shall be cut off but not for Himself; and the people of the prince who is to come (ANTICHRIST) shall destroy the city and the sanctuary. The end of it shall be with a flood, and till the end of the war desolations are determined."

- Jerusalem will be the location of the final battle of [9]_____, mankind's most severe war.

    Zechariah 12:2-4, "Behold, I will make Jerusalem a cup of drunkenness to all the surrounding peoples, when they lay siege against Judah and Jerusalem. 3)And it shall happen in that day that I will make Jerusalem a very heavy stone for all peoples, all would heave it away will surely be cut in pieces, though all nations of the earth are gathered against it. 4)In that day, says the Lord, I will strike every horse with confusion, and its rider with madness; I will open My eyes on the house of Judah, and will strike every horse with blindness."

- Jerusalem, glorified and remodeled, will be the location of [10]_____ millennial kingdom.

Isaiah 1:26, "I will restore your judges as at the first, and your counselors as at the beginning. Afterward you shall be called the city of righteousness, the faithful city."

Isaiah 4:3-4, "And it shall come to pass that he who is left in Zion and remains in Jerusalem will be called holy - everyone who is recorded among the living in Jerusalem. 4)When the Lord has washed away the filth of the daughter of Zion, and purged the blood of Jerusalem from her midst, by the spirit of judgment and by the spirit of burning."

Isaiah 62:2, 4, 11-12, "The Gentiles shall see your righteousness, and all kings your glory. You shall be by a new name, which the mouth of the Lord will name. 4)You shall no longer be termed Forsaken, nor shall your land any more be termed Desolate; but you shall be called Hephzibah, and your land Beulah; for the Lord delights in you, and your land shall be married. 11)Indeed the Lord has proclaimed to the end of the world; say to the daughter of Zion, surely your salvation is coming; behold, His reward is with Him, and His work before Him. 12)And they shall call them The Holy People, the Redeemed of the Lord; and you shall be called Sought Out, A City Not Forsaken."

- An unfathomable [11]_____ will be in the millennial Jerusalem someday! Livestock, perhaps even [12]_____ will be there!

Zechariah 2:2-4, "So I said, 'Where are you going?' And he said to me, 'To measure Jerusalem, to see what is its width and what is it length.' 3)And there was the angel who talked with me, going out; and another angel was coming to meet him, 4)who said to him, 'Run, speak to this young man, saying: "Jerusalem shall be inhabited as towns without walls, because of the multitude of men and livestock in it."'"

Zechariah 2:12, "And the Lord will take possession of Judah as His inheritance in the Holy Land, and will again choose Jerusalem."

"A WALL OF FIRE AROUND HER": God's Protection
- Zechariah 2:4-5

Zechariah 2:5, "'For I,' says the Lord, 'will be a wall of fire all around her, and I will be the glory in her midst.'"

- The Jews in burned-down Jerusalem were safer than their [13]_____ counterparts behind Babylon's massive walls!
- The Jews enjoyed [14]_____ years of protection from God until Nehemiah rebuilt the walls of Jerusalem.
- When we are walking in obedience, [15]_____ is "a wall of fire around us" always protecting us. Spiritually, are you in Babylon or Jerusalem?

2 Kings 6:15-17, "And when the servant of the man of God arose early and went out, there was an army, surrounding the city with horses and chariots. And his servant said to him, 'Alas, my master! What shall we do?' 16)So he

answered, 'Do not fear, for those who are with us are more than those who are with them.' 17)And Elisha prayed, and said, 'Lord, I pray, open his eyes that he may see.' Then the Lord opened the eyes of the young man and he saw. And behold, the mountain was full of horses and chariots of fire all around Elisha."

LAND OF THE NORTH: God's Punishment - 2:7-8

Zechariah 2:6-7, "'Up, up! Flee from the land of the north,' says the Lord; 'for I have spread you abroad like the four winds of heaven,' says the Lord. 7)Up, Zion! Escape, you who dwell with the daughter of Babylon."

- Who dispersed the disobedient people? [16]_____
- To the disobedient still in Babylon, the command was clear: [17]_____.
- They should have departed in 536 BC.! In [18]_____ B.C. Persia decimated Babylon, many died!

    Zechariah 2:8-9, "For thus says the Lord of hosts: 'He sent Me after glory, to the nations which plunder you; for he who touches you touches the apple of His eye. 9)For surely I will shake My hand against them, and they shall become spoil for their servants."

GOD'S MAN: The Messiah - 2:1, 8-11

Zechariah 2:1, "Then I raised my eyes and looked, and behold, a man with a measuring line in his hand." Zechariah 2:8, "... He sent Me after glory ...." Zechariah 2:9b, "Then you will know that the Lord of hosts has sent Me." Zechariah 2:10, "'Sing and rejoice, O daughter of Zion! For behold, I am coming and I will dwell in your midst,' says the Lord." Zechariah 2:11b, "Then you will know that the Lord of hosts has sent Me to you."

- The "Man with a measuring line" is unquestionably [19]_____ _____, who we see repeatedly throughout the book of Zechariah.

GOD'S ULTIMATE VICTORY: Christ 's Kingdom – 2:11-12

Zechariah 2:11-13, "Many nations shall be joined to the Lord in that day, and they shall become My people. And I will dwell in your midst. Then you will know that the Lord of hosts has sent Me to you. 12)And the Lord will take possession of Judah as His inheritance in the Holy Land, and will again choose Jerusalem. 13)Be silent, all flesh, before the Lord, for He is aroused from His holy habitation."

- The millennial kingdom (1,000 years) will take place in [20]_____ _____ after the battle of Armageddon concluded by Christ's Second Coming. (cf. Isaiah 49:19; 44:26; Jeremiah 31:23-25)
- Jesus, God's Messiah, will reign in His temple in the new Jerusalem.

Answers

16. God 17. Escape 18. 518 19. Jesus Christ 20. Jerusalem
Armageddon 10. Jesus 11. multitude 12. pets 13. disobedient 14. 66 15. God
9. Jerusalem 8. one 7. Jesus 6. Tyre 5. Zechariah's 4. Nuclear 3. round 2. Sea 1.

224

The Angel of the Lord:
Who is it ?

Message #5 in the series, Mr. Z and Jesus

Bible Text: Zechariah 3:1-10

THE 10 GREATEST PROPHECIES REGARDING ISRAEL/JEWS

1. Jesus prophesied the [1]_____ would be destroyed.
- Bible text: Matthew 24:1-2
- Recorded: approx. 30 A.D.
- Fulfilled: 70 A.D.

2. Jesus said [2]_____ would be destroyed.
- Bible text: Luke 21:24
- Recorded: approx. 30 A.D.
- Fulfilled: 70 A.D.

3. Daniel foretold the destruction of Jerusalem and the Temple.
- Bible text: Daniel 9:26
- Written: about 530 B.C.
- Fulfilled: 70 A.D.

4. Jerusalem would be destroyed and "plowed like a [3]_____."
- Bible text: Micah 3:11-12
- Written: sometime between 750-686 B.C.
- Fulfilled: 135 A.D.

5. The Bible foreshadowed [4]_____ destruction of Israel.
- Bible passage: Deuteronomy 28:49-52
- Written: about 1400 B.C.
- Fulfilled: 70 A.D.

6. [5]_____ would become a wasteland.
- Bible Text: Deuteronomy 29:23
- Written: about 1400 B.C.
- Fulfilled: 135 – 1800s A.D.

7. The people of [6]_____ would be exiled, scorned and ridiculed.
- Bible Text: Deuteronomy 28:36-37
- Written: about 1400 B.C.
- Fulfilled: 135-1900s A.D.

8. The [7]_____ of Israel would be inhabited by enemies.
- Bible Text: Leviticus 26:31-32
- Written: about 1400 B.C.
- Fulfilled: 135 A.D. to today

9. The [8]_____ of Israel will never cease to be a nation.
- Bible Text: Jeremiah 31:35-36
- Written: sometime from 626 to about 586 B.C.

10. The exiled people of Israel would return to [9]_____.
- Bible Text: Jeremiah 32:37-41
- Written: about 626 to about 586 B.C.

THE CLEANSING & RESTORATION OF ISRAEL

- The first [10]_____ visions deal primarily with the physical elements of the temple; the [11]_____ vision speaks to Israel's future cleansing and restoration.

> "This vision of Joshua the high priest actually goes beyond the man himself. We will learn that this vision gives us the answer to a very difficult question. This is the problem: We have learned so far that God is going to return the nation of Israel to the land and that He will dwell in the midst of them. They will be totally restored as His people. That hasn't happened yet, but He says He is going to do that." -Dr. J. Vernon McGee, *Thru the Bible, Volume III Proverbs - Malachi*

> Zechariah 3:1-2, "Then he showed me Joshua the high priest standing before the Angel of the Lord, and Satan standing at his right hand to oppose him. 2)And the Lord said to Satan, 'The Lord rebuke you, Satan! The Lord who has chosen Jerusalem rebuke you! Is this not a brand plucked from the fire.'"

THE ACCUSED – Joshua the high priest

> Exodus 19:6, "And you shall be to Me a kingdom of priests and a holy nation."

- Joshua ("Jehovah saves") is the same person as Jeshua in Ezra and Nehemiah (Haggai 1:1; Ezra 5:1; Zechariah 6:11). He was the current high priest at the time.
- Joshua represents the sinful nation of [12]_____ and believers today.

> Zechariah 3:8, "Hear, O Joshua, the high priest, you and your companions who sit before you, for they are a wondrous sign; for behold, I am bringing forth My servant the BRANCH."

- Joshua and the other priests are [13]_____ of the nation of Israel, viewed as covered with sin!

> "He represents and practically impersonates Israel in his holy office. For the nation he prays; for it he enters the Holy Place, he bears the nation's guilt. We must, therefore, not refer the issues and implications of this chapter to Joshua as an individual, nor merely to Joshua, the high priest. We must conclude that his condition is Israel's condition, his acquittal a typical way of expressing theirs; the words of comfort and assurance given him apply with equal validity to them." -H. C. Leupold, Exposition of Zechariah.

- "Joshua the high priest standing before" (3:1) - this term describes the priestly [14]_____ or ministry (Dt. 10:8; Judges 20:28; Ezekiel 44:15; 2 Chron. 29:11). It describes his official ministry which is sacrifice, sprinkling the blood of atonement and daily interceding as he offers incense before the veil.

> Zechariah 3:3-5, "Now Joshua was clothed with filthy garments, and was standing before the Angel. 4)Then He answered and spoke to those who stood before Him, saying, 'Take away the filthy garments from Him.' And to him

He said, 'See, I have removed your iniquity from you, and I will clothe you with rich robes.' 5)And I said, 'Let them put a clean turban on his head.' So they put a clean turban on his head, and they put the clothes on him. And the Angel of the Lord stood by."

- Look at the symbolism: Joshua is covered in excrement! The word for filth here is the strongest word the Hebrew language possesses. It is the filth of a loathsome character.

- The filthy garments are removed and ¹⁵_____ garments put on – even festive garments! Why?

  Zechariah 3:2b, "The Lord who has chosen Jerusalem rebuke you! Is this not a brand plucked from the fire."

  Zechariah 3:6-7, "Then the Angel of the Lord admonished Joshua, saying, 7)'Thus says the Lord of hosts: 'If you will walk in My ways, and if you will keep My command, then you shall also judge My house, and likewise have charge of My courts; and I will give you places to walk among these who stand here.'"

- There is cleansing when there is genuine repentance: IF YOU WALK IN MY WAYS; IF YOU KEEP MY COMMAND ... THEN!

  "Joshua represented not only the nation of Israel, he represents us today. In him we see the sin of the believer. Joshua was a priest before God – God appointed priests in the Old Testament. In our day every believer is a priest before God, but some of us are standing in dirty garments." -J. Vernon McGee, *Thru the Bible, Volume III*, p. 918.

- God replaces our sin with his ¹⁶_____.

THE ACCUSER – SATAN

  Zechariah 3:1, "Then he showed me Joshua the high priest standing before the Angel of the Lord, and Satan standing at his right hand to oppose him."

- Satan is no myth ... Zechariah ¹⁷_____ him!

- It reads: "THE Satan standing at his right hand to satanize him." "The opposer to oppose him," "the accuser to accuse him." The name Satan means ¹⁸_____ _____, it describes his primary work against believers.

  Revelation 12:10, "Then I heard a loud voice saying in heaven, 'Now salvation, and strength, and the kingdom of our God, and the power of His Christ have come, for the accuser of our brethren who accused them before our God day and night, has been cast down.'"

- The most appropriate response to demonic warfare in your life: The ¹⁹_____ _____ rebuke you, Satan!

  Zechariah 3:2, "And the Lord said to Satan, 'The Lord rebuke you, Satan! The Lord who has chosen Jerusalem rebuke you! Is this not a brand plucked from the fire?"

- What a picture of the Godhead: "The (Angel of the) Lord (Jesus Christ)" calling on "The Lord (God the Father)" to rebuke ²⁰_____.

THE ANGEL OF THE Lord – JESUS CHRIST

  Zechariah 3:8-10, "Hear, O Joshua, the high priest, you and your companions who sit before you, for they are a wondrous sign; for behold, I am bringing forth My servant the BRANCH. 9) For behold, the stone that I have laid before Joshua; upon the stone are seven eyes. Behold, I will engrave its inscription, says the Lord of hosts, 'And I will remove the iniquity of that land in one day. 10)In that day, says the Lord of hosts, 'Everyone will invite his neighbor under his vine and under his fig tree.'"

- THE BRANCH speaks of [21]_____ the Messiah!

  Isaiah 11:1-2, "There shall come forth a Rod from the stem of Jesse, and a Branch shall grow out of his roots. 2)The Spirit of the Lord shall rest upon Him, the Spirit of wisdom and understanding, the Spirit of counsel and might, the Spirit of knowledge and of the fear of the Lord.'"

  Jeremiah 23:5-6, "'Behold, the days are coming,' says the Lord, 'That I will raise to David a Branch of righteousness; a King shall reign and prosper, and execute judgment and righteousness in the earth.' 6)In His days Judah will be saved, and Israel will dwell safely; now this is His name by which He will be called."

- "The Stone" represents [22]_____ the Messiah! Jesus is the foundation and chief cornerstone of the church (Ephesians 2:19-22).

  Daniel 2:34-35, "You watched while a stone was cut out without hands, which struck the image on its feet of iron and clay, and broke them in pieces. 35)Then the iron, the clay, the bronze, the silver, and the gold were crushed together, and became like chaff from the summer threshing floors; the wind carried them away so that no trace of them was found. And the stone that struck the image became a great mountain and filled the whole earth."

- To the Jews at His first coming, Jesus, was a stumbling stone and [23]_____ _____ of offense (Isaiah 8:13-15; Psalm 118:22-23; Matthew 21:42; I Peter 2:7-8).
- "Seven eyes" – speaks of the [24]_____ of the Holy Spirit or Godhead and would be symbolic of infinite intelligence and omniscience.
- "I will remove the iniquity of the land in one day" – how?

  1) [25]_____ – when Jesus died for our sins;

  2) [26]_____ coming of Jesus Christ.

  Romans 11:26-27, "And so all Israel will be saved, as it written: 'The Deliverer will come out of Zion, and He will turn away ungodliness from Jacob; 27)For this is My covenant with them, when I take away their sins.'"

the Thrilling Prophecies of
Mr. Z and Jesus
Jerusalem, the Jew, and You

God's Two Olive Trees
Anointed Ones on Mission
Message #6 the series, Mr. Z and Jesus

Bible Text: Zechariah 4:1-14

EIGHT INTRIGUING QUESTIONS IN CHAPTER 4

1) "What do you see?" (v. 1)
2) "What are these, my lord?" (v. 3)
3) "Do you know what these are?" (v. 5)
4) "Who are you, O great mountain?" (v. 7)
5) "For who has despised the day of small things?" (v. 10)
6) "What are the two olive trees – at the right of the lampstand and at its left?" (v. 11)
7) "What are these two olive branches that drip into the receptacles of the two gold pipes from which the golden oil drains?" (v. 12)
8) "Do you know what these are?" (v. 13)

WHY WAS ZECHARIAH ASLEEP? (4:1)

Zechariah 4:1, "Now the angel who talked with me came back and awakened me as a man who is wakened out of his sleep."

"At this point he already had six tremendous visions. He was working the swing shift and the night shift and it was time to have a little rest. So after he had been given the sixth vision, he dozed off. Now the angel has to wake him up because he is not to be given this vision in a dream; he will see every bit of it." *-Thru the Bible with Dr. J. Vernon McGee*, Thomas Nelson Publishers, Nashville, TN, C, 1982, Volume III, p. 921.

Message, Zechariah 4:1, "The Messenger-Angel again called me to attention. It was like being wakened out of deep sleep."

NLT, Zechariah 4:1, "Then the angel who had been talking with me returned and woke me, as though I had been asleep."

• Zechariah's spiritual exhilaration of the previous [1]_____ visions wore him out – he fell asleep!

Daniel 10:9, "Yet I heard the sound of his words; and while I heard the sound of his words I was in a deep sleep on my face, with my face to the ground."

WHY THE UNIQUE LAMPSTAND? (4:2-4)

Zechariah 4:2-4, "And he said to me, 'What do you see?' So I said, 'I am looking, and there is a lampstand of solid gold with a bowl on top of it, and on the stand seven lamps with seven pipes to the seven lamps. 3)Two olive trees are by it, one at the right of the bowl and the other at its left. 4)So I answered and spoke to the angel who talked with me, saying, 'What are these, my lord?'"

- The lampstand represented Israel as a nation for which God will fulfill His
2_____.

- The lampstand represents the true Light of the world, 3_____.

> Isaiah 49:5-6, "And now the Lord says, Who formed Me from the womb to be His Servant, to bring Jacob back to Him, so that Israel is gathered to Him (for I shall be glorious in the eyes of the Lord, and My God shall be My strength), 6)Indeed He says, 'It is too small a thing that You should be My servant to raise up the tribes of Jacob, and to restore the preserved ones of Israel; I will also give You as a light to the Gentiles, that You should be My salvation to the ends of the earth."

> Luke 1:78, "Through the tender mercy of our God, with which the Dayspring from on high has visited us."

> Luke 2:32, "A light to bring revelation to the Gentiles, and the glory of Your people Israel."

> John 8:12, "Then Jesus spoke to them again, saying, 'I am the light of the world. He who follows Me shall not walk in darkness, but have the light of life.'"

- The bowl full of oil symbolizes the 4_____.
- The 5_____ channels symbolize an unlimited supply of 6_____ from the Holy Spirit.
- Oil 7_____, 8_____, 9_____ and is a sign of joy!

> Romans 14:17, "For the kingdom of God is not eating and drinking, but righteousness and peace and joy in the Holy Spirit."

WHO ARE THE OLIVE TREES? (4:3, 11-14)

Zechariah 4:3, 11-14, "Two olive trees are by it, one at the right of the bowl and the other at its left. 11)Then I answered and said to him, 'What are these two olive trees - at the right of the lampstand and at its left?' 12)And I further answered and said to him, 'What are these two olive branches that drip into the receptacles of the two gold pipes from which the golden oil drains?' 13)Then he answered me and said, 'Do you not know what these are?' And I said, 'No, my lord.' 14)So he said, 'These are the two anointed ones, who stand beside the Lord of the whole earth.'"

- Two passages crucial to understand this text: 10_____ &
11_____.

- Historically, the two olive trees could have been 12_____ and Haggai. Some say Zerubbabel and Joshua, the High Priest.

> "The two olive trees were identified in Zechariah's day. Zerubbabel, who was the king in the line of David, is one of the olive trees. The other olive tree was Joshua, the high priest. They would be the two instruments God would use to bring light back into the nation Israel and make them a light to the world."
> -*Thru the Bible with Dr. J. Vernon McGee*, Thomas Nelson Publishers, Nashville, TN, C, 1982, Volume III, p. 922.

- Prophetically they speak of [13]_____ and Elijah or Isaiah in the Tribulation era (see Revelation 11).

WHY THE IGNORANCE? (4:5)

Zechariah 4:5, "Then the angel who talked with me answered and said to me, 'Do you not know what these are?' and I said, 'No, my lord.'"

- Ignorance of Bible [14]_____ will leave you overcome by all types of spiritual opposition.

WHO WAS ZERUBBABEL? (4:6-10)

Zechariah 4:6-10, "So he answered and said to me: This is the word of the Lord to Zerubbabel: 'Not by might nor by power, but by My Spirit,' says the Lord of hosts. 7)'Who are you, O great mountain? Before Zerubbabel you shall become a plain! And he shall bring forth the capstone with shouts of Grace, grace to it!' 8)Moreover the word of the Lord came to me saying: 9)'The hands of Zerubbabel have laid the foundations of this temple; his hands shall also finish it. Then you will know that the Lord of hosts has sent Me to you. 10)For who has despised the day of small things? For these seven rejoice to see the plumb line in the hand of Zerubbabel. They are the eyes of the Lord, which scan to and from throughout the whole earth.'"

- Zerubbabel served as the [15]_____ head of Jerusalem. Joshua the high priest served as the religious head.

Message, Zechariah 4:6, "Then he said, 'This is God's Message to Zerubbabel: You can't force these things. They only come about through my Spirit,' says God-of-the-Angel-Armies. 'So, big mountain, who do you think you are? Next to Zerubbabel you're nothing but a molehill. He'll proceed to set the Cornerstone in place, accompanied by cheers: Yes! Yes! Do it!'"

- "might" – signifies the strength of [16]_____
- "power" signifies "[17]_____ great one"

WHAT IS YOUR "MOUNTAIN"? (4:7)

Zechariah 4:7, "Who are you, O great mountain? Before Zerubbabel you shall become a plain! And he shall bring forth the capstone with shouts of 'Grace, grace to it.'"

- [18]_____ records the "mountain" of opposition Zerubbabel faced and overcame by God's Spirit. (See Ezra 3:8-11; 4:1-6, 24-25).
- You can overcome [19]_____ your opposition through Jesus Christ!

Philippians 4:13, "I can do all things through Christ who strengthens me."

WHO HAS DESPISED THE DAY OF SMALL THINGS?

Zechariah 4:10, "For who has despised the day of small things?"

- God's greatest work always begins in [20]_____ things.

The Flying Scroll:
What in the World is It ?

Message #7 in the series Mr. Z and Jesus

Bible Text: Zechariah 5:1-11

Psalm 9:7-8, "But the Lord shall endure forever; He has prepared His throne for judgment. 8)He shall judge the world in righteousness, and He shall administer judgment for the peoples in uprightness."

Psalm 96:13, "For He is coming to judge the earth. He shall judge the world with righteousness, and the peoples with His truth."

Ecclesiastes 3:17, "I said in my heart, 'God shall judge the righteous and the wicked; for there is a time for every purpose and for every work.'" Ecclesiastes 11:9, "Rejoice, O young man in your youth, and let your heart cheer you in the days of your youth; walk in the ways of your heart, and in the sight of your eyes; but know that for all these God will bring you into judgment." Ecclesiastes 12:14, "For God will bring every work into judgment, including every secret thing, whether good or evil."

Ezekiel 18:20, "The soul who sins shall die." Amos 4:12, "Therefore thus will I do to you, O Israel; because I will do this to you, Prepare to meet your God, O Israel."

Matthew 3:12, "His winnowing fan is in His hand, and He will thoroughly clean out His threshing floor, and gather His wheat into the barn; but He will burn up the chaff with unquenchable fire." Matthew 13:30, "Let both grow together until the harvest, and at the time of harvest I will say to the reapers, 'First gather together the tares and bind them in bundles to burn them, but gather the wheat into my barn.'"

Matthew 22:13, "Then the king said to the servants, 'Bind him hand and foot, take him away, and cast him into outer darkness; there shall be weeping and gnashing of teeth.'"

Luke 12:2-5, "For there is nothing covered that will not be revealed, nor hidden that will not be known. 3)Therefore whatever you have spoken in dark will be heard in the light, and what you have spoken in the ear in inner rooms will be proclaimed on the housetops. 4)And I say to you, My friends, do not be afraid of those who kill the body, and after that have no more that they can do. 5)But I will show you whom you shall fear: Fear Him who, after He has killed, has power to cast into hell; yes, I say to you, fear Him!"

Acts 10:42, "And He commanded us to preach to the people, and to testify that it is He who was ordained by God to be Judge of the living and the dead."

Acts 17:31, "Because He has appointed a day on which He will judge the world in righteousness by the Man whom He has ordained. He has given assurance of this to all by raising Him from the dead."

Acts 24:25, "Now as he (Paul) reasoned about righteousness, self-control, and the judgment to come, Felix was afraid and answered, 'Go away for now; when I have a convenient time I will call for you.'"

2 Thessalonians 1:7-8, "And give you who are troubled rest with us when the Lord Jesus is revealed from heaven with His mighty angels, 8)in flaming fire taking vengeance on those who do not know God, and on those who do not obey the gospel of our Lord Jesus Christ."

Hebrews 9:27, "And as it is appointed for men to die once, but after this the judgment."

I Peter 4:5, "They will give an account to Him who is ready to judge the living and the dead."

2 Peter 2:9, "Then the Lord knows how to deliver the godly out of temptations and to reserve the unjust under punishment for the day of judgment."

Revelation 20:11-12, 15 "Then I saw a great white throne and Him who sat on it, from whose face the earth and the heaven fled away. And there was found no place for them. 12)And I saw the dead, small and great, standing before God, and the books were opened. And another book was opened, which is the Book of Life. And the dead were judge according to their works, by the things which were written in the books. 15) And anyone not found written in the Book of Life was cast into the lake of fire."

- Zechariah chapter [1]_____ teaches the inevitability of God's judgment.
- God's judgment is based upon God's [2]_____.

Zechariah 's Eight Night Visions

1) The Rider on the Red Horse – 1:7-17
2) The Four Horns & Four Craftsmen – 1:18-21
3) Man with the Measuring Line – 2:1-13
4) The Clothing of Joshua the High Priest – 3:1-10
5) The Gold Lampstand & Two Olive Trees – 4:1-14
6) The Flying Scroll – 5:1-14
7) The Woman in the Ephah (Basket) – 5:5-11
8) The Four Chariots – 6:1-8

Zechariah 's Sixth Vision – The Flying Scroll (5:1-4)

Zechariah 5:1-4, "Then I turned and raised my eyes, and saw there a flying scroll. 2)And he said to me, 'What do you see?' So I answered, 'I see a flying scroll. Its length is twenty cubits and its width ten cubits.' 3)Then he said to me, 'This is the curse that goes out over the face of the whole earth: Every thief shall be expelled, according this side of the scroll; and, Every perjurer shall be expelled, according to that side of it. 4)I will send out the curse,' says the Lord of hosts; 'It shall enter the house of the thief and the house of the one who swears falsely by My name. It shall remain in the midst of his house and consume it, with its timber and stones.'"

MESSAGE, 5:1-4, "I looked up again and saw – surprise! – a book on the wing! A book flying! The Messenger-Angel said to me, 'What do you see now?' I said, 'I see a book flying, a huge book – thirty feet long and fifteen feet wide!' He told me, 'This book is the verdict going out worldwide against thieves and liars. The first half of the book disposes of everyone who steals; the second half takes care of everyone who lies. I launched it' – Decree of God-of-Angel-Armies – 'and so it will fly into the house of every thief and every liar. It will land in each house and tear it down, timbers and stones.'"

- "a flying scroll" – signifies [3]_____.

  Ezekiel 2:8-10, "But you, son of man, hear what I say to you. Do not be rebellious like that rebellious house; open your mouth and eat what I give you. 9)Now when I looked, there was a hand stretched out to me; and behold, a scroll of a book was in it. 10)Then He spread it before me; and there was writing on the inside and on the outside, and written on it were lamentations and mourning and woe." (cf. Rev. 5:1-14; 10:1-11)

- The size of the scroll: 15 x 30 feet; the exact same dimensions of the [4]_____
  _____ of the Tabernacle (I Kings 6:3), and Solomon's Porch of the Temple where the Law was proclaimed.

- "this side," "that side" – the Law was written on [5]_____ sides. This signifies the completeness of the coming judgment. It is all based on the totality of [6]_____.

  Romans 2:1-2, 5-9 "Therefore you are inexcusable, O man, whoever you are who judge, for in whatever you judge another you condemn yourself; for you who judge practice the same things. 2)But we know that the judgment of God is according to truth against those who practice such things. 5)But in accordance with your hardness and your impenitent heart you are treasuring up for yourself wrath in the day of wrath and revelation of the righteous judgment of God, 6)who will render to each one according to his deeds: 7)eternal life to those who by patient continuance in doing good seek for glory, honor, and immortality; 8)but to those who are self-seeking and do not obey the truth, but obey unrighteousness – indignation and wrath, 9)tribulation and anguish, on every soul of man who does evil, of the Jew first and also the Greek."

- "This is the curse that goes out over the face of the whole earth" –signifies the
  [7]_____ of God's judgment … no one will escape it!

- "every thief," "every perjurer," ("who swears falsely by My name," v. 4) - a reference to the [8]_____ and [9]_____ commandment; sin against [10]_____
  _____ and sin against [11]_____. They are representative of all the sins that break the Law of God.

- "'I will send out the curse,' says the Lord of hosts" (5:4a) - reveals the terrible, certain, complete judgment of God coming to every nonbeliever.

  Jude 14-15, "Now Enoch, the seventh from Adam, prophesied about these men also, saying, 'Behold, the Lord comes with ten thousands of His saints, 15)to execute judgment on all, to convict all who are ungodly among them of all their ungodly deeds which they have committed in an ungodly way, and of all the harsh things which ungodly sinners have spoken against Him.'"

- "It shall remain in the midst of his house and consume it, with its timber and stones" (5:4b) - Christ comes judging the [12]_____; during His millennial Kingdom He will judge sin [13]_____; and at the end of the Millennium the [14]_____ judgment will occur.

Zechariah's Seventh Vision – Woman in the Basket (5:5-11)

Zechariah 5:5-11, "Then the angel who talked with me came out and said to me, 'Lift your eyes now, and see what this is that goes forth.' 6)So I asked, 'What is it? And he said, 'It is a basket that is going forth.' He also said, 'This is their resemblance throughout the earth: 7)Here is a lead disc lifted up, and this is a woman sitting inside the basket; 8)then he said, 'This is Wickedness! And he thrust her down into the basket, and threw the lead cover over its mouth. 9)Then I raised my eyes and looked, and there were two women, coming with the wind in their wings; for they had wings like the wings of a stork, and they lifted up the basket between the earth and heaven. 10)So I said to the angel who talked with me, 'Where are they carrying the basket?' 11)And he said to me, 'To build a house for it in the land of Shinar; when it is ready, the basket will be set there on its base.'"

- "the basket" (5:6) – the ephah (the largest dry measure used by the Hebrews to measure grain), or basket, was a commercial measuring device. Here it is full and confirms the sinfulness of the nations and the need for [15]_____.
- "The ephah was a common measure in Israel, but no ephah would be large enough to house a person, so, like the huge scroll, this was a special ephah. The woman attempted to get out of the ephah, so a heavy lead cover was put on the ephah to keep her in. A talent of lead would weigh from seventy-five to one hundred pounds." -*The Bible Exposition Commentary*, Warren W. Wiersbe.
- It refers to [16]_____ wickedness... a worldwide system for materialism and the lust for money.
- The "woman" symbolizes the embodiment of all kinds of sin including religious sins (see Revelation chapters 17 & 18). "Wickedness" (5:8) is feminine in Hebrew and denotes moral, religious, and civil evil.

  Revelation 17:3-5, "So he carried me away in the Spirit into the wilderness. And I saw a woman sitting on a scarlet beast which was full of names of blasphemy, having seven heads and ten horns. 4)The woman was arrayed in purple and scarlet, and adorned with gold and precious stones and pearls, having in her hand a golden cup full of abominations and the filthiness of her fornication. 5)And on her forehead a name was written: MYSTERY, BABYLON THE GREAT, THE MOTHER OF HARLOTS AND OF THE ABOMINATIONS OF THE EARTH."

- "two women" – may refer to strong [17]_____ deceiving the world systems in its lust of materialism. The stork, a migratory bird having long and wide wings (5:9) is an unclean bird, Leviticus 11:19.
- "the land of Shinar" (5:11) – same as the location of Babel, namely, [18] _____.

Answers

1.5 2. Word 3. judgment 4. Holy Place 5. both 6. God's Word 7. totality 8. 3rd 9. 8th 10. man 11. God 12. lost 13 immediately 14 final 15. judgment 16. economic 17. demons 18. Babylon

236

the Thrilling Prophecies of
Mr. Z and Jesus
Jerusalem, the Jew, and You

The Millennial Temple and Its King
Message #8 in the series Mr. Z and Jesus

Bible Text: Zechariah 6:1-15

GOD'S INSTRUMENTS OF JUDGMENT – ANGELS

- 1 _____ Beings - Psalm 103:20
- 2 _____ Beings - Matthew 26:53
- 3 _____ Intelligence - 2 Samuel 14:17, 20
- 4 _____ Beings - Deuteronomy 33:2
- 5 _____ and Guard Believers - Psalm 91:11
- Execute 6 _____ at God's Direction - Ps. 103:20

ZECHARIAH'S 8TH VISION – The Four Chariots Zechariah 6:1-8

Zechariah 6:1-2, 4-8, "Then I turned and raised my eyes and looked, and behold, four chariots were coming from between two mountains, and the mountains were mountains of bronze. 2)With the first chariot were red horses, with the second chariot black horses, with the third chariot white horses, and with the fourth chariot dappled horses - strong steeds. 4)Then I answered and said to the angel who talked with me, 'What are these, my lord?' 5)And the angel answered and said to me, 'These are four spirits of heaven, who go out from their station before the Lord of all the earth. 6)The one with the black horses is going to the north country, the white are going after them, and the dappled are going toward the south country.' 7)Then the strong steeds went out, eager to go, that they might walk to and fro throughout the earth. And He said, 'Go, walk to and fro throughout the earth.' So they walked to and fro throughout the earth. 8)And He called to me, and spoke to me, saying, 'See, those who go toward the north country have given rest to My Spirit in the north country.'"

THE ANGELIC EXECUTION OF JUDGMENT

- "four chariots" represent 7 _____ chariots; God's vehicles of Divine judgment.
- "two mountains" represent Mount 8 _____ and the Mount of 9 _____. (Definite article in Hebrew, "THE TWO MOUNTAINS.") This would locate these four chariots down in the Kidron Valley.

Zechariah 14:4, "And in that day His feet will stand on the Mount of Olives, which faces Jerusalem on the east. And the Mount of Olives shall be split in two, from east to west, making a very large valley; half of the mountain shall move toward the north and half of it toward the south."

Joel 3:2, "I will also gather all nations, and bring them down to the Valley of Jehoshaphat; and I will enter into judgment with them there on account of My

237

people, My heritage Israel, whom they have scattered among the nations; they have also divided up My land."

- "mountains of bronze" – throughout Scripture [10]_____ appears as a symbol of [11]_____.
- "four spirits of heaven" – are [12]_____ God is using to bring judgment in the final battle.

> Zechariah 6:5, "And the angel answered and said to me, 'These are four spirits of heaven, who go out from their station before the Lord of all the earth.'"

> Daniel 7:10, "A fiery stream issued and came forth from before Him. A thousand thousands ministered to Him; ten thousand times ten thousand stood before Him. The court was seated, and the books were opened."

> Luke 1:19, "And the angel answered and said to him, 'I am Gabriel, who stands in the presence of God, and was sent to speak to you and bring you these glad tidings.'"

> Revelation 7:1, "After these things I saw four angels standing at the four corners of the earth, holding the four winds of the earth."

> Zechariah 4:14, "So he said, 'These are the two anointed ones, who stand before the Lord of the whole earth.'"

- "north country" – may represent [13]_____ attacking Israel in the Tribulation.
- "south country" – no doubt refers to [14]_____.

COLOR OF HORSES

1) [first chariot] "red horses" – represent [15]_____ and bloodshed.

> Revelation 6:4, "Another horse, fiery red, went out. And it was granted to the one who sat on it to take peace from the earth, and that people should kill one another; and there was given to him a great sword."

2) [second chariot – NORTH COUNTRY] "black horses" – represent famine conditions in war.

> Revelation 6:5-6, "When He opened the third seal, I heard the third living creature say, 'Come and see.' So I looked, and behold, a black horse, and he who sat on it had a pair of scales in his hand. 6)And I heard a voice in the midst of the four living creatures saying, 'A quart of wheat for a denarius, and three quarts of barley for a denarius; and do not harm the oil and the wine.'"

3) [third chariot – NORTH COUNTRY] "white horses" – represent [16]_____ _____ and conquest.

> Revelation 6:1-2, "Now I saw when the Lamb opened one of the seals; and I heard one of the four living creatures saying with a voice like thunder, 'Come and see.' 2)And I looked, and behold, a white horse He who sat on it had a bow; and a crown was given to him, and he went out conquering and to conquer."

4) [fourth chariot – SOUTH COUNTRY] "dappled (gray) horses" – represent [17]_____ and hell.

> Revelation 6:7-8, "When He opened the fourth seal, I heard the voice of the four living creatures saying, 'Come and see.' 8)So I looked, and behold, a pale

horse. And the name of him who sat on it was Death and Hades followed with him. And power was given to them over a fourth of the earth, to kill with sword, with hunger, with death, and by the beasts of the earth."

- WHEN? At the [18]_____ of the seven-year Tribulation.
- SCOPE? This judgment will include all the [19]_____ of the earth.

> Zechariah 6:7, "Then the strong steeds went out, eager to go, that they might walk to and fro throughout the earth. And He said, 'Go, walk to and fro throughout the earth.' So they walked to and fro throughout the earth."

JESUS CROWNED KING & PRIEST

Zechariah 6:9-15, "Then the word of the Lord came to me, saying: 10)'Receive the gift from the captives – from Heldai, Tobijah, and Jedaiah, who have come from Babylon – and go the same day and enter the house of Josiah the son of Zephaniah. 11)Take the silver and gold, make an elaborate crown, and set it on the head of Joshua the son of Jehozadak, the high priest. 12)Then speak to him saying, "Thus says the Lord of hosts, saying: 'Behold, the Man whose name is the BRANCH! From His place He shall branch out, and He shall build the temple of the Lord; Yes, He shall build the temple of the Lord. He shall bear the glory, and shall sit and rule on His throne; so He shall be a priest on His throne, and the counsel of peace shall be between them both.'" 14)Now the elaborate crown shall be for a memorial in the temple of the Lord for Helem, Tobijah, Jedaiah, and Hen the son of Zephaniah. 15)Even those from afar shall come and build the temple of the Lord. Then you shall know that the Lord of hosts has sent Me to you. And this shall come to pass if you diligently obey the voice of the Lord your God.'"

CROWNING JOSHUA PICTURED THE MESSIAH

- "Behold, the Man whose name is the BRANCH!" (v. 12) – this is the [20]_____ _____ title for Jesus Christ.

> Zechariah 3:8, "Hear, O Joshua, the high priest, you and your companions who sit before you, for they are a wondrous sign; for behold, I am bringing forth My Servant the Branch."

- "From His place He shall branch out" (v. 12b) – [21]_____, the Messiah, will come from Israel, from His own people.

> Isaiah 53:2, "For He shall grow up before Him as a tender plant, and as a root out of dry ground."

> Luke 2:52, "And Jesus increased in wisdom and stature, and in favor with God and men."

- "And He shall build the temple of the Lord; Yes, He shall build the temple of the Lord" (v. 12c, 13a) – emphatic in Hebrew, "He HIMSELF." Jesus, the Messiah, will build His [22]_____ Temple. (See Ezekiel chapters 40 – 42.)
- "He shall bear the glory" (v. 13b) – the millennium will be the time for Christ to be [23]_____ on the earth!
- "And shall sit and rule on His throne" (v. 13c) – imagine a world where [24]_____ _____ alone rules!
- "So He shall be a priest on His throne" (v. 13d) – Jesus, who is King, will also be a [25]_____. No more separation of church and state!

239

Psalm 110:4, "The Lord has sworn and will not relent, You are a priest forever according to the order of Melchizedek."

- "Even those from afar shall come and build the temple of the Lord" (v. 15a) – 26_____ with Jews, all ethnic groups, will be in the Millennial Kingdom together because of Jesus' redemption.

> Isaiah 2:2, "Now it shall come to pass in the latter days that the mountain of the Lord's house shall be established on the top of the mountains, and shall be exalted above the hills; and all nations shall flow to it."

> Micah 4:1, "Now it shall come to pass in the latter days that the mountain of the Lord's house shall be established on the top of the mountains, and shall be exalted above the hills; and people shall flow to it."

- "Then you shall know that the Lord of hosts has sent Me to you" (15b) – 27_____ _____ Himself speaking here in the book of Zechariah!

OUR PARTICIPATION IS CONDITIONAL

> Zechariah 6:15c, "And this shall come to pass if you diligently obey the voice of the Lord your God."

- Before blessing there is always 28_____!
- The elaborate crown in Zerubbabel's temple was a reminder that God would send 29_____, His Messiah.

> Zechariah 6:14, "Now the elaborate crown shall be for a memorial in the temple of the Lord for Helem, Tobijah, Jedaiah, and Hen the son of Zephaniah."

Answers

1. Powerful 2. Swift 3. Superior 4. Innumerable 5. Guide 6. Judgment 7. war 8. Zion 9. Olives 10. bronze 11. judgment 12. angels 13. Russia 14. Egypt 15. war 16. victory 17. death 18. end 19. nations 20. Messianic 21. Jesus 22. millennial 23. exalted 24. Jesus 25. Priest 26. Gentiles 27. Jesus 28. obedience 29. Jesus

the Thrilling Prophecies of
Mr. Z and Jesus
Jerusalem, the Jew, and You

Rituals vs. Obedience

Message #9 in the series, Mr. Z and Jesus

Bible Text: Zechariah 7:1-8:23;

> "As the mainline has moved closer to flat lining, churches that have maintained allegiance to traditional Christian belief, comparatively speaking, have experienced membership increases. Some of those increases are quite dramatic. The old-time religion not only survives but prevails. The most recent 'Religious Congregations and Membership' study, published in 2000 by the Glenmary Research Center ... tells the statistical story. If we take losers first, we find that the Presbyterian Church USA (11,106 churches) has experienced decline of 11.6 percent over the previous ten years; the United Methodist Church (35,721 churches) was down 6.7 percent; and the Episcopal Church (7,314 churches) lost 5.3 percent of its membership. Also, the United Church of Christ (5,863 churches) declined 14.8 percent, while the American Baptist Churches USA were down 5.7 percent." –Exodus: Why Americans Are Fleeing Liberal Churches for Conservative Christianity by Dave Shiflett, Sentinel, NY, NY, C, 2005, pp. xiii, xiv.

RITUAL – a [1]_____ or form of rites; a solemn act.

- Tragically, rituals have replaced the teaching of the [2]_____ of God in many churches.

  > Acts 18:11, "And he (Paul) continued there a year and six months, teaching the word of God among them."

RITUALS – Right or Wrong ?

> Zechariah 7:1-3, "Now in the fourth year of King Darius it came to pass that the word of the Lord came to Zechariah, on the fourth day of the ninth month, Chislev, 2)when the people sent Sherezer, with Regem-Melech and his men, to the house of God, to pray before the Lord, 3)and to ask the priests who were in the house of the Lord of hosts, and the prophets, saying, 'Should I weep in the fifth month and fast as I have done for so many years.'"

- The date the "word of the Lord" came to Zechariah? December 4, 518 B.C., nearly [3]_____ years after the eight visions.
- The delegation from Bethel wanted to know if they should continue the ritual of [4]_____, observed in exile, now that the temple was being rebuilt.

1) When the [5]_____ is pure, the ritual is pure.

  > Zechariah 7:4-7, "Then the word of the Lord of hosts came to me saying, 5)'Say to all the people of the land, and to the priests: "When you fasted and mourned in the fifth and seventh months during these seventy years, did you really fast for Me – for Me? 6)When you eat and when you drink, do you not

eat and drink for yourselves? 7)Should you not have obeyed the words which the Lord proclaimed through the former prophets when Jerusalem and the cities around it were inhabited and prosperous, and the South and the Lowland were inhabited."" [Regarding the 70 years reference, remember much earlier the prophet Jeremiah had warned the Jews they were going into captivity for 70 years because of their sin ... see Jeremiah 25:1-11].

VARIOUS RITUALISTIC FASTS

Zechariah 8:19, "Thus says the Lord of hosts: 'The fast of the fourth month, the fast of the fifth, the fast of the seventh, and the fast of the tenth, shall be joy and gladness and cheerful feasts for the house of Judah. Therefore love truth and peace.'"

- "Fast of the fourth month" - the day when the city walls were breached (ninth of Tammuz), 2 Kings 25:3-4; Jer. 39:2.
- "Fast of the fifth month" - when the house of God was destroyed by fire (ninth of Ab), 2 Kings 25:8-10.
- "Fast of the seventh month" - the anniversary of the assassination of Gedaliah the son of Ahikam (third of Tishri), 2 Kings 25:25; Jer. 41:2.
- "Fast of the tenth month" - the day Nebuchadnezzar laid siege to Jerusalem (tenth of Tebeth), 2 Kings 25:1; Ezek. 24:2. It was now [6]_____ years later, the Temple was almost rebuilt, and the questioned was, ""Are these ritualistic fasts necessary?" Notice, they did not inquire about the one and only [7]_____ fast each year on Yom Kippur, the Day of Atonement.

2) When the motive is [8]_____, the ritual is impure.

Zechariah 7:8-12, 14, "Then the word of the Lord came to Zechariah, saying, 9)Thus says the Lord of hosts: 'Execute true justice, show mercy and compassion everyone to his brother. 10)Do not oppress the widow or the fatherless, the alien or the poor. Let none of you plan evil in his heart against his brother.' 11)But they refused to heed, shrugged their shoulders, and stopped their ears so that they could not hear. 12)Yes, they made their hearts like flint, refusing to hear the law and the words which the Lord of hosts had sent by His Spirit through the former prophets. Thus great wrath came from the Lord of hosts. 14)But I scattered them with a whirlwind among all the nations which they had not known. Thus the land became desolate after them, so that no one passed through or returned; for they made the pleasant land desolate."

- Rituals are no replacement for [9]_____ in our lives.
- Rituals are no replacement for [10]_____ for Jesus Christ.

John 21:17, "He said to him the third time, 'Simon, son of Jonah, do you love me?' Peter was grieved because He said to him the third time, 'Do you love Me?'"

- Rituals can give [11]_____ assurance spirituality and can belong to a system of works which God rejects.

Colossians 2:20-23, "Therefore, if you died with Christ from the basic principles of the world, why, as though living in the world, do you subject yourselves to regulations - 21)'Do not touch, do not taste, do not handle,' 22)which all concern things which perish with the using – according to the commandments of and doctrines of men? 23)These things indeed have an appearance of wisdom in self-imposed religion, false humility, and neglect of the body, but are of no value against the indulgence of the flesh."

There are only [12]_____ the church is to practice: believer's [13]_____ and the Lord's [14]_____.

- Zechariah chapter 7 is a call to [15]_____ and authentic worship to God!

ISRAEL'S RESTORATION & KINGDOM – 8:1-23

- "The word of the Lord" appears [16]_____ times in chapter 8; v. 1, 3-4, 6-7, 9, 14, 18, 20, & v. 23.
- There are two basic divisions in chapter 8: v.v. 1 - 17 & v.v. 18 - 23. 1 [17]_____ _____ on Israel enemies.

Zechariah 8:1-2, "Again, the word of the Lord of hosts came, saying, 2)Thus says the Lord of hosts: 'I am zealous for Zion with great zeal; with great fervor I am zealous for her.'"

- "zealous" – [18]_____ (perfect tense in Hebrew) indicating a state of mind. The [19]_____ of God in the midst of Israel in the Millennial Kingdom.

Zechariah 8:3, "Thus says the Lord: 'I will return to Zion, and dwell in the midst of Jerusalem. Jerusalem shall be called the City of Truth, The Mountain of the Lord of hosts, The Holy Mountain.'"

3) God's [20]_____ will characterize the millennial kingdom.

Zechariah 8:4, "Thus says the Lord of hosts: 'Old men and old women shall again sit in the streets of Jerusalem, each one with his staff in his hand because of great age. The streets of the city shall be full of boys and girls playing in the streets.'"

4) God's [21]_____ will cause the millennial kingdom to happen.

Zechariah 8:6, "Thus says the Lord of hosts: 'If it is a marvelous in the eyes of the remnant of this people in these days, will it also be marvelous in My eyes?' says the Lord of hosts."

- "marvelous" – "difficult," or "[22]_____"

Genesis 18:14, "Is anything too hard for the Lord?"

5) God will [23]_____ His people, Israel, and the millennial kingdom will be based in Jerusalem.

Zechariah 8:7-8, "Thus says the Lord of hosts: 'Behold, I will save My people from the land of the east and from the land of the west; 8)I will bring them back, and they shall dwell in the midst of Jerusalem. They shall be My people and I will be their God, in truth and righteousness.'"

Isaiah 43:5-6, "Fear not, for I am with you; I will bring your descendants from the east, and gather you from the west; 6)I will say to the north, 'Give them up!' Bring My sons from afar, and My daughters from the ends of the earth."

Jeremiah 32:38-39, "They shall be My people, and I will be their God; 39)then I will give them one heart and one way, that they may fear Me forever, for the good of them and their children after them."

6) God's blessing of [24]_____ will characterize the millennial kingdom. Zechariah 8:9-13

7) God will [25]_____ Israel and she will be redeemed.

Zechariah 8:14-15, "For thus says the Lord of hosts: 'Just as I determined to punish you when your fathers provoked Me to wrath,' says the Lord of hosts, 'And I would not relent, 15)So again in these days I am determined to do good to Jerusalem and to the house of Judah. Do not fear.'"

What Will the Millennial Kingdom Be Like ?

- Perfect [26]_____

Zechariah 8:19b, "Shall be joy and gladness and cheerful feasts for the house of Judah. Therefore love truth and peace."

- Perfect [27]_____ with God

Zechariah 8:21, "The inhabitants of one city shall go to another, saying, 'Let us continue to go and pray before the Lord, and seek the Lord of hosts. I myself will go also.'"

- Perfect [28]_____

Zechariah 8:22-23, "Yes, many peoples and strong nations shall come to seek the Lord of hosts in Jerusalem, and to pray before the Lord.' 23)Thus says the Lord of hosts: 'In those days ten men from every language of the nations shall grasp the sleeve of a Jewish man, saying, "Let us go with you, for we have heard that God is with you."'"

OUR BEHAVIOR

Zechariah 8:16-17, "'These are the things you shall do: speak each man the truth to his neighbor give judgment in your gates for truth, justice, and peace; 17)Let none of you think evil in your heart against your neighbor; and do not love a false oath. For all these are things that I hate,' says the Lord."

Message, 8:16-17, "And now here's what I want you to do: Tell the truth, the whole truth, when you speak. Do the right thing by one another, both personally and in your courts. Don't cook up plans to take unfair advantage of others. Don't do or say what isn't so. I hate all that stuff. Keep your lives simple and honest.' Decree of God."

Answers

1. ceremonial 2. Word 3. two 4. fasting 5. motive 6. 86 7. required 8. impure 9. obedience 10. love 11. false 12. sacraments 13. baptism 14. Supper 15. repentance 16. 10 17. Punishment 18. jealous 19. presence 20. peace 21. power 22. impossible 23. regather 24. prosperity 25. restore 26. pleasure 27. communion 28. positioning

the Thrilling Prophecies of
Mr. Z and Jesus
Jerusalem, the Jew, and You

Alexander the Great in Zechariah?
Amazing Prophecies You Must Know!
Message #10 in the series Mr. Z and Jesus
Bible Text: Zechariah 9:1-17

WHEN GOD USES THE UNGODLY 9:1-7

"The testimony of the oldest translation of the Old Testament (which is the Greek) and the compilers of the Jewish canon are in favor of the genuineness of these chapters. The arguments, of the liberals are untenable and can be refuted. We can rest assured that the Spirit of God used one author for all fourteen chapters ... In verses 1 to 8 of chapter 9, the campaign of Alexander the Great is sketched. His successes are recounted in verses 1-7, and verse 8 notes the deliverance of Jerusalem. After the Battle of Issus, Alexander quickly conquered Damascus, Sidon, Tyre (after seven months it was burned), Gaza, Ashkelon, Ashdod, and Ekron. The course of his victories in 332 B.C. was from northern Syria south by the valley of the Orontes River to Damascus, then along the Phoenician and Philistine Coast." *-Zechariah: Israel's Comfort and Glory* by Charles Lee Feinberg, C, The Minor Prophets, C, 1990, p. 314.

"The scene described in 9:1-8 is the course of the invasion and conquest by Alexander the Great and the beginning of the Grecian world empire ... It is quite remarkable indeed that in all this Jerusalem should have been spared. The Jewish historian Josephus sees this as the result of a dream Alexander had. Whether this was so or not, verse 8 plainly declares that it was the Lord's will to spare the city and He caused the enemy to bypass Jerusalem. So God makes His enemies carry out His purposes." *-Jehovah Remember: Studies in Zechariah* by Nathan J. Stone, B.D., Th.M., Moody Bible Institute, Chicago, IL, C, 1966, Part II, p. 6.

"Alexander the Great was unwittingly God's instrument of judgment. His forces subjugated 'the land of Hadrach,' taking key towns, Damascus and Hamath. Damascus was the capital of Syria and still is today. Also, it continues to cause Israel a great deal of difficulty. The cities mentioned in verses 1-7 trace the march of Alexander's great army down into the Promised Land. It is history now, but when it was written, it was prophecy. Its literal fulfillment makes it one of the most remarkable accounts we find in the Word of God. This is so disturbing to the liberal theologian that he attempts to move the timing of the writing of Zechariah up to the time of Alexander the Great!" *-Zechariah* by J. Vernon McGee, Thru the Bible Books, Pasadena, CA, C, 1979, p. 124.

LESSONS TO LEARN

1) God is ¹_____.
2) God uses the just and the unjust to accomplish His purpose.
3) No person or influence can 2_____ God's plan.

ALEXANDER'S TRAIL OF DESTRUCTION

Zechariah 9:1, "The burden of the word of the Lord against the land of Hadrach, and Damascus its resting place (For the eyes of men and all the tribes of Israel are on the Lord)."

NLT, 9:1, "This is the message from the Lord against the land of Aram and the city of Damascus, for the eyes of humanity, including all the tribes of Israel, are on the Lord."

TOWNS OF DESTRUCTION

1) 1 JUDGMENT IN SYRIA: Hadrach (Hattarika) and ³_____ (the capitol city), both towns of ⁴_____.

Zechariah 9:2-4, "Also against Hamath which borders on it, and against Tyre and Sidon though they are very wise. 3)For Tyre built herself a tower, heaped up silver like the dust, and gold like the mire of the streets. 4)Behold, the Lord will cast her out; He will destroy her power in the sea, and she will be devoured by fire."

2) THE DOOM OF PHOENICIA: ⁵_____ and ⁶_____, famous Phoenician cities (southern Lebanon area of today).

• ⁷_____ had already prophesied the doom of Tyre and identified ⁸_____ as the energizing force behind her! He also predicted the doom of Sidon. (See Ezekiel 28:1-19, further Ezekiel 26:4-12, 27:27; Sidon - 28:20-24.)

3) THE CONQUEST OF PHILISTIA: ⁹_____, Gaza, Ekron, and ¹⁰_____, all Philistine coastal cities.

Zechariah 9:5-6, "Ashkelon shall see it and fear; Gaza also shall be very sorrowful; and Ekron for He dried up her expectation. The king shall perish from Gaza, and Ashkelon shall not be inhabited. 6)A mixed race shall settle in Ashdod, and I will cut off the pride of the Philistines."

"Special mention is made by a contemporary of Alexander that the king of Gaza was brought alive to the conqueror after the city was taken; the satrap, or petty 'king' of the city, was bound to a chariot and dragged around the city to his death. Thus did the city lose its independence." –*The Minor Prophets* by Charles L. Feinberg, Moody Press, Chicago, IL, C, 1990, p. 316.

MILLENNIAL PROMISE

Zechariah 9:7, "I will take away the blood from his mouth, and the abominations from between his teeth. But he who remains, even he shall be for our God, and shall be like a leader in Judah, and Ekron like a Jebusite."

JERUSALEM PROTECTED FROM ALEXANDER

Zechariah 9:8, "I will camp around My house because of the army, because of him who passes by and him who returns. No more shall an oppressor pass through them, for now I have seen with My eyes."

- The early Jewish historian Flavius Josephus wrote about the miraculous protection of [11]_____ from Alexander the Great.
- Alexander passed through Jerusalem more than once in his military campaigns without harming it.

ISRAEL'S COMING DELIVERER

Zechariah 9:9, "Rejoice greatly O daughter of Zion! Shout, O daughter of Jerusalem! Behold, your King is coming to you; He is just and having salvation, lowly and riding on a donkey, a colt, the foal of a donkey."

- [12]_____ quoted Zechariah – an indisputable reference to Christ's triumphal entry in Jerusalem. John quoted Zechariah as well (see John 12:12-16).

Matthew 21:1-5, "Now when they drew near Jerusalem, and came to Bethphage, at the Mount of Olives, then Jesus sent two disciples, 2)saying to them, 'Go into the village opposite you, and immediately you will find a donkey tied, and a colt with her. Loose them and bring them to Me. 3)And if anyone says anything to you, you shall say, "The Lord has need of them," and immediately he will send them.' 4)All of this was done that it might be fulfilled which was spoken by the prophet, saying: 5)'Tell the daughter of Zion, "Behold, your King is coming to you, lowly, and sitting on a donkey; a colt, the foal of a donkey."'"

- Jesus came riding into Jerusalem on an animal of [13]_____ because He is the Prince of peace.
- The next verse refers to the [14]_____ coming of Jesus Christ, God's Messiah and his future Millennial Kingdom.

Zechariah 9:10, "I will cut off the chariot of Ephraim and the horse from Jerusalem; the battle bow shall be cut off. He shall speak peace to the nations; His dominion shall be from sea to sea, and from the River to the ends of the earth."

- How fascinating: the Millennial Kingdom of Jesus although based in Jerusalem will cover the entire [15]_____!

Psalm 72:8, "He shall have dominion also from sea to sea, and from the river to the ends of the earth."

THE BLOOD OF HIS COVENANT

Zechariah 9:11-12, "As for you also, because of the blood of your covenant, I will set your prisoners free from the waterless pit. 12)Return to the stronghold, you prisoners of hope. Even today I declare that I will restore double to you."

- When we have been washed in the Blood of Jesus Christ, God restores MORE than [16]_____ to us!

THE MACCABEAN PERIOD & THE TRIBULATION

Zechariah 9:13-17

"The only time historically in which the Jews fought the Greeks was during

247

the Maccabean period (175-135 B.C.). The Greek kingdom, known as the Seleucid Dynasty, was ruling Syria. Under Antichus IV (Epiphanes), the Jews were pressured to conform to the Greek religion. While a number of Jews were willing to go along with the program, a rebellion broke out that was led by the Hasmonaean family (Mattathias and his sons, the most famous of which was Judas Maccabaeus, called 'the hammer'). Information for this period is found in Daniel 11:1- 35; the Books of Maccabees, and Josephus' Antiquities of the Jew ... Even though this section depicts God's protection of His people during the Maccabean period, it also prefigures the Great Tribulation and the Millennium to follow." –*Zechariah* by Homer Heater, Jr. Lamplighter Books, Zondervan Publishing House, Grand Rapids, MI, C, 1987, pp. 98-99.

Answers

1. sovereign 2. stop 3. Damascus 4. Syria 5. Tyre 6. Sidon 7. Ezekiel 8. Satan 9. Ashkelon 10. Ashdod 11. Jerusalem 12. Matthew 13. peace 14. SECOND 15. earth 16. double

The Time of the Latter Rain: What Does it Mean ?

Message #11 in the series, Mr. Z and Jesus

Bible Text: Zechariah 10:1-12

ASK THE Lord FOR RAIN – 10:1

Zechariah 10:1, "Ask the Lord for rain in the time of the latter rain. The Lord will make flashing clouds; He will give them showers of rain, grass in the field for everyone."

- Sadly, many Christians don't ask the [1]_____ for all their needs!

    James 4:2, "You lust and do not have. You murder and covet and cannot obtain. You fight and war. Yet you do not have because you do not ask."

- Zechariah prophecy promises literal rain, a literal kingdom to come; and it promises [2]_____ rain of blessings to come!

    Hosea 6:1-3, "Come, and let us return to the Lord; for He has torn, but He will heal us; He has stricken, but He will bind us up. 2)After two days He will revive us; on the third day He will raise us up, that we may live in His sight. 3)Let us know, let us pursue the knowledge of the Lord. His going forth is established as the morning; He will come to us like the rain, like the later and former rain to the earth."

- God has an ultimate plan for Israel ... their [3]_____.

    Romans 11:1, 26-27, "I say then, has God cast away His people? Certainly not! 26)And so all Israel will be saved, as it is written: 'The Deliverer will come out of Zion, and He will turn away ungodliness from Jacob; 27)For this is My covenant with them, when I take away their sins.'"

    Isaiah 59:20-21, "The Redeemer will come to Zion, and to those who turn away from transgressions in Jacob, says the Lord. 21)As for Me, says the Lord, this is My covenant with them: My Spirit who is upon you, and My words which I have put in your mouth, shall not depart from your mouth, nor from the mouth of your descendants, for from the mouth of your descendants' descendants' says the Lord, 'from this time and forevermore.'"

TERAPHIM AND FALSE SHEPHERDS – 10:2-3

Zechariah 10:2-3, "For the idols speak delusion; the diviners envision lies, and tell false dreams; they comfort in vain. Therefore the people wend their way like sheep; they are in trouble because there is no shepherd. 3)My anger is kindled against the shepherds, and I will punish the goatherds. For the Lord of hosts will visit His flock, the house of Judah, and will make them as His royal horse in the battle."

NASB, Zechariah 10:2-3, "For the teraphim speak iniquity, and the diviners see lying visions, and tell false dreams; they comfort in vain. Therefore the people wander like sheep, they are afflicted, because there is no shepherd."

- The teraphim were household [4]_____.

"The teraphim were household gods used for the purpose of divination, probably in the form of human beings. They were like the household gods of the Romans. (See Gen. 31:19, 30.) They were kept at shrines (Judg. 17:5) and in private homes (I Sam. 19:13, 16)." –*The Minor Prophets* by Charles L. Feinberg, Moody Press, Chicago, IL, C, 1990, p. 320.

- False shepherds were a problem to Israel just as they are to the [5]_____ _____ today!
- God has a special [6]_____ reserved for false shepherds! [See Ezekiel 34:6-10.]

THE CORNERSTONE JESUS – 10:4

Zechariah 10:4, "From him comes the cornerstone, from him the tent peg, from him the battle bow, from him every ruler together."

- Zechariah reminds the people that the [7]_____ is coming!

JESUS IS:

1) The [8]_____.

Isaiah 28:16, "Therefore thus says the Lord God: 'Behold, I lay in Zion a stone for a foundation, a tried stone, a precious cornerstone, a sure foundation; whoever believes will not act hastily.'"

Romans 9:33, "As it is written: 'Behold, I lay in Zion a stumbling stone and rock of offense, and whoever believes on Him will not be put to shame.'"

Ephesians 2:20, "Having been built on the foundation of the apostles and prophets, Jesus Christ Himself being the chief cornerstone."

2) The [9]_____ – all the glory of the Kingdom rests on Him.

Isaiah 22:23-24, "I will fasten him as a peg in a secure place, and he will become a glorious throne to his father's house. 24)They will hang on him all the glory of his father's house, the offspring and the posterity...."

   • Eliakim was a prototype of the Messiah to come.

1) The [10]_____.

Zechariah 10:4, "... from him the battle bow."

ISRAEL IN THE TRIBULATION – 10:5-8

Zechariah 10:5-8, "They shall be like mighty men, who tread down their enemies in the mire of the streets in the battle. They shall fight because the Lord is with them, and the riders on horses shall be put to shame. 6)'I will strengthen the house of Judah, and I will save the house Joseph. I will bring them back, because I have mercy on them. They shall be as though I had no cast them aside; for I am the Lord their God, and I will hear them. 7)Those of Ephraim shall be like a mighty man, and their heart shall rejoice as if with wine. Yes, their children shall see it and be glad; their heart shall rejoice in the Lord. 8)I will whistle for them and gather them, for I will redeem them;

and they shall increase as they once increased."

- Before the Messiah can establish His Kingdom He must first deliver and restore [11]_____.

WHAT JESUS DOES FOR US:

1) I will strengthen (10:6a)
2) I will save (10:6b)
3) I will bring them back (10:6c)
4) I have mercy on them (10:6d)
5) I will hear them (10:6e)

God is going to [12]_____ for Israel's victory during the tumult of the Tribulation.

DISPLACEMENT AGAIN FOR ISRAEL? – 10:9

Zechariah 10:9, "I will sow them among the peoples, and they shall remember Me in far countries; they shall live, together with their children, and they shall return."

- Is it possible that Israel may be [13]_____ out of their land yet again?

"It is the current belief of several outstanding expositors that the nation of Israel is not now in that land permanently. I'm not sure but what the accurate interpretation of the Word of God is that they will again be put out of the land of Israel and that subsequently God Himself will return them to the land." –*Zechariah* by Dr. J. Vernon McGee, Thru the Bible, Box 100, Pasadena, CA 91109, C, 1979, p. 147.

ISRAEL'S PERMANENT REGATHERING – 10:10-12

Zechariah 10:10-12, "I will also bring them back from the land of Egypt, and gather them from Assyria. I will bring them into the land of Gilead and Lebanon, until no more room is found for them. 11)He shall pass through the sea with affliction, and strike the waves of the sea: All the depths of the River shall dry up. Then the pride of Assyria shall be brought down, and the scepter of Egypt shall depart. 12)'So I will strengthen them in the Lord, and they shall walk up and down in His name,' says the Lord."

- [14]_____ is part of the promised Land – so we know Israel, now, does not have all their Land.
- Again, there is the hint of a future [15]_____ again!

"'I will bring them back from the land of Egypt.' There are very few Jews in the land Egypt in our day. I believe this refers to future dispersion ... I do not think that the wildest interpretation of prophecy in our day would dare say that the present return of Israel to Palestine is a fulfillment of this Scripture. It could not possibly be. It clearly refers to a future regathering" –*Zechariah* by Dr. J. Vernon McGee, Thru the Bible, C, 1979, pp. 150-151

Answers

1. Lord 2. spiritual 3. salvation 4. idols 5. church 6. punishment 7. Messiah 8. Cornerstone 9. Nail 10. Battle Bow 11. Israel 12. whistle 13. kicked 14. Lebanon 15. regathering

251

the Thrilling Prophecies of
Mr. Z and Jesus
Jerusalem, the Jew, and You

Thirty Pieces of Silver in Zechariah?
Message #12 in the series, Mr. Z & Jesus

Bible Text: Zechariah 11:1-17

John 1:10-11, "He was in the world, and the world was made through Him, and the world did not know Him. 11)He came to His own, and His own did not receive Him."

NLT, John 1:11, "He came to his own people, and even they rejected him."

MESAGE, John 1:11, "He came to His own people, but they didn't want Him."

THE TRAGIC RESULT OF REJECTING JESUS

John 3:36, "He who believes in the Son has everlasting life; and he who does not believe in the Sonshall not see life, but the wrath of God abides on Him."

"The chapter is undoubtedly the darkest of Israel's history ... the context of the rest of the chapter is determining and it points unmistakably to the judgment which resulted from the rejection of the Shepherd of Israel, that destruction which overtook the land and people in A.D. 70." *–Zechariah: Israel's Comfort and Glory* by Charles Lee Feinberg, Moody Press, Chicago, IL, C, 1990, p. 325.

"This chapter also presents the Good Shepherd of His people, the Good Shepherd who will give His life for the sheep. Then another shepherd is presented, the foolish shepherd, who will come much later. He pictures the Antichrist, the one who will shear the sheep and kill them for food." *–Thru the Bible by J. Vernon McGee, Volume III Proverbs - Malachi*, Thomas Nelson Publishers, Nashville, TN, C, 1982, p. 965.

ISRAEL 'S TRAGIC INVASION – 11:1-3

Zechariah 11:1, 3, "Open your doors, O Lebanon, that fire may devour your cedars. Wail, O cypress, for the cedar has fallen, because the mighty trees are ruined. Wail, O oaks of Bashan, for thick forest has come down. 3)There is the sound of wailing shepherds! For their glory is in ruins. There is the sound of roaring lions! For the pride of the Jordan is in ruins."

- Here is a tragic prediction of Israel being attacked from an invader of the north, the [1]_____ army. This occurred in A.D. 70 - over 1,000,000 Jews were killed.
- [2]_____ had predicted this devastation as had Zechariah's prophecy.

Matthew 23:37-39, "O Jerusalem, Jerusalem, the one who kills the prophets

253

and stones those who are sent to her! How often I wanted to gather your children together, as a hen gathers her chicks under her wings, but you were not willing! 38)See! Your house is left to you desolate; 39)for I say to you, you shall see Me no more till you say, 'Blessed is He who comes in the name of the Lord!'"

"FEED THE FLOCK FOR SLAUGHTER " - 11:4-14

Zechariah 11:4-5, "Thus says the Lord my God, 'Feed the flock for slaughter, 5)whose owners slaughter them and feel no guilt; those who sell them say, "Blessed by the Lord, for I am rich"; and their shepherds do not pity them.'"

- Zechariah portrayed a shepherd leading his flock to [3]_____. Why? Israel's false shepherds had rejected the True Shepherd, Jesus Christ.

    Zechariah 11:6, "For I will no longer pity the inhabitants of the land, says the Lord. 'But indeed I will give everyone into his neighbor's hand and into the hand of his king. They shall attack the land, and I will not deliver them from their hand.'"

- The [4]_____ attacked the land of Israel and enacted devastating defeat. The "king" was Caesar!

    John 19:15, "But they cried out, 'Away with Him, away with Him! Crucify Him!' Pilate said to them, 'Shall I crucify your King!' The chief priests answered, 'We have no king but Caesar!'"

THE MINISTRY OF THE TRUE SHEPHERD - 11:7-8

Zechariah 11:7-8, "So I fed the flock for slaughter, in particular the poor of the flock. I took for myself two staffs: the one I called Beauty, and the other I called Bonds; and I fed the flock. 8)I dismissed the three shepherds in one month. My soul loathed them, and their soul abhorred me."

- Those "poor in spirit" recognized the need for the [5]_____.
- Shepherds carried two staffs: one to protect against wild beasts; and the other to help the sheep in difficult places. "Beauty" refers to [6]_____ and "Bonds" refers to the [7]_____ - the Christ, the Good Shepherd, heals and forgives His people.
- The loathsome three shepherds? Perhaps the priests, elders, and [8]_____ of Israel - all who rejected Jesus Christ.

    Zechariah 11:9, "Then I said, 'I will not feed you. Let what is dying die, and what is perishing perish. Let those that are left eat each other's flesh.' 10)And I took my staff, Beauty, and cut it in two, that I might break the covenant which I had made with all the peoples. 11)So it was broken on that day. Thus the poor of the flock, who were watching me, knew that it was the word of the Lord."

- Those who refused to believe God set aside to [9]_____ (v. 9). Cannibalism occurred in Jerusalem's defeat of A.D. 70.
- God providential care of Israel was set aside because of her [10]_____.
- Jesus' followers, spread throughout the earth, [11]_____ our Lord's prediction of Jerusalem when it occurred!

"THIRTY PIECES OF SILVER " – 11:12-14

Zechariah 11:12-14, "Then I said to them, 'If it is agreeable to you, give me my wages; and if not, refrain.' So they weighed out for my wages thirty pieces of silver. 13)And the Lord said to me, 'Throw it to the potter – that princely price they set on me.' So I took the thirty pieces of silver and threw them into the house of the Lord for the potter. 14)Then I cut in two my other staff, Bonds, that I might break the brotherhood between Judah and Israel."

- To the Christ-rejecting Jews of Jesus day He was worth only the price of a 12)_____.
- Zechariah 11:13 is an exact fulfillment of Matthew 13)_____.
- The breaking of the staff, Bonds, was a declarative statement that the nation Israel would be 14)_____ when the Romans invaded in A.D. 70.

THE EVIL SHEPHERD TO COME – 11:15-17

Zechariah 11:15-17, "And the Lord said to me, 'Next, take for yourself the implements of a foolish shepherd. 16)For indeed I will raise up a shepherd in the land who will not care for those who are cut off, nor seek the young, nor heal those that are broken, nor feed those that still stand. But he will eat the flesh of the fat and tear their hooves in pieces. 17)Woe to the worthless shepherd, who leaves the flock! A sword shall be against his right eye; His arm shall completely wither, and his right eye shall be totally blinded.'"

- "Foolish shepherds" represent all the false 15)_____ that plagued Israel and the church.
- The false shepherd to come is the 16)_____!

2 Thessalonians 2:7-12, "For the mystery of lawlessness is already at work; only He who now restrains will do so until He is taken out of the way. 8)And then the lawless one will be revealed, whom the Lord will consume with the breath of His mouth and destroy with the brightness of His coming. 9)The coming of the lawless one is according to the working of Satan, with all power, signs, and lying wonders, 10)and with all unrighteous deception among those who perish, because they did not receive the love of the truth, that they might be saved. 11)And for this reason God will send them strong delusion, that they should believe the lie, 12)that they all may be condemned who did not believe the truth but had pleasure in unrighteousness."

Answers

1. Roman 2. Jesus 3. slaughter 4. Romans 5. Messiah 6. favor 7. unity 8. scribes 9. judgment 10. sin 11. remembered 12. slave 13. 27:3-10 14. broken 15. teachers 16. Antichrist

255

the Thrilling Prophecies of
Mr. Z and Jesus
Jerusalem, the Jew, and You

The Deceit of the Antichrist
Message #13 in the series, Mr. Z and Jesus
Bible Text: Zechariah 11:15-17

> I John 2:18, "Little children, it is the last hour; and as you have heard that the Antichrist is coming, even now many antichrists have come, by which we know that it is the last hour."

- Because Israel rejected the True Shepherd, tragically, they will receive the [1]_____ _____ Shepherd, the Antichrist.

> "But who is meant by this foolish or wicked shepherd? Jewish commentators interpret of Herod; some Christian interpreters ... apply it to 'all the evil native Jewish rulers collectively,' who, subsequent to the rejection of Christ, oppressed and devoured the flock ... others again indentify him with the imperial Roman power ... But ... the full and final fulfillment of this solemn prophecy will take place in the final phase of the development of the fourth great world power (i.e., the Roman), when amid the ten horns, or kingdoms, there shall come up 'a little horn' who shall be master of them all." –*Zechariah A Commentary on His Visions and Prophecies* by David Baron , Kregel Publications, Grand Rapids, MI, C, Hebrew Christian Testimony to Israel, London, 1918, ppp. 415-416.

The Deceitful Character of the Antichrist

> Zechariah 11:15, "And the Lord said to me, 'Next, take for yourself the implements of a foolish shepherd.'"

- "foolish" is a synonym for [2]_____ – diabolical in his intentions and actions.

> Zechariah 11:16, "For indeed I will raise up a shepherd in the land who will not care for those who are cut off, nor seek the young, nor heal those that are broken, nor feed those that still stand. But he will eat the flesh of the fat and tear their hooves in pieces."

1) Antichrist operates in [3]_____ sovereign plan.

> Zechariah 11:16a, "I will raise up a shepherd in the land."

2) Antichrist capitalizes on [4]_____ misery in the Tribulation period.

> Zechariah 11:16b, "... who will not care for those who are cut off, nor seek the young, nor heal those that are broken, nor feed those that still stand."

3) Many [5]_____ will die and experience a horrendous fate because of the Antichrist.

Zechariah 11:16c, "But he will eat the flesh of the fat and tear their hooves n pieces."

The Condemnation of the Antichrist

Zechariah 11:17, "Woe to the worthless [idol] shepherd, who leaves the flock! A sword shall be against his arm and against his right eye; His arm shall completely wither, and his right eye shall be totally blinded."

1) "Woe" signifies a [6]_____. The Hebrew word is "hoy," and it denotes trouble! At the appointed hour, God will remove the power of the Antichrist.

2) The arm is the emblem of [7]_____ and the eye of [8]_____ _____. God will give the Antichrist delusions at the appointed time.

"The false shepherd, the Antichrist, will actually be the one who brings in the Great Tribulation in all its fury. In the first part of the Tribulation Israel will be deceived into thinking that Antichrist is their Good Shepherd, but by the time they discover his real character, he will be the world dictator, and the armies of the world will come against Jerusalem." –*Thru the Bible, Proverbs - Malachi* with J. Vernon McGee, Thomas Nelson Publishers, Nashville, TN, C, 1982, p. 970.

Fascinating Facts About the Antichrist

1) The Holy Spirit [9]_____ the Antichrist at present. After the Rapture, the Antichrist is revealed and his sinister work begins.

2 Thessalonians 2:6-8, "And now you know what is restraining, that he may be revealed in his own time. 7)For the mystery of lawlessness is already at work; only He who now restrains will do so until He is taken out of the way. 8)And then the Lawless one will be revealed, whom the Lord will consume with the breath of His mouth and destroy with the brightness of His coming."

2) The Antichrist will rise from the [10]_____ empire, the nation which destroyed Jerusalem.

Daniel 9:26, "And after sixty-two weeks Messiah shall be cut off, but not for Himself, and the people of the prince who is to come shall destroy the city and the sanctuary. The end of it shall be with a flood, and till the end of the war desolations are determined."

3) The Antichrist will be the head of a [11]_____-nation European Confederacy.

Revelation 13:1, "Then I stood on the sand of the sea. And I saw a beast rising up out of the sea, having seven heads and ten horns, and on his horns ten crowns, and on his heads a blasphemous name."

Revelation 17:12-13, "The ten horns which you saw are ten kings who have received no kingdom as yet, but they receive authority for one hour as kings with the beast. 13)These are of one mind, and they will give their power and authority to the beast."

4) In his rise to worldwide power the Antichrist will have [12]_____ three rulers.

Daniel 7:8, 24, "I was considering the horns, and there was another horn, a little one, coming up among them, before whom three of the first horns were plucked out by the roots. And there, in this horn, were eyes like the eyes of a man, and a mouth speaking pompous words. 24)The ten horns are ten kings who shall arise from this kingdom. And another shall rise after them; He shall be different from the first ones, and shall subdue three kings."

Daniel 11:36, "Then the king shall do according to his own will: he shall exalt and magnify himself above every god, shall speak blasphemies against the God of gods, and shall prosper till the wrath has been accomplished; for what has been determined shall be done."

5) The Antichrist will exude charm, [13]_____, oration, persuasiveness, and political and commercial skill unequalled.

Daniel 7:20, "And the ten horns that were on its head, and the other horn which came up, before which three fell, namely, that horn which had eyes and a mouth which spoke pompous words, whose appearance was greater than his fellows."

Daniel 8:23-24, "And in the latter time of their kingdom, when the transgressors have reached their fullness, a king shall arise, having fierce features, who understands sinister schemes. 24)His power shall be mighty, but not by his own power; He shall destroy fearfully, and shall prosper and thrive; he shall destroy the mighty, and also the holy people."

6) In his ascent to power the Antichrist will survive an [14]_____ attempt.

Revelation 13:3, 7-8, "And I saw one of his heads as if it had been mortally wounded, and his deadly wound was healed. And all the world marveled and followed the beast. 7)It was granted to him to make war with the saints and to overcome them. And authority was given him over every tribe, tongue, and nation. 8)All who dwell on the earth will worship him, whose names have not been written in the Book of Life of the Lamb slain from the foundation of the world."

7) In the middle of the Tribulation the Antichrist [15]_____ the covenant with the Jews and proclaims himself as god.

Daniel 7:25, "He shall speak pompous words against the Most High, shall persecute the saints of the Most High, and shall intend to change times and law. Then the saints shall be given into his hand for a time and times and half a time."

Daniel 9:27, "Then he shall confirm a covenant with the many for one week; but in the middle of the week he shall bring an end to sacrifice and offering. And on the wing of abominations shall be one who makes desolate, even until the consummation, which is determined, is poured out on the desolate."

Daniel 11:36-37, "Then the king shall do according to his own will: he shall exalt and magnify himself above every god, shall speak blasphemies against the God of gods, and shall prosper till the wrath has been accomplished; for what has been determined shall be done. 37)He shall regard neither the God of his fathers nor the desire of women, nor regard any god; for he shall exalt himself above them all."

8) The Antichrist will be energized by [16]_____ and deception will characterize humanity.

> Revelation 13:4, "So they worshiped the dragon who gave authority to the beast; and they worshiped the beast, saying, 'Who is like the beast? Who is able to make war with him?'"

> 2 Thessalonians 2:9-12, "The coming of the lawless one is according to the working of Satan, will all power, signs, and lying wonders, 10)and with all unrighteous deception among those who perish, because they did not receive the love of the truth, that they might be saved. 11)And for this reason God will send them strong delusion, that they should believe the lie, 12)that they all may be condemned who did not believe the truth but had pleasure in unrighteousness."

9) At Jesus Christ's Second Coming the Antichrist will be [17]_____.

> Revelation 19:19-20, "And I saw the beast, the kings of the earth, and their armies, gathered together to make war against Him who sat on the horse and against His army. 20)Then the beast was captured and with him the false prophet who worked signs in his presence, by which he deceived those who received the mark of the beast and those who worshiped his image. These two were cast alive in the lake of fire burning with brimstone."

Answers

17. destroyed

1. False 2. wicked 3. God's 4. Israel's 5. Jews 6. curse 7. might 8. intelligence 9. hinders 10. Roman 11. 10 12. destroyed 13. intelligence 14. assassination 15. breaks 16. Satan

the Thrilling Prophecies of
Mr. Z and Jesus
✡
Jerusalem, the Jew, and You

The Coming War Against Jerusalem
Message #14 in the series, Mr. Z and Jesus
Bible Text: Zechariah 12:1-14; p. 1541 in the Nelson Study Bible

FOUR AMAZING FACTS ABOUT CHAPTERS 12-14

Zechariah 12:1, "The burden of the word of the Lord against Israel. Thus says the Lord, who stretches out the heavens, lays the foundation of the earth, and forms the spirit of man within him."

1) [1]_____ will be the focal point of the world at the Second Coming of Christ.

• [2]_____ is mentioned 10 times in Zechariah chapter 12.

2) The final battle, Armageddon (Rev. 16:16), will be a major military build-up from the [3]_____ corners of the globe against Jerusalem (Daniel 11:36-45).

3) The [4]_____ Coming of Christ will end this battle of all battles (Rev. 19:11-21).

• "in that day" – is cited [5]_____ times in Zechariah chapter 12-14. It is a reference to "The Day of the Lord" which begins with the Great Tribulation period and continues until the end of the Final Judgment (after the Millennium).

"THE DAY OF THE LORD"...

• Occurs 18 times in Zechariah
• Is the theme of the book of Joel
• Is NOT a 24-hour period
• Is a PERIOD OF TIME
• Begins with the Rapture of the Church

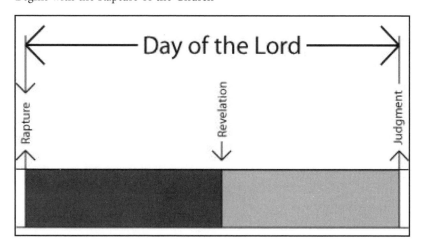

I Thessalonians 5:2, "For you yourselves know perfectly that the day of the Lord so comes as a thief in the night."

4) God will fulfill His plan with [6]_____ during the Tribulation – a day of spiritual salvation and victory.

Daniel 12:1, "At that time Michael shall stand up, the great prince who stands watch over the sons of your people; and there shall be a time of trouble, such as never was since there was a nation, even to that time. And at that time your people shall be delivered."

Matthew 24:21, "For then there will be great tribulation, such as has not been since the beginning of the world until this time, no, nor ever shall be."

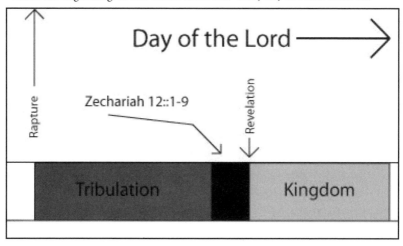

JERUSALEM WILL BE ... 12:2-4

Zechariah 12:2-3, "Behold, I will make Jerusalem a cup of drunkenness to all the surrounding peoples, when they lay siege against Judah and Jerusalem. 3)And it shall happen in that day that I will make Jerusalem a very heavy stone for all peoples; all who would heave it away will surely be cut in pieces, though all nations of the earth are gathered against it."

- "a cup of drunkenness" – a large basin everyone can drink from (Hebrew, saph) ... attacking nations will be like a drunkard who cannot walk the straight line!

  "The thought is this: Jerusalem and Judah will both become a cup or goblet which causes intoxication. This will result in staggering. Like men greedy with their drink from a glass of wine and ending up hopelessly drunk, so will God make those nations which besiege Jerusalem! They will reel in their attempt to overthrow the city." –Raymond Hyman Saxe

- "heavy stone" – refers to a heavy stone used in weightlifting contests. [7]_____ _____ will give a hernia to any nation that tries to gain victory over it!

- "cut in pieces" – refers to the completeness of [8]_____ (Lev. 21:5).

  Isaiah 54:17, "No weapon formed against you shall prosper, and every tongue which rises against you in judgment you shall condemn. This is the heritage of the servants of the Lord, and their righteousness is from Me, says the Lord."

"The final target of God-hate on this planet will be the Jew and Jerusalem. As the nations of the last days work on getting rid of the last lingering reminders of the Judeo-Christian ethic, they will concentrate their efforts on Jerusalem. The Jews will refuse to surrender their city and will defend it with fanatical zeal. The nations will be so obsessed with Jerusalem that they will be like drunkards who tarry too long at the cup." –Exploring the Minor Prophets by John Phillips, Kregel Publications, Grand Rapids, MI, C, 1998, p. 296

THE INVADING ARMIES – 12:4-6

Zechariah 12:4-6, "In that day, says the Lord, 'I will strike every horse with confusion, and its rider with madness; I will open My eyes on the house of Judah, and will strike every horse of the peoples with blindness. 5)And the governors of Judah shall say in their heart, "The inhabitants of Jerusalem are my strength in the Lord of hosts, their God." 6)In that day I will make the governors of Judah like a firepan in the woodpile, and like a fiery torch in the sheaves; they shall devour all the surrounding peoples on the right hand and on the left, but Jerusalem shall be inhabited again in her own place – Jerusalem.'"

THE FOUR ARMIES AT ARMAGEDDON:

- The army from the [9]_____ (Dan. 7:7-8, 24; Rev. 17:12-14), the European Confederacy, the revived Roman Empire made up of 10 nations led by the Antichrist.
- The army from the [10]_____ (Ezek. 38:1-6, 14- 16) which would be Russia and her allies, i.e., Persia, Cush, Put, Gomer, and Togermah, ancient names of modern Arab states.
- The army from the [11]_____ (Dan. 11:40-44) which would be Egypt and her Arab allies.
- The army from the [12]_____ (Rev. 9:13-16; 16:12- 16) an army of 200,000,000! God will send [13]_____ to the invaders!

   Zechariah 12:4a, "...I will strike every horse with confusion, and its rider with madness..."

   Zechariah 12:4c, "...and will strike every horse of the people with blindness."

   "Humanly speaking, there will be no reason for the world dictator, with vast military resources at his command, not to be able to conquer the troublesome city. But the besiegers will be up against God Himself. No matter what strategies they employ or what armies they summon, they will be incapacitated by God's direct intervention." –*Exploring the Minor Prophets* by John Phillips, Kregel Publications, Grand Rapids, MI, 1998, p. 297

In the midst of the battle Israel spiritual [14]_____ will be opened supernaturally by God!

   Zechariah 12:4b, "I will open My eyes on the house of Judah..."

Jews outside of Jerusalem will be [15]_____ and reminded of

God's covenant to them!

> Zechariah 12:6, "...I will make the governors of Judah shall say in their heart, 'The inhabitants of Jerusalem are my strength in the Lord of hosts, their God.'"

Supernaturally, God is going to [16]_____ Israel to defeat her enemies!

> Zechariah 12:7, "The Lord will save the tents of Judah first, so that the glory of the house of David and the glory of the inhabitants of Jerusalem shall not become greater than that of Judah."

The [17]_____ people outside of Jerusalem will be protected insuring victory for the city!

> Zechariah 12:8, "In that day the Lord will defend the inhabitants of Jerusalem; the one who is feeble among them in that day will be like David, and the house of David shall be like God, like the Angel of the Lord before them."

Israel in her most difficult moment will be infused with the strength of [18]_____ _____ the Conqueror!

> Zechariah 12:9, "It shall be in that day that I will seek to destroy all the nations that come against Jerusalem."

"Will seek" speaks of the precision of a [19]_____. God will "pick off" the nations attacking His people!

> "There will be a converging of all the nations against Jerusalem which we see in a great deal of detail in the book of Revelation. All of these great prophecies are like trains or planes coming into a train station or airport. All of these great themes of prophecy which originate elsewhere in the Bible converge into the book of Revelation like a great airport or Union Station."
> -J. Vernon McGee

> Zechariah 12:10, "And I will pour on the house of David and on the inhabitants of Jerusalem the Spirit of grace and supplication; then they will look on Me whom they pierced. Yes, they will mourn for Him as one mourns for his only son, and grieve for Him as one grieves for a firstborn."

When Israel's eyes focus on God ... she will finally see God incarnate, [20]_____ _____ the Messiah!

When Israel Views the Pierced One

Message #15 in the series, Mr. Z and Jesus

Bible Text: Zechariah 12:10-13:6

GOD'S PLAN TO REDEEM ISRAEL

Zechariah 12-14 teaches God will save and [1]_____ Israel – His purpose will be accomplished. See Luke 14:15-24; Matthew 21:33-46

> Micah 7:18-19, "Who is a God like You, pardoning iniquity and passing over the transgression of the remnant of His heritage? He does not retain His anger forever, because He delights in mercy. 19)He will again have compassion on us, and will subdue our iniquities. You will cast all our sins into the depths of the sea."

> Psalm 103:12-13, "As far as the east is from the west, so far has He removed our transgressions from us. 13)As a father pities his children, so the Lord pities those who fear Him."

> Jeremiah 31:34b, "For I will forgive their iniquity, and their sin I will remember no more."

TWO BURDENS OF ZECHARIAH - 9:1; 12:1

> Zechariah 9:1, "The burden of the word of the Lord against the land of Hadrach, and Damascus its resting place (For the eyes of men and all the tribes of Israel are on the Lord)."

The first burden of Zechariah's prophecy covers chapters [2]_____.

> Zechariah 12:1, "The burden of the word of the Lord against Israel. Thus says the Lord, who stretches out the heavens, lays the foundation of the earth and forms the spirit of man within him."

The second burden of Zechariah's prophecy covers chapters [3]_____.

> "In the remainder of Zechariah 12, the prophet sets forth, as nowhere else in Scripture with such vividness and power, the conversion of Israel to the Lord. Nothing in Israel's past history can be interpreted as the fulfillment of this passage." –*The Minor Prophets* by Charles L. Feinberg, Moody Press, Chicago, IL, C, 1948, p. 332

ISRAEL'S DAY OF SALVATION/CLEANSING

> Zechariah 12:10, "And I will pour on the house of David and on the inhabitants of Jerusalem the Spirit of grace and supplication; then they will look on Me whom they have pierced. Yes, they will mourn for Him as one mourns for his only son, and grieve for Him as one grieves for his firstborn."

> "The great grief is spoken of as the most intense kind of sorrow, like that for

an only son. This is especially forceful, because childlessness was considered a curse and dishonor. Their hearts will be smitten with grief like that for the firstborn in the home, a peculiar sorrow to loving parents. The mourning has been compared to the greatest private sorrow; now it is likened to the most intense public grief exhibited in Israel." –*The Minor Prophets* by Charles L. Feinberg, Moody Press, Chicago, IL, C, 1948, p. 333

Zechariah 12:11, "In that day there shall be a great mourning in Jerusalem, like the mourning at Hadad Rimmon in the plain of Megiddo."

Hadad, Rimmon, the names of Syrian gods, west of Esdraelon, near [4]_____ _____, where godly King Josiah was killed (609 B.C. clash with Pharaoh-neco of Egypt) his death was a national tragedy. Israel wept bitterly (2 Chronicles 35:22-25) and will weep again!

Zechariah 12:12-14, "And the land shall mourn, every family by itself: the family of the house of David by itself, and their wives by themselves; the family of the house of Nathan by itself, and their wives by themselves; 13)the family of the house of Levi by itself, and their wives by themselves; the family of Shimei by itself, and their wives by themselves; 14)all the families that remain, every family by itself, and their wives by themselves."

This is truly Israel's day of [5]_____, forgiveness, and mourning over sin. David and Levi, representing the kingly and priestly lines, Nathan (2 Sam. 5:14) and Shimei (Num. 3:18), also represent the kingly and priestly lines, are cited. Everyone is included – the people will follow the example of the leaders – and mourn!

Hosea 3:4-5, "For the children of Israel shall abide many days without king or prince, without sacrifice or sacred pillar, without ephod or teraphim. 5)Afterward the children of Israel shall return and seek the Lord their God and David their king. They shall fear the Lord and His goodness in the latter days."

[6]_____ times it is mentioned that their wives mourn apart from their husbands! The reality of their sin, realizing they had rejected the Messiah, is overwhelming!

WHEN REVIVAL COMES TO ISRAEL

Zechariah 13:1, "In that day a fountain shall be opened for the house of David and for the inhabitants of Jerusalem, for sin and for uncleanness."

"In that day" refers to the [7]_____ of the Lord, when Christ returns and Israel is saved!

"The house of David and for the inhabitants of Jerusalem"– all 12 tribes in [8]_____ _____, everyone in Israel is impacted!

Ezekiel 36:24-25, "For I will take you in from among the nations, gather you out of all countries, and bring you into your own land. 25)Then I will sprinkle clean water on you, and you shall be clean; I will cleanse you from all your filthiness and from all your idols."

"A fountain shall be opened" – "fountain" (maqor) refers to a spring of water. "Opened" conveys the idea of a [9]_____, permanent opening – this REVIVAL is not going to STOP!

Romans 11:26-27, "And so all Israel will be saved, as it is written: 'The Deliverer will come out of Zion, and He will turn away ungodliness from Jacob; 27)For this is My covenant with them, when I take away their sin.'"

"For sin" (chattath) refers to that which misses the mark or goes the [10]_____ _____ way.

"Uncleanness" identifies something to be [11]_____ ... ceremonial impurity such as touching a dead body, etc.

> Romans 10:3, "For they being ignorant of God's righteousness, and seeking to establish their own righteousness, have not submitted to the righteousness of God."

ISRAEL CLEANSED OF FALSE PROPHETS

> Zechariah 13:2, "It shall be in that day says the Lord of hosts, that I will cut off the names of the idols from the land, and they shall no longer be remembered. I will also cause the prophets and the unclean spirits to depart from the land."

Israel's two besetting sins: [12]_____ and false [13]_____ _____.

> Psalm 96:5, "For all the gods of the people are idols, but the Lord made the heavens."

> Psalm 106:36, "They served their idols, which became a snare to them."

> Psalm 115:4, "Their idols are silver and gold, the work of men's hands."

> Hosea 2:17, "For I will take from her mouth the names of Baals, and they shall be remembered by their name no more."

> "Zechariah did not name the idols, but we know that one of them will be the blasphemous image of the antichrist, which the false prophet (a Jew) will place in the rebuilt temple in Jerusalem (Revelation13). Perhaps the antichrist will consider it sound policy to set up other idols in Jerusalem, his religious capital – Shinto idols from Japan and images of Buddha and the multitudinous gods of the Hindus, for example. As long as worship of his image is paramount, he may not care if other idols are worshiped too. Perhaps the antichrist will take sardonic satisfaction in establishing a pantheon of all the world's false gods to exacerbate Jewish monotheistic sensibilities. When the Lord comes, He will cleanse His beloved Jerusalem of all its images and put an end to all idolatry." -*Exploring the Minor Prophets* by John Phillips, Kregel Publications, Grand Rapids, MI, C, 1998, p. 299

The deception energizing false prophets is unclean [14]_____ (the only mention in the OT).

> Deuteronomy 18:20-22, "But the prophet who presumes to speak a word in My name, which I have not commanded him to speak, or who speaks in the name of other gods, that prophet shall die. 21)And if you say in your heart, 'How shall we know the word which the Lord has not spoken?' 22)when a prophet speaks in the name of the Lord, if the thing does not happen or come to pass, that is the thing which the Lord has not spoken; the prophet has spoken presumptuously; you shall not be afraid of him."

> Jeremiah 14:14-15, "And the Lord said to me, 'The prophets prophesy lies

in My name. I have not sent them, commanded them, nor spoken to them; they prophesy to you a false vision, divination, a worthless thing, and the deceit of their heart. 15)Therefore thus says the Lord concerning the prophets who prophesy in My name, whom I did not send, and who say, 'Sword and famine shall not be in this land' – 'By sword and famine those prophets shall be consumed!'"

"A robe of coarse hair to deceive" (v. 4) – exterior holiness (I Kings 19:13, 19), inner [15]_____ control!

THE END OF THE MILLENNIUM?

Zechariah 13:3-6, "It shall come to pass that if anyone still prophesies, then his father and mother who begot him will say to him, 'You shall not live, because you have spoken lies in the name of the Lord.' And his father and mother who begot him shall thrust him through when he prophesies. 4)And it shall be in that day that every prophet will be ashamed of his vision when he prophesies; they will not wear a robe of coarse hair to deceive. 5)But he will say, 'I am no prophet, I am a farmer; for a man taught me to keep cattle from my youth.' 6)And one will say to him, 'What are these wounds between your arms?' Then he will answer, 'These with which I was wounded in the house of My friends."

• Offspring of the Tribulation redeemed will turn from God and receive [16]_____
_____.

"Or perhaps the focus is on the later years of the millennium. Countless millions of children, grand-children, and greatgrandchildren will be born; all these will know nothing of war, woe, pestilence, famine, and injustice. They will make annual pilgrimages to Jerusalem to see the wonders of the capital, to catch a glimpse of the King, and to see the heavenly Jerusalem above (in stationary orbit over the earthly Jerusalem) shining like a diamond in the sky. In spite of these ideal conditions and in spite of the ease with which a person born in the millennium can be born again, an ever increasing number of people will remain unregenerate ... We know from Revelation 20:7-10 that at the end of the millennium Satan will be released from his prison to fan these flames into a universal conflagration. It may be that the prophecy in Zechariah 13:2b-5 refers to the first tentative sparks of a final outbreak of rebellion." –*Exploring the Minor Prophets* by John Phillips, Kregel Publications, Grand Rapids, MI, C, 1998, pp. 300-301

Answers

1. cleanse 2. 9-11 3. 12-14 4. Megiddo 5. repentance 6. Five 7. day 8. Israel 9. continuous 10. wrong 11. shunned 12. idols 13. prophets 14. spirits 15. demonic 16. Judgment

the Thrilling Prophecies of
Mr. Z and Jesus
Jerusalem, the Jew, and You

When & Where Jesus Quoted Zechariah?
Message #16 in the series, Mr. Z and Jesus

Bible Text: Zechariah 13:7-9

JESUS QUOTED ZECHARIAH, MATTHEW 26:31

Matthew 26:31, "Then Jesus said to them, 'All of you will be made to stumble because of Me this night, for it is written: '"I will strike the Shepherd, and the sheep of the flock will be scattered."'"

- TIMETABLE: After He predicted Peter's denial prior to His arrest in Gethsemane.

  "Even Jesus applied this verse to Himself at the Last Supper (Matthew 26:31). His prophecy was fulfilled when the disciples fled." *-Zechariah* by Homer Heater, Jr. Lamplighter Books, Zondervan Publishing House, Grand Rapids, MI, C, 1987, p. 110

SEVEN GREAT TRUTHS IN ZECHARIAH 13:7-9

Zechariah 13:7, "'Awake, O sword, against My Shepherd, against the Man who is My Companion,' says the Lord of hosts. 'Strike the Shepherd, and the sheep will be scattered; then I will turn My hand against the little ones.'"

1) God is speaking to a ¹_____, an instrument of death.

   Zechariah 13:7a, "Awake, O sword against My Shepherd....'"

2) The sword is against, My Shepherd, ²_____.

- In the sovereignty of God, the Lord allowed the ³_____ of His Son for our redemption.

  2 Corinthians 5:21, "For He made Him who knew no sin to be sin for us, that we might become the righteousness of God in Him."

  Isaiah 53:10, "Yet it pleased the Lord to bruise Him; He has put Him to grief. When You make His soul an offering for sin, He shall see His seed, He shall prolong His days, and the pleasure of the Lord shall prosper in His hand."

  Acts 2:23, "Him (Jesus), being delivered by the determined purpose and foreknowledge of God, you have taken by lawless hands, have crucified, and put to death."

  "The shepherd of Jehovah, whom the sword is to smite, is therefore no other than the Messiah, who is also identified with Jehovah in ch. Xii. 10; or the good shepherd, who says of Himself, 'I and My Father are one (John x. 30).'" -Keil, *The Twelve Minor Prophets*, vol. 2 in Biblical Commentary on the Old Testament, p. 397

3) We see a beautiful picture of the ⁴_____.

Zechariah 13:7b, "Against the Man who is My Companion, says the Lord of hosts...."

- "Man" is an uncommon word; it refers to a [5]_____ man, not an ordinary man.
- "Companion" refers to a [6]_____ associate. God identifies Jesus Christ as the mighty man of His union.
- The verse could read: "THE MIGHTY MAN [JESUS] WHO IS CO- EQUAL WITH ME."

> "No angel in the sky, no anointed cherub, no archangel, or shining seraph could be called God's 'fellow' – His equal. The word translated 'fellow' occurs elsewhere in Scripture only in Leviticus (6:2; 19:11, 15, 17, for instance). Often translated 'neighbor,' the word conveys the thought of one united together by the possession of common nature, rights, and privileges." –*Exploring the Minor Prophets* by John Phillips, Kregel Publications, Grand Rapids, MI, C, 1998, pp. 302-303

4) After the crucifixion, the Jewish nation was decimated and the [7]_____ _____ began, A.D. 70.

> "The Lord God is the speaker, and Christ, the Messiah, is the person spoken of. The term, 'the man that is my fellow' would be better translated, 'the man my equal' or 'the man of my union.' This is an unmistakable Old Testament reference to the deity of Christ." –*Zechariah* by J. Vernon McGee, Thru the Bible Books, Box 100, Pasadena, CA 91109, C, 1979, p. 190

> Zechariah 13:7c, "Strike the Shepherd, and the sheep will be scattered...."

> "And Zechariah foresaw the sword bared at Calvary. He saw the glittering blade sheathed in the soul of the Savior and the burning flame extinguished in His blood. God's wrath has thus been eternally disarmed for all who trust the Savior ... The crime of Calvary loomed up before Zechariah as he viewed the sword and the Shepherd. Man's side of the cross was sad and sordid. But there was another side. The time had come for God to deal to His own eternal satisfaction with the problem of sin." –*Exploring the Minor Prophets* by John Phillips, Kregel Publications, Grand Rapids, MI, C, 1998, p. 303

5) A vivid prediction of an unthinkable [8]_____ toll (during the Tribulation).

> Zechariah 13:7d-8, "Then I will turn My hand against the little ones. 8)And it shall come to pass in all the land,' says the Lord, 'That two-thirds in it shall be cut off and die, but one third shall be left in it.'"

WHO ARE "THE LITTLE ONES"?

- The disciples of the first century.
- Jews of the centuries dispersed throughout the world.
- The Jews of the Tribulation.

> Jeremiah 30:7, "Alas! For that day is great, so that none is like it; and it is the time of Jacob's trouble, but he shall be saved out of it."

> Matthew 24:21, "For then there will be great tribulation, such as has not been since the beginning of the world until this time, no, nor ever shall be."

"The third shall be left therein' refers to the same remnant that shall ask, 'What are these wounds in thine hands?' They will have come through the horrors of the great tribulation period in which two-thirds of their people have perished." –*Zechariah* by Dr. J. Vernon McGee, p. 191

"The fulfillment of this promise is the Tribulation, when Israel will undergo a time of trouble hitherto unknown (Matthew 24:21). Two-thirds will be cut off and die (13:8, the two-thirds probably should be taken as 'majority'), and one third will be left. Then the remaining third will be tested as silver and gold (13:9), and the results will be glorious. Israel will call on the name of the Lord, and He will answer her." –*Zechariah* by Dr. Homer Heater, Jr., Lamplighter Books, Zondervan Publishing House, Grand Rapids, MI, C, 1987, p. 110

6) God sends [9]_____ to His people who He loves.

Zechariah 13:8b-9a, "But one-third shall be left in it: 9a)I will bring the one-third through the fire, will refine them as silver is refined, and test them as gold is tested.'"

Revelation 7:2-4, "Then I saw another angel ascending from the east, having the seal of the living God. And he cried with a loud voice to the four angels to whom it was granted to harm the earth and the sea, 3)saying, 'Do not harm the earth, the sea, or the trees till we have sealed the servants of our God on their foreheads.' 4)And I heard the number of those who were sealed. One hundred and forty-four thousand of all the tribes of the children of Israel were sealed."

Revelation 7:13-14, "Then one of the elders answered, saying to me, 'Who are these arrayed in white robes, and where did they come from?' 14)And I said to him, 'Sir, you know.' So he said to me, 'These are the ones who come out of the great tribulation, and washed their robes and made them white in the blood of the Lamb.'"

WHY GOD ALLOWS TRIALS IN OUR LIFE

I Peter 1:6-7, "In this you greatly rejoice, though now for a little while, if need be, you have been grieved by various trials, 7)that the genuineness of your faith, being much more precious than gold that perishes, though it be tested by fire, may be found to praise, honor, and glory at the revelation of Jesus Christ."

"Trials" (peirasmois) – the term denotes a process of testing for the purpose of displaying the nature or [10]_____ of the thing or person tested.

- To [11]_____ us (2 Corinthians 12:7-10)

- To increase [12]_____ values (John 16:33)

- To cause us to help the [13]_____ (2 Cor. 1:3-7)

- To [14]_____ us because of our sin (Heb. 12:5-12)

- To [15]_____ our spiritual character (James 1:2-4)

271

7) God will save [16]_____ by the Second Coming of Jesus Christ.

> Zechariah 13:9b, "And I will answer them. I will say, 'This is My people'; and each one will say, 'The Lord is my God.'"

Our Thousand Year Reign:
Why We Reject Amillennialism
Message #17 in the series, Mr. Z and Jesus

Bible Text: Revelation 20:1-9

> "The Millennium is God's answer to the prayer, 'Thy Kingdom come.'
> When we pray the prayer which we mistakenly call the Lord's Prayer, we
> say, 'Thy kingdom come ... in earth, as it is heaven' (Matthew 6:10). That
> is the kingdom which He is going to establish on earth, and it is called the
> Millennium." –*Thru the Bible with J. Vernon McGee, Volume V*, Thomas Nelson
> Publishers, Nashville, TN, C, 1983, pp. 1054-1055

POSTMILLENNIALISM – man will bring in the 1,000 kingdom by preaching the
Gospel. Eventually the world will embrace Christianity. (Unitarian minister, Daniel
Whitby (1638-1726), popularized this theory which faded after WW I, II, and the
Nazi genocide).

AMILENNNIALISM – teaches there will be [1]_____ thousand-year reign of
Christ on earth and no earthly Kingdom of God. Rather, the New Testament church
inherits all of the spiritual promises and prophecies of Old Testament Israel.

PREMILLENNIALISM – holds that Christ will [2]_____ and bodily
return to earth before the 1,000 Kingdom begins. Clement of Rome (A.D. 40-100);
Ignatius (50-115); Polycarp (70-167); Justin Martyr (100-168); Irenaeus (140-202); and
Tertullian (150-220) all embraced this view. In the fourth century, with the rise of the
Roman Catholic Church, which viewed herself as God's instrument to usher in the
promised glory, premillennialism faded.

- Millennium comes from the Latin word that means [3]_____.
- In Revelation 20:1-9 the word for 1,000 years is repeated [4]_____ times.

WHY THE MILLENNIUM & ISRAEL?

1) God's covenant with [5]_____ – the land and posterity are
   fulfilled in the Millennium:
- Abraham's seed (Israel) would become a mighty nation (Gen. 12:1-3; 13:16; 15:5;
  17:7; 22:17-18).
- Abraham seeds would someday own Palestine forever. (Gen. 12:7; 13:14-17; 15:7,
  18-21; 17:8)
2) God's covenant with [6]_____ – a three-fold promise:
- From David would come an everlasting throne. (2 Chronicles 13:5; 2 Sam. 7:12-
  16; 23:5)
- From David would come an everlasting kingdom.
- From David would come an everlasting King.
3) God's covenant with Israel to possess the [7]_____. (Palestinic cov-

enant) - fulfilled in the Millennial kingdom (Isa. 11:11-12; 65:9, Ezek. 16:60-63; 36:28-29, 39:28; Hos. 1:10-2:1; Mic. 2:12; Zech. 10:6)

4) God's promise of a [8]_____ covenant:
- A new heart.
- The forgiveness of sin.
- The filling of the Spirit all fulfilled in Israel's conversion & the millennial age. (Jer 31:31-34; 32:35-39; Ezek. 11:18-20; 16:60-63; 37:26; Rom. 11:26-29)

NAMES OF THE MILLENNIUM

1) The [9]_____ to come.

   Hebrews 2:5, "For He has not put the world to come, of which we speak, in subjection to angels."

2) The kingdom of [10]_____.

   Matthew 5:10, "Blessed are those who are persecuted for righteousness' sake, for theirs is the kingdom of heaven."

3) The kingdom of [11]_____.

   Mark 1:14, "Now after John was put in prison, Jesus came to Galilee, preaching the gospel of the kingdom of God."

4) The last [12]_____.

   John 6:40, "And this is the will of Him who sent Me, that everyone who sees the Son and believes in Him may have everlasting life; and I will raise him up at the last day."

5) The [13]_____.

   Matthew 19:28, "So Jesus said to them, 'Assuredly I say to you, that in the regeneration, when the Son of Man sits on the throne of His glory, you who have followed Me will also sit on twelve thrones, judging the twelve tribes of Israel.'"

- "regeneration" - means "[14]_____," the earth will be made new and different.

THE LOCATION OF THE MILLENNIUM

   Isaiah 2:2-4, "Now it shall come to pass in the latter days that the mountain of the Lord's house shall be established on the top of the mountains, and shall be exalted above the hills; and all nations shall flow to it. 3)Many people shall come and say, 'Come, and let us go up to the mountain of the Lord, to the house of the God of Jacob; He will teach us His ways, and we shall walk in His paths.' For out of Zion shall go forth the law, and the word of the Lord from Jerusalem. 4)He shall judge between the nations, and rebuke many people; they shall beat their swords into plowshares, and their spears into pruning hooks; nations shall not lift up sword against nation, neither shall they learn war anymore."

- [15]_____ will become the center of the millennium earth. (Jer. 31:6; Mic. 4:1; Zech. 2:10-11)
- Jerusalem will become the center of [16]_____ of Jesus Christ, the King. (Jer. 30:16-21; 31:6, 23; Joel 3:17; Zech. 8:8, 20-23)
- Jerusalem will endure [17]_____. (Isa. 9:7; 33:20-21; 60:15;

Joel 3:19-21; Zech. 8:4)

- Jerusalem will occupy an [18]_____ site.

    Zechariah 14:10, "All the land shall be turned into a plain from Geba to Rimmon south of Jerusalem. Jerusalem shall be raised up and inhabited in her place from Benjamin's Gate to the place of the First Gate and the Corner Gate, and from the Tower of Hananel to the king's winepress."

THE PURPOSE OF THE MILLENNIUM

1) To [19]_____ believers.

    Psalm 58:11, "So that men will say, 'Surely there is a reward for the righteous; surely He is God who judges in the earth.'"

    Proverbs 11:18, "The wicked man does deceptive work, but he who sows righteousness will have a sure reward."

    Matthew 16:27, "For the Son of Man will come in the glory of His Father with His angels, and then He will reward each according to His works."

    Matthew 25:34, "Then the King will say to those on His right hand, 'Come, you blessed of My Father, inherit the kingdom prepared for you from the foundation of the world.'"

2) To fulfill Jesus' model [20]_____.

    Luke 11:2, "So He said to them, 'When you pray, say: Our Father in heaven, Hallowed be Your name. Your kingdom come. Your will be done on earth as it is in heaven.'" (cf. Matt. 6:9-13)

3) To redeem the physical [21]_____.

    Romans 8:19, 22, "For the earnest expectation of the creation eagerly waits for the revealing of the sons of God. 22)For we know that the whole creation groans and labors with birth pangs together until now."

THE GLORY OF THE MILLENNIAL KINGDOM

Daniel 7:27, "Then the kingdom and dominion, and the greatness of the kingdoms under the whole heaven, shall be given to the people, the saints of the Most High. His kingdom is an everlasting kingdom, and all dominions shall serve and obey Him."

- There will be [22]_____. (Isa. 2:4; 9:4-7; 11:6-9; 32:17-18; 33:5-6; 54:13; 55:12; 60:18; 65:25; 66:12; Ez. 28:26; 34:25, 28; Hos. 2:18; Mic. 4:2-3; Zech. 9:10)
- There will be [23]_____. (Isa. 9:3-4; 12:3-6; 14:7-8; 25:8-9; 30:29; 42:1, 10-12; 52:9; 60:15; 61:7, 10; 65:18-19; 66:10-14; Jer. 30:18-19; 31:13-14; Zeph. 3:14-17; Zech. 8:18-19; 10:6-7)
- There will be [24]_____. (Isa. 1:26-27; 4:3-4; 29:18-23; 31:6-7; 35:8-9; 52:1; 60:21; 61:10; Jer. 31:23; Ezek. 36:24-31; 37:23-24; 43:7-12; 45:1; Joel 3:21; Zeph. 3:11, 13; Zech. 8:3; 13:1-2; 14:20-21)
- There will be [25]_____. (Isa. 12:1-2; 29:22-23; 30:26; 40:1-2; 49:13; 51:3; 61:3-7; 66:13-14; Jer. 31:23-25; Zeph. 3:18-20; Zech. 9:11-12; Rev. 21:4)
- There will be [26]_____. (Isa. 9:7; 11:5; 32:16; 42:1-4; 65:21-23; Jer. 23:5; 31:23; 31:29-30)
- There will be full [27]_____. (Isa. 11:1-2, 9; 41:19-20; 54:13; Hab. 2:14)

- There will be 28_____. (Isa. 2:2-3; 12:3-6; 25:9; 29:17- 24; 30:20-21; 32:3-4; 49:10; 52:8; Jer. 3:14-15; 23:1-4; Mic. 4:2)
- The curse will be 29_____. (Isa. 11:6-9; 35:9; 65:25)
- 30_____ will be eliminated. (Isa. 33:24; Jer. 30:17; Ezek. 34:16)
- There will be 31_____. (Isa. 41:8-14; 62:8-9; Jer. 32:27; 23:6; Ezek. 34:27; Joel 3:16-17; Amos 9:15; Zech. 8:14-15; 9:8; 14:10-11)
- There will be 32_____. Children are specifically mentioned in Scripture in the Millennial kingdom. (Jer. 30:20; 31:29; Ezek. 47:22; Zech. 10:8)

    Isaiah 11:6, 8, "The wolf also shall dwell with the lamb, the leopard shall lie down with the young goat, the calf and the young lion and the fatling together; and a little child shall lead them. 8)The nursing child shall play by the cobra's hole, and the weaned child shall put his hand in the viper's den."

- There will be purposed 33_____. (Isa. 62:8-9; 5:21-23; Jer. 31:5; Ezek. 48:18-19)
- There will be an increase of 34_____. (Isa. 4:5; 30:26; 60:19-20; Zech 2:5)
- There will unified 35_____. (Isa. 45:23; 52:1, 7-10; 66:17-23; Zech 13:2; 14:16; 8:23; 9:7; Zeph. 3:9; Mal. 1:11; Rev. 5:9-14)
- There will be the full presence of 36_____. (Ezek. 37:27-28; Zech. 2:2, 10-13; Rev. 21:3)
- There will be the fullness of the 37_____. (Isa. 32:13-15; 41:1; 44:3; 59:19, 21; Ezek. 36:26-27; 37:14: 39:29; Joel 2:28-29; Ezek. 11:19-20)
- There will be the privilege of 38_____ with Christ.

    Revelation 20:4, 6, "And I saw thrones, and they sat on them, and judgment was committed to them. Then I saw the souls of those who had been beheaded for their witness to Jesus and for the word of God, who had not worshiped the beast or his image, and had not received his mark on their foreheads or on their hands. And they lived and reigned with Christ for a thousand years. 6)Blessed and holy is he who has part in the first resurrection. Over such the second death has no power, but they shall be priests of God and of Christ, and shall reign with Him a thousand years."

THE CLOSE OF THE MILLENNIUM

Revelation 20:7-8, "Now when the thousand years have expired, Satan will be released from his prison 8)and will go out to deceive the nations which are in the four corners of the earth, Go and Magog, to gather them together to battle, whose number is as the sand of the sea."

- Incredibly, after 1,000 utopia with Jesus Christ some will defect and be 39_____ _____.

Answers

39. deceived.

32. reproduction 33. labor 34. light 35. worship 36. God 37. Holy Spirit 38. reigning

18. elevated 19. reward 20. prayer 21. creation 22. peace 23. joy 24. holiness 25. com-fort 26. justice 27. knowledge 28. instruction 29. removed 30. Sickness 31. protection

11. God 12. day 13. regeneration 14. recreation 15. Jerusalem 16. worship 17. forever

1. no 2. literally 3. 1,000 4. 6 5. Abraham 6. David 7. land 8. new 9. world 10. heaven

What the World Will Be Like Someday

Message #18 in the series, Mr. Z and Jesus

Bible Text: Zechariah 14:1-21

THE DAY OF TH E LORD – 14:1-2

Zechariah 14:1-2, "Behold, the day of the Lord is coming, and your spoil will be divided in your midst. 2)For I will gather all nations to battle against Jerusalem; the city shall be taken, the houses rifled, and the women ravished. Half of the city shall go into captivity, but the remnant of the people shall not be cut off from the city."

Zechariah 12:2-3, "Behold, I will make Jerusalem a cup of drunkenness to all the surrounding peoples, when they lay siege against Judah and Jerusalem. 3)And it shall happen in that day that I will make Jerusalem a very heavy stone for all peoples; all who heave it away will surely be cut in pieces, though all nations of the earth are gathered against it."

Zechariah 13:8, "And it shall come to pass in all the land, says the Lord, that two-thirds in it shall be cut off and die, but one-third shall be left in it." [Here is the "remnant"].

- "The Day of the Lord" is a great and terrible day because it is THE day of the judgment of the [1]_____.

Joel 2:1-3, "Blow the trumpet in Zion, and sound an alarm in My holy mountain! Let all the inhabitants of the land tremble; for the day of the Lord is coming, for it is at hand: 2)A day of darkness and gloominess, a day of clouds and thick darkness, like the morning clouds spread over the mountains. A people come, great and strong, the like of whom has never been; nor will there ever be any such after them, even for many successive generations. 3)A fire devours before them, and behind them a flame burns; the land is like the Garden of Eden before them, and behind them a desolate wilderness; surely nothing shall escape them."

Joel 1:15, "Alas for the day! For the day of the Lord is at hand; it shall come as destruction from the Almighty."

THE SECOND COMING OF CHRIST – 14:3-5

Zechariah 14:3-5, "Then the Lord will go forth and fight against those nations, as He fights in the day of battle. 4)And in that day His feet will stand on the Mount of Olives, which faces Jerusalem on the east. And the Mount of Olives shall be split in two, from the east to west, making a very large valley; half of the mountain shall move toward the north and half of it toward the south. 5)Then you shall flee through My mountain valley, for the mountain valley shall reach to Azal. Yes, you shall flee as you fled from the earthquake in the days of Uzziah king of Judah. Thus the Lord my God will come, and all the saints with You."

- Jesus will return at His Second Coming where He left at His first coming: the
  2 _____.

> Acts 1:11-12, "Who also said, 'Men of Galilee, why do you stand gazing up into heaven? This same Jesus, who was taken up from you into heaven, will so come in like manner as you saw Him go into heaven.' 12)Then they returned to Jerusalem from the mount called Olivet, which is near Jerusalem, a Sabbath day's journey."

> "At the present time the mount of Olives is at the center of a mile-long line of hills that dominate Jerusalem. The mount of Olives stands 187 feet above mount Zion, 245 feet above mount Moriah, and 443 feet above Gethsemane. Located to the east of Jerusalem, toward the sunrise, the mount of Olives is separated from the city by the narrow Kidron valley. On the other side of the mountain is the wilderness that runs down to the Dead Sea. The road to Bethany and the Jordan river run around the side of the mountain. The valley created by the coming convulsion will be a miraculous escape route for the desperate Jewish survivors in Jerusalem." –John Phillips

WHEN JESUS RETURNS

- The Mount of Olives will 3_____ in two.
- A large new valley of 4_____ will be created.
- Innumerable 5_____ will return with Christ! (This proves that the Church, believers in Christ, will not endure the Tribulation. You can return with Christ if you are IN the Tribulation!)

> Zechariah 12:10b, "...Then they will look on Me whom they pierced...."

> I Thessalonians 3:13, "So that He may establish your hearts blameless in holiness before our God and Father at the coming of our Lord Jesus Christ with all His saints."

> Colossians 3:4, "When Christ who is our life appears, then you also will appear with Him in glory."

> Jude 14, "Now Enoch, the seventh from Adam, prophesied about these men also, saying, 'Behold, the Lord comes with ten thousands of His saints.'"

> Revelation 19:19, "And I saw the beast, the kings of the earth, and their armies, gathered together to make war against Him who sat on the horse and against His army."

THE STRANGEST DAY – 14:6-8

> Zechariah 14:6-7, "It shall come to pass in that day that there will be no light; the lights will diminish. 7)It shall be one day which is known to the Lord – neither day nor night. But at evening time it shall happen that it will be light."

- Some kind of weird "6_____ zone" – a day that is not a day, a night that is not a night, a strange kind of darkness and light. When

Jesus returns the world changes!

Zechariah 14:12-15, "And this shall be the plague with which the Lord will strike all the people who fought against Jerusalem. There flesh shall dissolve while they stand on their feet, their eyes shall dissolve in their sockets, and their tongues shall dissolve in their mouths. 13)It shall come to pass in that day that a great panic from the Lord will be among them. Everyone will seize the hand of his neighbor's hand; 14)Judah also will fight at Jerusalem. And the wealth of al the surrounding nations shall be gathered together: Gold, silver, and apparel in great abundance. 15)Such also shall be the plague on the horse and the mule, on the camel and the donkey, and on all the cattle will be in those camps. So shall this plague be."

JERUSALEM'S NEW RIVER - 14:8

Zechariah 14:8, "And in that day it shall be that living waters shall flow from Jerusalem, half of them toward the eastern sea; and half of them toward the western sea, in both summer and winter it shall occur."

"In other words, this will be a spring that will gush up water, and I think it means literal water. Apparently, Jerusalem, which has been an inland city, will suddenly become a seagoing city, that is, a port town." -*Zechariah* by J. Vernon McGee, Thru the Bible, Box 100, Pasadena, CA 91109, C, 1979, p. 201

- [7]_____ will flow out of Jerusalem and stream into the Dead Sea and the Mediterranean. In today's JERUSALEM there is no river! But at the ushering in of the Millennial 1000-year age not only will there be a river in Jerusalem, but also the death-giving Dead Sea will come alive! It will be alive with its banks lined with all kinds of trees for food, always fruit-bearing, and fishermen on its shores (Ezekiel 47:8-10, 12).

"As a result of the Lord's triumph several things follow: Living waters flow from Jerusalem to the Dead Sea and to the Mediterranean (Joel 3:18; Ezek. 47:1-12). This will have been caused by the earthquake which split the Mount of Olives. The water's flow will not be hindered summer or winter. It is healing and life-giving in the physical sense. But they may also have a spiritual meaning, typifying fullness of spiritual blessing (Rev. 22:1)." -*Jehovah Remembers* by Nathan J. Stone, Moody Bible Institute, 820 North LaSalle Street, Chicago, IL 60610, C, 1966, Part II, p. 28

- A great reminder, in heaven also will be a river of water of [8]_____.

Revelation 22:1-2, "And he showed me a pure river of water of life, clear as crystal, proceeding from the throne of God and of the lamb. 2)In the middle of its street, and on either side of the river, was the tree of life, which bore twelve fruits, each tree yielding its fruit every month. The leaves of the tree were for the healing of the nations."

THE MILLENNIAL KINGDOM 14:9-11, 20-21

Zechariah 14:9-11, "And the Lord shall be King over all the earth. In that day it shall be - 'The Lord is one, and His name one. 10)All the land shall be turned into a plain from Geba to Rimmon south of Jerusalem. Jerusa-

279

lem shall be raised up and inhabited in her place of the First Gate and the Corner Gate, and from the Tower of Hananel to the king's winepress. 11)The people shall dwell in it; and no longer shall there be utter destruction. But Jerusalem shall be safely inhabited.'"

Zephaniah 3:9, "For then I will restore to the people a pure language, that they all may call on the name of the Lord, to serve Him with one accord."

- The language ^{9}_____ will be gone! We will all speak the same heavenly language!
- After Jesus returns He will be ^{10}_____ as King over all the earth!

Revelation 9:15, "Now out of His mouth goes a sharp sword, that with it He should strike the nations. And He Himself will rule them with a rod of iron. He Himself treads the winepress of the fierceness and wrath of Almighty God."

WORLD WIDE WORSHIP 14:16-21

Zechariah 14:16-21, "And it shall come to pass that everyone who is left of all nations which came against Jerusalem shall go up from year to year to worship the King, the Lord of hosts, and to keep the Feast of Tabernacles. 17)And it shall be that whichever of the families of the earth do not come up to Jerusalem to worship the King, the Lord of hosts, on them there will be no rain. 18)If the family of Egypt will not come up and enter in, they shall have no rain; they shall receive the plague with which the Lord strikes the nations who do not come up to keep the Feast of Tabernacles. 19)This shall be the punishment of Egypt and the punishment of all the nations that do not come up to keep the Feast of Tabernacles. 20)In that day 'HOLINESS TO THE LORD' shall be engraved on the bells of the horses. The pots in the Lord's house shall be like the bowls before the altar. 21)Yes, every pot in Jerusalem and Judah shall be holiness to the Lord of hosts. Everyone who sacrifices shall come and take them and cook in them. In that day there shall no longer be a Canaanite in the house of the Lord of hosts."

- "Who is left of all the nations" – how encouraging ... there will be a saved remnant from ^{11}_____ the nations!
- "Feast of the Tabernacles" – is the feast the Israelites celebrated when they came out of ^{12}_____.
- "The pots" – everything in this Kingdom will be dedicated to God.
- "A Canaanite" – there will be ^{13}_____ hypocrites in this great Millennial Kingdom.

Revelation 21:27, "But there shall by no means enter it anything that defiles, or causes an abomination or a lie, but only those who are written in the Lamb's Book of life."

Revelation 22:15, "But outside are dogs and sorcerers and sexually immoral and murderers and idolaters, and whoever loves and practices a lie."

Answers

Notes

Chapter One *The Panorama of the Prophetic in Zechariah*

[1] Homer Heater, Jr.. *Zechariah: Bible Study Commentary*. (Grand Rapids: Zondervan, 1987).

[2] C. I. Scofield, *The Scofield Study Bible* (New York: Oxford University Press, 1909).

Chapter Three *The Times of the Gentiles: Horns, Craftsmen, and Israel*

[1] J. Dwight Pentecost, *Things to Come* (Grand Rapids: Zondervan, 1958), 213.

[2] Henry H. Halley, *Halley's Bible Handbook* (Grand Rapids: Zondervan, 1962), 347.

[3] Warren W. Wiersbe. Prophets. The Bible Exposition Commentary (Wheaton: Victor, 2002): 450.

[4] John Phillips, *Exploring the Minor Prophets* (Grand Rapids: Kregel, 1998), 275.

Chapter Five *The Angel of the Lord: Who Is It?*

[1] J. Vernon McGee, *Thru the Bible, Proverbs-Malachi, Vol. 3* (Nashville: Thomas Nelson Publishers, 1982), 917.

[2] H. C. Leupold, *Exposition of Zechariah* (Grand Rapids: Bak-

er Book House, 1965).

3 McGee, *Thru the Bible*, 918.

Chapter Ten *Alexander the Great in Zechariah?*

1 Charles Lee Feinbery, *Zechariah: Israel's Comfort and Glory* (New York: American Board of Missions to the Jews, 1990), 314.

2 Nathan J. Stone, *Jehovah Remembers: Studies in Zechariah, Part II* (Chicago: Moody Bible Institute, 1966), 6.

3 J. Vernon McGee, *Zechariah, Through the Bible Books* (Nashville: Thomas Nelson, 1979), 124.

4 Feinberg, *Zechariah*, 316.

5 Flavius Josephus, *Antiquities, XI.*

Chapter Eleven *The Time of the Latter Rain: What Does It Mean?*

1 The latter rain refers to spring rain, which is much needed for productive crops, while former rain comes in the fall.

2 Charles L. Feinberg, *The Minor Prophets* (Chicago: Moody Press, 1990), 320.

3 V. H. Matthews H. M. W. Chavalas, and J. H. Walton, *The IVP Bible background commentary: Old Testament, electronic ed.* (Downers Grove: InterVarsity Press).

Chapter Twelve *Thirty Pieces of Silver in Zechariah?*

1 Charles Lee Feinberg, *Zechariah: Israel's Comfort and Glory* (Chicago: Moody Press, 1990), 325

2 J. Vernon McGee, *Thru the Bible: Proverbs-Malachi, Vol.3*

(Nashville: Thomas Nelson Publishers, 1982), 965.

Chapter Thirteen *The Deceit of the Antichrist*

[1] David Baron, *Zechariah: A Commentary on His Visions and Prophecies* (Grand Rapids: Kregel Publications, 1918), 415-6.

[2] Homer Heater Jr., *Zechariah* (Grand Rapids: Zondervan, 1987), 97.

[3] Nathan Stone, *Jehovah Remembers, Part 2* (Chicago: Moody Bible Institute, 1966), 17.

[4] J. Vernon McGee, *Thru the Bible: Proverbs-Malachi* (Nashville: Thomas Nelson Publishers, 1982) 970.

Chapter Fourteen *The Coming War against Jerusalem*

[1] http://www.time.com/time/covers/1101020701/story.html

[2] Raymond Hyman Saxe, *Israel's Future Triumph* (Ann Arbor: Grace Bible Publications, 1978), 7.

[3] John Phillips, *Exploring the Minor Prophets* (Grand Rapids: Kregel Publications, 1998), 296.

[4] Ibid., 297.

Chapter Fifteen *When Israel Views the Pierced One*

[1] Charles L. Feinberg, *The Minor Prophets* (Chicago: Moody Press, 1948), 332.

[2] Ibid., 333.

[3] John Walvoord and Roy Zuck, eds., *The Bible knowledge*

commentary: *An Exposition of the Scriptures, electronic ed.* (Wheaton: Victor Books).

4 John Phillips, *Exploring the Minor Prophets* (Grand Rapids: Kregel Publications, 1998), 299.

5 Ibid., 300–1.

Chapter Sixteen *When & Where Jesus Quoted Zechariah?*

1 John Phillips, Exploring the Minor Prophets (Grand Rapids: Kregel Publications, 1998), 302–3.

2 J. Vernon McGee, Zechariah (Pasadena: Thru the Bible Books, 1979), 190.

3 J. F. Walvoord and R. B. Zuck, eds., The Bible Knowledge Commentary: An Exposition of the Scriptures (electronic edition).

4 Homer Heater, Zechariah (Grand Rapids: Zondervan, 1987), 110.

Chapter Eighteen *What the World Will Be Like Someday*

1 Craig Brian Larson, 750 Engaging Illustrations (Grand Rapids: Baker Book House, 2002), 318.

2 C. S. Lewis, The Chronicles of Narnia - More info

3 J. Vernon McGee, Zechariah (Pasadena: Thru the Bible, 1979), 201.

4 Nathan J. Stone, Jehovah Remembers (Chicago: Moody Bible Institute, 1966), 28.

Zechariah Bibliography

The following resources have proven invaluable in the preparation of the preceding chapters and are therefore commended to anyone seeking a deeper understanding of Zechariah and his message. However, the reader should be cautioned that not all of the texts listed here share the author's theological positions. As in all things, the reader is encouraged to exercise discernment and discretion when studying God's Word.

Baldwin, Joyce. "D.J. Wiseman." *Tyndale Old Testament Commentaries: Haggai, Zechariah, Malachi*. Downers Grove, IL: InterVarsity Press, 1972.

Barnes, W. Emery. *Cambridge Bible for Schools and Colleges: Haggai, Zechariah, Malachi*. Cambridge: University Press, 1917.

Baron, David. *Zechariah: A Commentary on His Visions and Prophecies*. Grand Rapids, MI: Kregel Publications, 1918.

Bentley, Michael. *Welwyn Commentary Series: Building For God's Glory*. Auburn, MA: Evangelical Press, 1989.

Brown, William P. *Westminster Bible Companion: Obadiah Through Malachi*. Louisville, KY: Westminster John Knox Press, 1996.

Dods, Marcus. *Hand-Books for Bible Classes: Haggai, Zechariah, and Malachi*. Edinburg: T&T Clark, 1938.

Feinberg, Charles L. *The Minor Prophets*. Chicago: Moody Press, 1987.

Gailey, J. H. *Layman's Bible Commentaries: Micah to Malachi*. London: SCM Press Ltd, 1962.

Gailey, James H., Jr. *The Layman's Bible Commentary. Vol. 15.* Richmond, VA: John Knox Press, 1962.

Hartman, Fred. *Zechariah: Israel's Messenger of the Messiah's Triumph.* Bellmawr, NJ: The Friends of Israel Gospel Ministry, Inc., 1994.

Ironside, H.A. *Notes on the Minor Prophets.* Neptune, NJ: Loizeaux Brothers, Inc.,1979.

Jamieson, Robert A., Fausset, R., and Brown, David. *Jamieson Fausset Brown Bible Commentary. Vol. 2*, Peabody, MA: Hendrickson Publishers, Inc., 2002.

Kelley, Page H. *Layman's Bible Book Commentary. Vol. 14.* Nashville, TN: Broadman Press 1984.

Leupold, H.C. *Exposition of Zechariah.* Grand Rapids, MI: Baker Book House, 1971.

MacArthur, John. *The Return and Reign of Jesus Christ: Zechariah 9-14.* Chicago: Moody Press, 1988.

Mackay, John L. *Focus on the Bible: Haggai, Zecharaiah, Malachi.* Scotland, Great Britain: Christian Focus Publications, 1994.

Mason, Rex. *The Cambridge Bible Commentary: The books of Haggai, Zechariah, and Malachi.* London: University Press, 1977.

McGee, J. Vernon. *Thru The Bible: Zechariah.* Pasadena, CA: 1979.

Meyer, F. B. *The Prophet of Hope.* New York: Fleming H. Revell Company, 1900.

Meyers, Carol L., and Meyers, Eric M. *The Anchor Bible. Vol. 25b and 25c.* New York: Doubleday, 1987.

Mitchell, Hinckley G., ed. *The International Critical Commentary: A Critical Commentary on Haggai & Zechariah.* New York: Charles Scribner's Sons, 1951.

Moore, Thomas V. *A Commentary on Zechariah*. London: The Banner of Truth Trust, 1961.

Moore, T. V. *The Geneva Series of Commentaries: Haggai, Zechariah, and Malachi*. London: Billing & Sons Limited, 1979.

Peterson, David L. *The Old Testament Library: Haggai and Zechariah 1-8*. Philadelphia, PA: The Westminster Press, 1984.

Peterson, David L. *The Old Testament Library: Zechariah 9-14 and Malachi*. Louisville, KY: Westminster Press, 1995.

Phillips, John. *Exploring The Minor Prophets*. Grand Rapids, MI: Kregel Publications, 2002.

Saxe, Raymond H. *Israel's Future Triumph: An Exposition of Zechariah 12-14*. Ann Arbor, MI: Grace Bible Publications, 1978.

Smith, Ralph L., ed. *World Biblical Commentary: Micah-Malachi. Vol. 32*, Nashville: Thomas Nelson Publishers, 1984.

Smith, Gary V. *An Introduction To The Hebrew Prophets: The Prophets As Preachers*. Nashville, TN: Broadman & Holman Publishers, 1994.

Stone, Nathan J. *Jehovah Remembers*. Chicago: Moody Bible Press, 1966.

Walker, Larry. "Frank Gaebelein", ed. *The Expositor's Bible Commentary. Vol. 7*. Grand Rapids, MI: Zondervan Publishing, 1985.

Wright, Charles Henry Hamilton. *Zechariah and His Prophecies*. Minneapolis, MN: Klock & Klock Christian Publishers, 1980.

Index

Scripture

Subject Index

A

B